The
Children's
Bible
Encyclopedia

The Childr B Encyclop

The Bible Made

WRITTEN BY MARK WATER

en's
ble
pedia

Simple and Fun!

ILLUSTRATIONS BY KAREN DONNELLY

COPYRIGHT © 1995 HUNT & THORPE
TEXT © MARK WATER
ILLUSTRATIONS © KAREN DONNELLY

Published by New Kids Media™ in association with Baker Book House Company, Grand Rapids, Michigan, under arrangement with Ottenheimer Publishers, Inc., Owings Mills, Maryland 21117 USA

Designed and produced by
THE BRIDGEWATER BOOK COMPANY
Designer: *Sarah Bentley*
Managing Editor: *Anna Clarkson*
Editor: *Fiona Corbridge*
Page make-up: *Chris Lanaway*
Text consultant: *Derek Williams*

ISBN 0-8010-4414-6
BI104MLKJIHGFEDCBA

Printed in Hong Kong

ACKNOWLEDGEMENTS
Bible quotations are from:
The Holy Bible, New International Version, © 1973, 1978, 1984 by International Bible Society. Used by permission of Hodder and Stoughton.
International Children's Bible, New Century Version (Anglicized Edition), © 1991 Word (UK) Ltd.
Used by permission.

CONTENTS

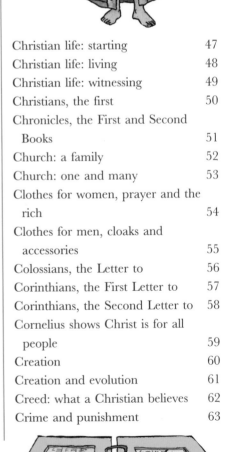

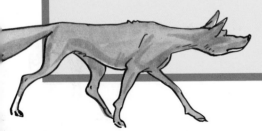

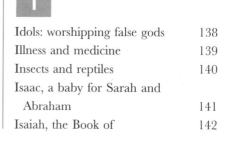

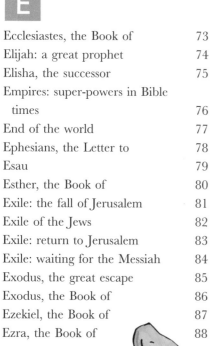

ABOUT THIS BOOK

This book is like a dictionary. All the subjects are in alphabetical order. This means that you don't have to start at the beginning: you can start anywhere, depending on what you want to read about. The title at the top of each page gives you the main subject for that page. You can find which page you need by looking in the contents pages, or in the index at the end of this book.

The Bible was written by many different people over a long period of time. This encyclopedia deals with four themes in the Bible. You can tell which theme you are reading about by the different colored boxes at the top of the page:

- Living in Bible Times (blue)
- People, Places and Events (green)
- The Bible (red)
- Teaching of the Bible (purple)

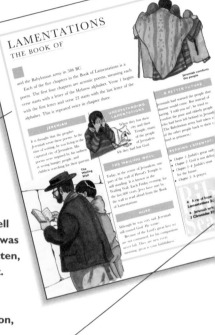

THE BIBLE

The pages on the Bible tell you about how the Bible was written, when it was written, and how to understand it. There is also a page for every book in the Bible, from Genesis to Revelation, so you can find out what each book is all about.

PEOPLE, PLACES AND EVENTS

In these pages you can read the whole story of the Bible, beginning with Adam, through to King David, Jesus and Paul. The pages are in alphabetical order, so you will need to follow the trail through the cross-references.

THE BIBLE

There are 66 books in the Bible. This may seem like a lot of pages, but there is an easy system for finding your way around:

- Each Bible book is split up into chapters, and each chapter has a number. Exodus 1 means the first chapter of the Book of Exodus. Usually these numbers are set at the top of each page in your Bible.
- Each chapter is split up into short sections of one or two lines. These are called verses. Verses also have numbers. The verse numbers are the small numbers on each page. So Exodus 1:12 means verse 12 of chapter 1 of the Book of Exodus.

BC refers to all the years before Jesus was born: 500 BC means 500 years before Jesus was born. AD refers to all the years after Jesus was born. All the dates of events in the Old Testament are 'BC'; all the dates in the New Testament are 'AD'.

How did people cook?

What sort of shoes did people wear?

What did a synagogue look like?

These pages tell you about everyday life in Bible times.

Many people argue about what Bible teaching means. What does the Bible actually say about Jesus Christ; about telling lies; about what to do when you're scared; about angels; about heaven? Look up the headings, or look in the index to find out.

On many pages you will see the words 'See also' or 'To find out more'. By turning to the suggested pages, you can follow a story or a subject through the encyclopedia. For example, read about Moses, then turn to Plagues, and then to Exodus, and so on.

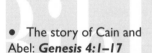

- The story of Cain and Abel: *Genesis 4:1–17*
- The way of Cain: *1 John 3:12*
- The way of Abel: *Hebrews 11:4*

When you read these pages you may think, 'Does the Bible really say that?' The best thing you can do is to find out for yourself! Most of the pages have a Bible Search so that you can look up the verses in your own Bible.

ANY QUESTIONS

These questions help you examine the text more closely, and to think about some of the Bible's teachings.

Enjoy the colorful, clearly drawn artwork–it shows you what people wore in Bible times, how they lived and traveled, and also what we think the different characters might have looked like.

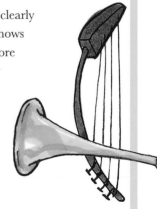

THE BIBLE LANDS

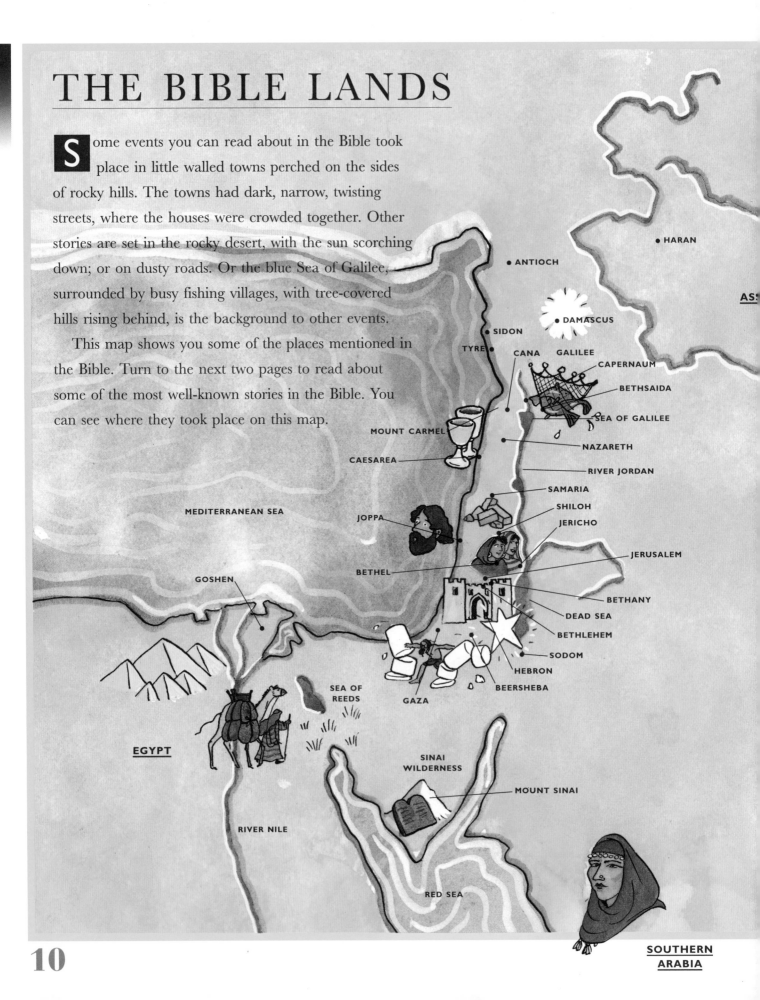

S ome events you can read about in the Bible took place in little walled towns perched on the sides of rocky hills. The towns had dark, narrow, twisting streets, where the houses were crowded together. Other stories are set in the rocky desert, with the sun scorching down; or on dusty roads. Or the blue Sea of Galilee, surrounded by busy fishing villages, with tree-covered hills rising behind, is the background to other events.

This map shows you some of the places mentioned in the Bible. Turn to the next two pages to read about some of the most well-known stories in the Bible. You can see where they took place on this map.

HARAN

ANTIOCH

AS⋮

DAMASCUS

SIDON

TYRE

CANA   GALILEE

CAPERNAUM

BETHSAIDA

SEA OF GALILEE

MOUNT CARMEL

NAZARETH

CAESAREA

RIVER JORDAN

SAMARIA

MEDITERRANEAN SEA

JOPPA

SHILOH

JERICHO

JERUSALEM

BETHEL

GOSHEN

BETHANY

DEAD SEA

BETHLEHEM

SODOM

HEBRON

BEERSHEBA

GAZA

SEA OF REEDS

EGYPT

SINAI WILDERNESS

MOUNT SINAI

RIVER NILE

RED SEA

SOUTHERN ARABIA

ARARAT MOUNTAINS

GREECE

TURKEY

ISRAEL

NORTH AFRICA

EGYPT

● NINEVEH

RIVER EUPHRATES

RIVER TIGRIS

BABYLON (BABEL)

BABYLONIA

UR ●

The story of the Bible is acted out in what we today call the Middle East. The Middle East has been described as the "seed-bed of the world". This is because it was in this part of the world that men and women first learned many important skills – such as writing, farming and metal-working.

THE OLD TESTAMENT TOP 20

Here are twenty of the best-known stories in the Old Testament. This list shows you the order in which they took place.

1 Creation. God makes the world. *Genesis 1*

2 The tower of Babel. The tower that pride built. *Genesis 11*

3 Adam and Eve. The first man and woman turn against God. *Genesis 2:1–3:24*

4 Noah's ark. The story of a flood and a floating zoo which ends up on the Ararat mountains. *Genesis 6:1–9:17*

5 Abraham and Isaac. Abraham's faith in God is put to the test. *Genesis 18:1–15; 21:1–7; 22:1–19*

6 Esau and Jacob. The twin brothers hate each other. Jacob ends up running away from Beersheba to Haran, and has a dream about angels. *Genesis 25:19–34; 27:1–28:22*

7 Joseph and his technicolor dreamcoat. The story of a family from the Hebron area: a father's favorite son and his jealous brothers. *Genesis 37; 39:1–47:31; 50:15–21*

8 Moses in the bulrushes. Miriam helps to save the life of her baby brother by the River Nile. *Exodus 2*

9 The Exodus. Moses saves the Israelites from the pharaoh's clutches. *Exodus 3:1–14:31*

10 The Ten Commandments. At Mount Sinai, God gives the people ten rules for living. *Exodus 19:1–20:21*

11 Joshua and the battle of Jericho. A surprising way to capture a city. *Joshua 2; 5:13–6:26*

12 Gideon. How 300 men beat thousands of desert fighters at the hill of Moreh. *Judges 6:1–7:24*

13 Samson and Delilah. Delilah makes Samson lose his great strength, and he is imprisoned in Gaza. *Judges 13–16*

14 Ruth. Ruth finds happiness and love when she goes to Bethlehem after she is widowed. *The Book of Ruth*

15 Samuel. One night at Shiloh, Samuel hears a voice calling his name. *1 Samuel 1; 3*

16 David and Goliath. "Kill me, and you'll win the war," roars the giant Samson at the army facing him. A shepherd boy steps forward. *1 Samuel 17*

17 Solomon. God gives Solomon the gift of wisdom. An Arabian queen comes to ask questions. *1 Kings 3:5–15; 10:1–13*

18 A blazing furnace. In Babylon, Shadrach, Meshach and Abednego will not bow down to a giant golden idol. The punishment is death by fire. *Daniel 3*

19 Daniel in the lions' den. In Babylon, Daniel's enemies fail to get rid of him. *Daniel 6*

20 Jonah. Jonah has a close encounter with a big fish in the sea near Joppa. *The Book of Jonah*

THE NEW TESTAMENT TOP 20

The stories in the New Testament took place after Jesus was born. The last four stories in this list are stories that Jesus himself told. Look at the map on pages 10 and 11. Can you find the places where these stories happened?

1 Christmas. The story of the angel and Mary, Jesus' birth in a stable in Bethlehem, the shepherds and the wise men. *Luke 2:1–20; Matthew 1:18–2:12*

2 Jesus as a boy. Jesus, aged twelve, goes missing in Jerusalem. *Luke 2:41–52*

3 Jesus is tempted. After Jesus is baptized, he spends 40 days in the wilderness, where the Devil tries to tempt him. *Luke 3:21–23; 4:1–13*

4 The wedding at Cana. The wedding guests drink all the wine before the party is over. *John 2:1–11*

5 The four friends. In Capernaum, four friends carry a sick man on a stretcher to be healed by Jesus. But the door is blocked by people. What can they do? *Mark 2:1–12*

6 Storm at sea. Jesus is asleep in a boat on the Sea of Galilee, when a violent storm blows up. *Mark 5:35–41*

7 Feeding of the 5,000. Near Bethsaida, a picnic that one boy will never forget. *John 6:1–15*

8 Jairus and his daughter. In Capernaum, Jairus' daughter becomes very ill and dies. Jairus rushes to find Jesus. *Luke 8:41–56*

9 Martha and Mary. What happens when two sisters invite Jesus for a meal at their house in Bethany. *Luke 10:38–42*

10 Zacchaeus up a tree. In Jericho, Zacchaeus can't see over the heads of the crowd. Then he has a bright idea. *Luke 19:1–10*

11 The Good Samaritan. A traveler is mugged on a mountain road from Jerusalem to Jericho, but nobody stops to help him. *Luke 10:25–37*

12 The lost son. Jesus' story of a son who left home in search of a good time. *Luke 15:11–32*

13 The lost sheep. A farmer with 100 sheep finds that one sheep is missing. *Luke 15:1–7*

14 The two houses. A man builds a house on sand. Another man builds a house on rock. Then the rains come. *Matthew 7:24–29*

15 Palm Sunday. Jesus rides into Jerusalem on a donkey. *Mark 11:1–11*

16 The Last Supper. Jesus eats his last meal in Jerusalem with his friends. It has to be in secret. *Mark 14:12–26*

17 Jesus is betrayed and killed. Judas gives Jesus away to his enemies. Jesus is put on trial, and crucified outside Jerusalem. *Luke 22:39–23:55*

18 Jesus rises again. The events of this exciting day start in a garden at dawn, in Jerusalem. *Luke 24:1–49*

19 Flames of fire. Jerusalem, the day the Christian Church began. *Acts 2:1–41*

20 Paul and the blinding light. Paul (who at that time was known as Saul) sets off from Jerusalem for Damascus, with plans to arrest every Christian. But Jesus has his own plans for Paul. *Acts 9:1–30*

AARON MIRIAM AND MOSES

Aaron was the brother of Miriam and Moses. The family lived in Egypt. Aaron and Miriam helped their brother Moses to lead the Israelite slaves out of Egypt. God chose Aaron to be the first priest of the Israelites. Miriam became a prophet.

Moses goes up Mount Sinai

A BASKET BOAT

The Israelites were treated as slaves by the Egyptian rulers. When Moses was a tiny baby, the pharaoh (king) ordered that all Israelite baby boys were to be put to death.

The family made a basket boat, put Moses in it, and hid it in the reeds by the River Nile. Miriam kept watch.

The pharaoh's daughter found the baby when she went to the river to bathe. Miriam left her hiding place and offered to find someone to look after the baby. The princess agreed and Miriam got her mother.

Moses was adopted by the princess, but thanks to Miriam's quick thinking, he was looked after by his mother. (Find out more on the page on Moses.)

ANY QUESTIONS
1 Why did the pharaoh order all Israelite baby boys to be put to death?
2 Why was Moses furious when he found the golden calf?

GIFT OF GAB

One day, when Moses was grown up, God told him to gather the people and rescue them from Pharaoh's clutches. Moses was almost dumbstruck. "But Lord, I get tongue-tied," he said.

God said, "Aaron is a good speaker." Aaron became Moses' spokesman. Whenever Moses went to the people or to the pharaoh, Aaron was at his side.

God made Aaron the High Priest, or chief priest, of the Israelites.

UP THE MOUNTAIN

Eventually, Moses led the Israelites out of Egypt. They set up camp in the Sinai desert. Moses went up to the top of Mount Sinai to talk to God. He was gone for a long time, and the people said to Aaron, "Moses has gone. Make us a god to lead us."

"Bring me your gold jewelry," Aaron said. He melted it down and made a golden calf. "Here is your god," he said. The people danced and celebrated their new god.

Then Moses came back. He was furious.

On another occasion, Miriam and Aaron grew jealous of Moses and spoke against him. Miriam became ill as a result, but Moses prayed for her to be healed, and she was.

Moses is found by the princess

- A basket boat: *Exodus 2:1–10*

- The golden calf: *Exodus 32*

- Aaron and Miriam oppose Moses: *Numbers 12*

Bible Search

ABRAHAM THE FATHER OF THE JEWISH NATION

Abraham

A braham lived in the city of Ur. One day, God told Abraham to leave Ur and travel far away to the country of Canaan, where he would make him the father of a great nation. Abraham trusted God and decided to do what he said. Abraham set off with his wife, Sarah, and his nephew, Lot. Other relations, servants and animals went too.

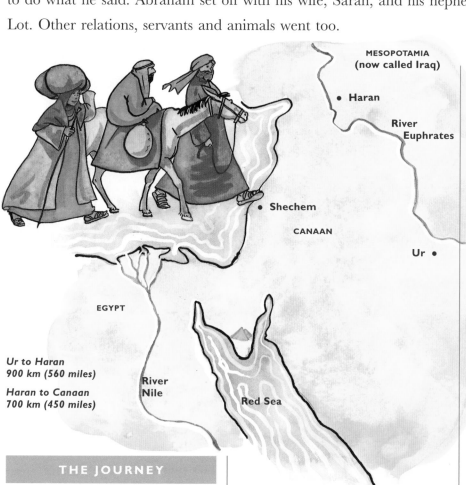

MESOPOTAMIA
(now called Iraq)

• Haran

River
Euphrates

• Shechem

CANAAN

Ur •

EGYPT

Ur to Haran
900 km (560 miles)

Haran to Canaan
700 km (450 miles)

River
Nile

Red Sea

A PROMISE

Abraham was to become the father, or founder, of the Jewish nation.

God told Abraham, "You will have as many descendants as stars in the sky." Abraham was surprised because he and Sarah were very old, and had no children. But soon Sarah did give birth to a son, called Isaac.

Bible Search

- Abraham leaves Ur:
Genesis 12:1–9

- A promise:
Genesis 13:16

- God's test:
Genesis 22:1–18

THE JOURNEY

Abraham and his people traveled for a long time, living in tents. Their first stop in Canaan was Shechem. Here God told Abraham, "I will give this land to you and your people."

God stopped Abraham from killing Isaac

ISAAC: A TEST

One day, God told Abraham to kill Isaac as a sacrifice, or offering, to God. It was a test to see if Abraham's faith in God was strong. Abraham was just about to kill his son when God said, "Stop!"

To find out more about Abraham, turn to the pages on Lot, Isaac and Sarah.

ACTS
OF THE APOSTLES

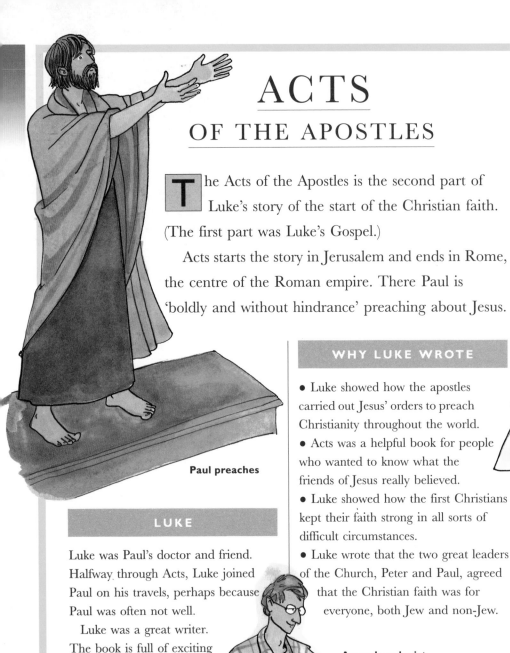

The Acts of the Apostles is the second part of Luke's story of the start of the Christian faith. (The first part was Luke's Gospel.)

Acts starts the story in Jerusalem and ends in Rome, the centre of the Roman empire. There Paul is 'boldly and without hindrance' preaching about Jesus.

Paul preaches

LUKE

Luke was Paul's doctor and friend. Halfway through Acts, Luke joined Paul on his travels, perhaps because Paul was often not well.

Luke was a great writer. The book is full of exciting stories and descriptions of the first Christians.

Archaeologists working in Bible lands have found items which have proved useful for checking Luke's story. Every time they have done this, they have discovered that the names and dates he gave are correct.

An archaeologist at work

WHY LUKE WROTE

• Luke showed how the apostles carried out Jesus' orders to preach Christianity throughout the world.
• Acts was a helpful book for people who wanted to know what the friends of Jesus really believed.
• Luke showed how the first Christians kept their faith strong in all sorts of difficult circumstances.
• Luke wrote that the two great leaders of the Church, Peter and Paul, agreed that the Christian faith was for everyone, both Jew and non-Jew.

Bible Search

• "You will be my witnesses": *Acts 1:8*
• Paul and Silas are put in prison: *Acts 16:16–34*
• Paul's sermon in Athens: *Acts 17:16–31*

Luke

THE ACTS OF THE HOLY SPIRIT

The Acts of the Apostles could also be called "The Acts of the Holy Spirit", because the book shows the Spirit in action. We see how the Spirit master-minded the spread of the good news of Jesus, through the first Christians.

READING ACTS

• *Chapter 1*: The Holy Spirit is received.
• *Chapter 2–7*: The good news in Jerusalem.
• *Chapter 8–12*: The good news spreads.
• *Chapter 13–21:26*: Paul's travels.
• *Chapter 21:27–28:31*: Paul is held prisoner.

ADAM AND EVE
FIRST MAN AND WOMAN

When God had made the Earth and its living creatures, he made a man. The man was called Adam. God didn't want Adam to be lonely, so he decided to make a partner for him. While Adam was asleep, God took one of his ribs and made it into a woman called Eve. Adam and Eve were both equally important to God. Neither Adam nor Eve wore clothes.

Adam and Eve were ashamed

Adam and Eve

THE GARDEN OF EDEN

Adam and Eve lived in the Garden of Eden, which was a beautiful place. The word *Eden* sounds like the Hebrew word *delight*. Eden was probably the land between the Tigris and Euphrates rivers, and the Garden, or park, was in the east.

GARDENERS

God put Adam and Eve in charge of looking after the Garden and all the animals.

God told them that they could eat from every tree in the Garden, except one. They must not eat fruit from the Tree of Knowledge (of good and evil), or they would die.

THE SERPENT

The Devil pretended to be a serpent, or snake. Slithering up to Eve, he told her that if she ate the forbidden fruit, she would be "like God", knowing good and evil. Tempted by the fruit and greedy for more power, Eve ate some. Then she gave fruit to Adam to eat too.

THE FALL

When they had eaten the fruit, Adam and Eve realized for the first time that they were naked, and they were ashamed. They stitched fig leaves together to make loincloths. When God came to the Garden, Adam and Eve hid. God saw that they had eaten from the Tree of Knowledge, and he threw them out of the Garden. They had 'fallen' from being perfect.

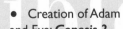

- Creation of Adam and Eve: *Genesis 2*
- The fall: *Genesis 3*

17

AMOS THE BOOK OF

A mos was a sheep-farmer from Tekoa, a small mountain village south of Jerusalem, in the southern kingdom of Judah.

Amos was sent by God to the northern kingdom of Israel, where he saw the wickedness of the rich people. He was angry and wanted everyone to know it.

THE FIERY MESSAGE

Amos had a lot to say:
- A builder uses a plumbline to make sure a wall is straight. Amos had a vision of God holding a plumbline against the crooked people.
- The rich people were rotten, like a basket of over-ripe fruit. Shopkeepers altered their scales. Judges took bribes.
- The rich lived in fine houses, with furniture made from costly wood and ivory. They had second homes in the country. They bought fine wines and rich foods.
- The poor were getting poorer. They had to sell their houses, and even sell themselves as slaves, to pay the money they owed.
- Religion was a sham. Most of the worshipers were thinking about making money, not about worshiping God. Some people were worshiping idols.

A rich woman

Some shopkeepers altered their scales

UNDERSTANDING AMOS

Amos shows us the goodness and greatness of God. God will not put up with selfish, greedy behavior and people who pretend to worship him.

Amos said, "Let justice flow like a river. Let goodness flow like a stream that never stops."

Amos prophesied that there would come a day when God would take action. It would be a day of doom, darkness and judgment.

READING AMOS

- *Chapter 1–2:* Judgement on the nations.
- *Chapter 3–6:* Three sermons on God's judgements.
- *Chapter 7:1–9:10:* Three visions.
- *Chapter 9:11–15:* Future hope for Israel.

A plumb-line

- Fat cows: ***Amos 4:1***
- Day of doom: ***Amos 4:2-3, 5:20***
- Rich living: ***Amos 3:15; 6:4-6***
- Plumb-line: ***Amos 7:7-8***
- Ripe fruit: ***Amos 8:1-6***

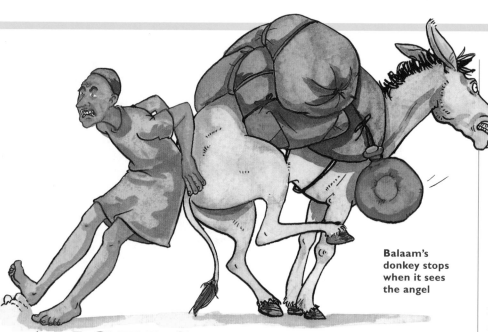

Balaam's donkey stops when it sees the angel

ANGELS GOD'S MESSENGERS

T he word angel comes from a Greek word meaning messenger. As far as we can tell, angels don't have wings! The angels who appeared in Jesus' tomb on Easter Sunday wore dazzling white clothes.

WHAT DO ANGELS DO?

- They pass on God's messages.
- They help God's people.
- They punish God's enemies.
- They explain God's plans.

DIFFERENT ANGELS

Gabriel
The angel Gabriel told Mary that Jesus was going to be born.

Michael
The archangel, or chief of the angels, was Michael. He was the commander in chief of God's army of angels.

Angels wore dazzling white clothes

Satan
Satan was an angel who decided to turn against God.

The angel of the Lord
This was the name given to an angel who often seemed to represent God himself. The angel of the Lord spoke to Moses out of a burning bush.

Guardian angels
Jesus said that children have their own angels.

TRAVELERS

Often angels were disguised as ordinary people. Abraham did not know that the three visitors, who came to tell him that he and his wife Sarah would have a baby, were angels.

BALAAM AND THE INVISIBLE ANGEL

Balaam was a fortune-teller. The king of the Moabites was frightened of the Israelites and sent for Balaam. He wanted him to put a curse on the Israelites so that the Moabites would be able to defeat them in battle.

When Balaam set off on his donkey, to travel to the king, the donkey stopped in the road. Balaam was furious. But the donkey had seen an angel holding a sword, blocking their way. Balaam couldn't see the angel, and beat the donkey. Then God made Balaam able to see the angel too. The angel said that the donkey had saved Balaam's life, because if it had continued on its way, the angel would have killed Balaam.

Bible Search

- Climbing a staircase: *Genesis 28:12*
- Cooking a meal: *1 Kings 19:5–7*
- In chariots of fire: *2 Kings 6:15–17*
- Passing on a battle plan: *Joshua 5:13–6:5*
- Helping Jesus: *Mark 1:13*

Guardian angels look after children

ANGER GOOD AND BAD

Jesus upsets the traders' tables at the Temple

Anger is a strong feeling that rises up inside us when something bad happens. Sometimes it's good to be angry. The Old Testament prophets were angry when the people disobeyed God, and so was Jesus.

It's wrong to be angry just because we can't get what we want, or if we want to hurt the person who made us angry.

Feeling angry

WHEN ANGER IS GOOD

Some children came to see Jesus, but the disciples tried to turn them away. Jesus was angry. "Let the children come to me," he said. We should be angry when we see innocent people treated unfairly, or when people get away with doing wrong.

USING ANGER

One day, Jesus went into the Temple, and saw that God's house of prayer had been turned into a market. He was very angry, and turned over the traders' tables and drove out the animals. Jesus used his anger to change things.

When we see something that is wrong, we too can try to put it right.

WHEN ANGER IS WRONG

Villagers send Jesus and the disciples away

Jesus sent his friends to a village in Samaria. "We don't want you here," the villagers said. James and John were angry. "Should we call fire down from heaven to kill these people?" they asked. But Jesus rebuked them, and said he had come to save people, not destroy them. Then he went to another town.

It's important to know how to deal with anger, in ourselves and in other people.

Bible Search

- David gets angry:
1 Samuel 25:1–13

- Abigail calms David:
1 Samuel 25: 14–35

- Jesus and children:
Mark 10:13–16

- Fire from heaven:
Luke 9:51–59

CALM DOWN

What should we do when someone is angry with us? The Bible gives some guidelines:
- Listen carefully. (See James 1:19.)
- Do something kind. (See Romans 12:20.)
- Reply gently. (See Proverbs 15:1.)
- Talk it over with other people. (See Matthew 18:15.)

Paul wrote: "Get rid of all bitterness and anger...be kind and tender-hearted to one another, and forgive one another as God has forgiven you..."

ANIMALS CARING FOR

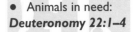

Many animals suffer at the hands of humans, often as the result of our greed. This is directly opposite to the teaching of the Bible.

Egg-laying hens are reared in cages, where they can't move. Animals are experimented on, to test cosmetics or household cleaners.

● Animals in need:
Deuteronomy 22:1–4

● Wild animals:
Leviticus 25:7

● Balaam's donkey:
Numbers 22:21–33

● New world:
Isaiah 11:6–9

Bible Search

ANY QUESTIONS

1 Why did God make Balaam's donkey able to speak?
2 What is unusual about a wolf living with a lamb?

BIBLE TEACHING

Jesus said that not even the tiniest sparrow died without God knowing about it. The Bible includes some rules which told people how to treat their animals:

● If a donkey falls down under its load, help it up, even if the donkey belongs to your enemy.

● Poor people and wild animals should be allowed to help themselves to food from fields and orchards.

AN ANGEL AND A DONKEY

Balaam was riding along the road on his donkey. Suddenly, an angel with a flaming sword appeared in front of him, blocking the way. Balaam could not see him, but his donkey could, and turned off the road into a field. Balaam beat the donkey in annoyance.

Twice more the angel appeared in the donkey's path, and the donkey stopped. Each time, Balaam beat it.

Then God made the donkey able to speak, and it asked Balaam: "What have I done to you? Why have you hit me?" Balaam replied furiously, "Because you disobeyed me."

Finally, God made Balaam able to see the angel. The angel told Balaam that the donkey had saved his life by moving out of the way.

The Bible said that a donkey must be helped if it fell

THE FUTURE

'The wolf will live with the lamb...'

The Bible pictures God's new world as a place where human beings and animals will live peacefully together.

'The leopard will lie down with the goat...'

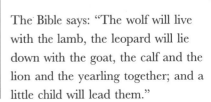

The Bible says: "The wolf will live with the lamb, the leopard will lie down with the goat, the calf and the lion and the yearling together; and a little child will lead them."

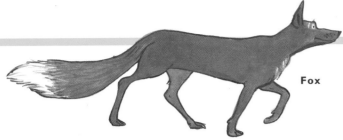
Fox

Rock hyrax

ANIMALS WILD

T he Bible refers to over seventy different animals: farm animals, working animals and wild animals. You can still see many of these in Israel today. Others, such as lions, bears and wild oxen, no longer live there.

Ibex

Lion

DOGS, FOXES AND JACKALS

In Palestine, dogs were despised. If you wanted to insult someone, you said, "You dog!"

Dogs ran wild and carried diseases because they hunted in piles of garbage for food. These wild dogs could be scared off with a stick.

Foxes hunted alone. Besides killing small animals, they spoiled crops by eating fruit and damaging grape vines.

Jackals hunted in packs, scavenging for scraps of food.

Dog

LIONS, LEOPARDS AND BEARS

Lions had short curly manes and were smaller than African lions. They killed sheep and sometimes people.

Leopards were feared even more than lions, as they seemed more intelligent and savage. Their spotted coats were a perfect camouflage.

Syrian brown bears roamed the hills of Israel.

The mountain goat, or ibex, lived in rocky mountainous areas. Males had large, backward-curving horns.

The rock hyrax, also known as cony or rock badger, was a small shy animal about the size of a rabbit. It lived in groups in holes on the mountainside. Powerful suction pads on its feet helped it to cling to the steepest rocks.

Gazelles were common. They were only 2 feet high and 3 feet long. Some girls were named Dorcas, meaning 'gazelle'.

Leopards

Bear

Bible Search

- Samson and 300 jackals:
Judges 15:4-5

- David kills a lion and bear:
1 Samuel 17:34-35

- Ibex and rock hyrax:
Psalm 104:18

- Mountain goat:
Job 39:1, 1 Samuel 24:2

ANIMALS FARM AND WORKING

People and animals lived and worked together. Animals were not usually kept as pets. In the New Testament, there is one reference to small dogs under a table, which could be pet dogs. And in the Old Testament, we can read about a pet lamb.

Donkey

ANIMAL TRAVEL

Today we have cars, but in Bible times, people used animals to travel around. Many families had a donkey. They could travel 19 miles a day. Kings rode on donkeys when they wanted to show that they came in peace.

Horses were only owned by kings and warriors.

Although they were bad-tempered and stubborn, camels were perfect for traveling in the desert. Their humps stored fat. They could go for a week without drinking, as each of their three stomachs held 13 pints of water. Long eyelashes protected their eyes from sand. The Arabian camel (a one-humped fast riding camel) could travel 160 miles in a day.

SHEEP

Sheep's wool was used to make warm clothes. Their skins were tanned for leather, and their horns were turned into musical instruments and jugs for oil. (To find out more, turn to the page on Shepherds.)

Lambs were important for sacrifices. You can read about this on the page on Sacrifices.

Horse and chariot

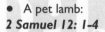

GOATS

Goats could eat twigs and leaves. This made them easier to keep than sheep, which only ate grass. Goats' strong black hair was woven into ropes and cloth for tents. Their skins were made into water-bottles.

Water-bottle

- A pet lamb:
2 Samuel 12: 1-4
- A journey with camels:
Genesis 24: 10-33
- Sheep and goats together:
Matthew 25: 31-33
- A market for animals:
John 2: 13-16

Bible Search

Sheep

CATTLE

Cattle were kept for their milk, meat and skins. Bulls, cows and especially oxen were used to pull wagons, plough fields and thresh grain.

Milking a cow

23

APOCRYPHA
BOOKS AND TEACHINGS

A Roman soldier

The "Apocrypha" is a group of Jewish books written to teach people to trust and serve God.

The Apocrypha were written after 300 B.C. During this time, the Greek army and then the Roman army conquered the Jews and their land.

A Greek soldier

A Greek translation of the Old Testament

THE APOCRYPHA

These books are not included in Jewish Hebrew Bibles. But they were in the Greek translation of the Old Testament. They are also in the Latin (Roman Catholic) translation of the Old Testament, since this was based on the Greek.

CHRISTIAN CHURCHES

The Roman Catholic and Eastern Orthodox churches think some of the books of the Apocrypha should be treated as equal to all the other Old Testament books. Some other Christians think that the Apocryphal books are helpful to read.

Judith fights for her country

Some or all of the following Apocryphal books are included in some Bibles:

1 and 2 Esdras ● Additions to the Old Testament Book of Ezra.
Tobit ● A story about blind Tobit who lived in Nineveh.
Judith ● A story about Judith, a Jewish girl who saved her country.
Additions to the Old Testament Book of Esther ● These include a dream, and some prayers.
The Wisdom of Solomon ● A book in praise of wisdom.

Ecclesiasticus ● A book of wise sayings.
Baruch ● Prayers and short sermons to help people to trust God in difficult times.
The Letter of Jeremiah ● An attack on idol worship.
Additions to the Old Testament Book of Daniel ● A hymn of praise sung by Shadrach, Meshach and Abednego and a prayer by Azariah.
Susanna ● Susanna was falsely accused of adultery.
Bel and the Dragon ● Two stories about Daniel.
The Prayer of Manasseh ● A beautiful prayer for forgiveness.
1 and 2 Maccabees ● History books about the Jews' brave fight against the Greeks who took over their land.

BABEL THE TOWER OF

People spoke in different languages

T he tower of Babel was never finished. Babel was an ancient city in Babylonia (the country now called Iraq). It is thought that the city of Babylon may have been built on the ruins of the city of Babel.

A TALL TALE

Hundreds of years after the Flood, Noah's descendants were living in the land of Babylonia. Everyone spoke the same language. The people decided to build a city with a tower that touched the sky. They thought it would make them famous. "If they do that," said God, "they will think they can do anything." So God turned their one language into many different languages. The half-built city became known as Babel, a word which sounded like a Hebrew word meaning "confused," or "babble." Now that nobody knew what anyone else was saying, they couldn't work together and finish building the city. People left Babel and God scattered them throughout the world.

God scattered people throughout the world

STAIRWAYS TO HEAVEN

The tower at Babel was probably an early type of ziggurat. The word *ziggurat* means "temple tower." A ziggurat was a gigantic man-made hill. It had a square base and sides like massive steps. Some ziggurats had five or seven steps, but most had three. Each step was joined to the next by a staircase. Ziggurats were solid, unlike pyramids, and at the top was a small temple.

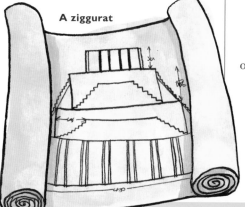

A ziggurat

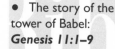

- The story of the tower of Babel: *Genesis 11:1–9*
- Building materials: *Genesis 11:3*
- The story of Noah: *Genesis 6, 7, 8, 9*

People left Babel

Traces have been found of over thirty ziggurats, all made from earth and brick. The king of the Babylonians, Nebuchadnezzar, had a ziggurat at Babylon. It was about 300 feet square at its base and 300 feet high. It had five steps.

BAPTISM ENTERING THE CHRISTIAN FAITH

The word baptism comes from a Greek word meaning to dip (in water). When you are baptized, water is put on your body as a sign to show you are made clean from sin. Before Jesus went back to heaven, he told his disciples, "Go and make disciples of all nations, baptizing them in the name of the Father and of the Son and of the Holy Spirit…"

Christians from all over the world

PETER'S SERMON

The apostle Peter's conclusion, at the end of his first sermon, was "Repent (turn away from your sins) and be baptized, every one of you… in the name of Jesus Christ for the forgiveness of your sins." Three thousand people became followers of Jesus that day, and were baptized.

A PRISON OFFICER

Paul and Silas had been beaten and thrown in prison for teaching Christianity. One day, there was an earthquake, and the prison doors flew open. But Paul and Silas didn't try to escape. The prison officer was so impressed with their courage that he asked if he could be a Christian. That night, he and all his family were baptized.

Bible Search

- Bronze basin:
  Exodus 30:17–21

- Jesus' words:
  Matthew 28:19–20

- Peter's first sermon:
  Acts 2:14–41

- In prison:
  Acts 16:16–34

After listening to Peter's sermon, many people wanted to be baptized

BAPTISM TODAY

Some people are baptized as babies. They have a few drops of water dabbed on their foreheads from a font (often a stone basin) in the church. Their parents make promises to God for them. When the baby has grown up, he or she makes the promises for him or herself. This second service is often called confirmation.

A baptism

ADULT BAPTISM

Some people say that baptism only makes sense if the person baptized understands what is happening, and so there is no point in being baptized as a baby. So instead, they often hold a church service to say thank you to God when a baby is born. Baptism only takes place later on, when a person has decided to follow Jesus.

In some churches, during an adult's baptism, the person's whole body is ducked beneath the water.

BEGGARS AND LEPERS

A beggar

There were no hospitals in Bible times, and no hostels, pensions, unemployment benefits or state aid. So people who were disabled, or too ill to work, had to beg. There were many beggars and lepers in Palestine in the time of Jesus.

HELP YOURSELF

The law said that it was the duty of every Jew to give money and food to beggars. Every farmer had to leave corn on the edges of his fields, and fruit on his trees, and poor people and beggars were allowed to help themselves. However, it was forbidden for the poor to take a sickle to the cornfields, or a basket to the orchards, probably so that they couldn't take too much!

Beggars were allowed to take food from farmers

Bible Search

- Old Testament lepers: *Leviticus 13:45–46*
- Jesus heals a leper: *Mark 1:40–44*
- Bartimaeus: *Mark 10:46–52*

BLIND BARTIMAEUS

Jesus was passing through Jericho when a voice in the crowd shouted out, "Son of David, have mercy on me!" It was a blind beggar called Bartimaeus, sitting by the roadside. "Be quiet!" people hissed at Bartimaeus, but Jesus stopped. Bartimaeus felt his way to Jesus. "What do you want me to do?" Jesus asked. "Teacher, I want to see," replied Bartimaeus. Jesus said, "Your faith has healed you," and Bartimaeus was able to see.

Bartimaeus

LEPROSY

In the Bible the word *leprosy* is used for a number of skin diseases. Many of the skin diseases could be cured, but real leprosy was incurable, and slowly killed the sufferer. Today, doctors know how to cure leprosy.

Leprosy was infectious, so lepers had to live apart from everybody else. They were allowed to live together in groups to help each other.

There were laws to make sure that everyone knew who had leprosy. Lepers had to:
- Tear their clothes.
- Leave their heads uncovered, and not brush their hair.
- Cover the lower part of their faces.
- Call "Unclean! Unclean!" whenever they saw anyone.

Lepers

BIBLE
THE BIBLE LIBRARY

The Bible is a library of books

There are many surprises in the Bible. The first surprise is that it's not one book, but a library of books. There are 66 books in the Bible.

More than 35 people wrote the books of the Bible. Some were wealthy and powerful, others were uneducated people with ordinary jobs. They wrote with God's help, about the things God had said and done.

TWO PARTS

The Bible is divided into two: the Old Testament and the New Testament. The Old Testament was written before Jesus was born; the New Testament after he was born. The Old Testament has 39 books, and the New Testament has 27 books.

THE OLD TESTAMENT

The word *Testament* means "agreement". The Old Testament is about God's agreement with the people of Israel. It shows his plan to save the world from the results of sin.

There are four groups of books in the Old Testament. These are: the Law, history, poetry and prophets.

• **Law**
The first five books are about the making of the world, the fall of the first man and woman into sin, and God's choice of a group of people descended from Abraham (the Israelites or people of Israel, later called the Jews). These books include the giving of the Ten Commandments.

The taste of knowledge

The Ten Command-ments

• **History**
Books that tell the story of God's chosen people.

The story of God's people

• **Poetry**
Songs, poetry, and wise sayings about the right way to live.

Songs from the Bible

• **Prophets**
The writings of the prophets or preachers. They gave God's message to the people and explained God's plan to send a rescuer who would save the people from sin.

ANY QUESTIONS
1 Which Bible books were written before Jesus was born?
2 How did these help people to live as God wanted?

THE NEW TESTAMENT

The New Testament was written after Jesus was born. It is about God's new agreement made with the people who trusted Jesus, the Christian Church. There are three groups of books in the New Testament:

● History
The first four books tell us about Jesus: his birth, life, death and raising from the dead. The Book of Acts is about the start of the Christian Church.

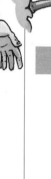

The story of Jesus unfolds in the New Testament

● Letters
21 books of the New Testament are letters. They were written by friends and followers of Jesus, to help Christians understand how to live with Jesus.

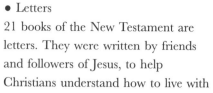

Friends and followers of Jesus wrote the New Testament

● Prophecies
The Book of Revelation contains some short letters addressed to churches in what is now Turkey. But most of Revelation is about the praise given to Jesus in heaven, and about future events at the end of the world.

Praising Jesus in heaven

SOME BIBLE WRITERS

MOSES A prince, then a shepherd.

DAVID A shepherd, then a musician, then a king.

AMOS A farmer, then a prophet, then a farmer again.

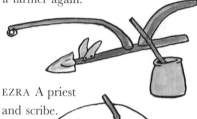

EZRA A priest and scribe.

MATTHEW A civil servant.

LUKE A doctor.

JOHN A fisherman.

PAUL A tentmaker and a Pharisee.

29

BIBLE TIME LINE

T he books of the Bible cover a period of between 1,500 and 2,000 years. In the Old Testament, the books are grouped by subject. (History, poetry and preaching books are all together.) On this time line, each book is placed near to the period of time it refers to.

Creation

Genesis

The Exodus

Entry into Canaan

Joseph

Exodus

Numbers

Leviticus

Deuteronomy

40 years in the wilderness

Joshua

Judges

Ruth

1 & 2 Kings

1 & 2 Samuel

David

Judah

The kingdom splits

Psalms
Proverbs
Song of Songs
Micah
Isaiah
Nahum
Zephaniah
Habakkuk
Jeremiah
Lamentations
Joel
Obadiah

Israel

1 & 2 Chronicles

Amos

Jonah

Hosea

The fall of Jerusalem

Luke

John

Exile in Babylonia
Ezekiel
Daniel
1st return from exile
Esther
Job
Ecclesiastes
Haggai
Zechariah

Mark

Matthew

Books of the Apocrypha

Samaria is destroyed

Temple rebuilt

Jesus is born

Acts

End of Old Testament

Jesus is killed

Malachi

Paul's letters

Nehemiah

Ezra

Other letters

Revelation

Jerusalem destroyed

KEY
Books of the Bible are underlined

(About 2000 B.C.) Abraham leaves Ur.

(About 1730 B.C.) Joseph goes to Egypt.

(About 1280 B.C.) The Exodus. Israelites spend 40 years in the wilderness

(About 1240 B.C.) Entry into Canaan.

(About 1011 B.C.) David crowned king.

(About 931 B.C.) The kingdom splits.

(760 B.C.) Amos

(760 B.C.) Jonah

(755 B.C.) Hosea

(742 B.C.) Micah

(722 B.C.) Samaria falls.

(587 B.C.) Fall of Jerusalem. Exile in Babylonia.

(586 B.C.) Obadiah

(About 538 B.C.) First return from exile. Rebuilding of Jerusalem.

(520 B.C.) Haggai

(460 B.C.) Malachi

(About 433 B.C.) End of the Old Testament.

(About 6 B.C.) Jesus is born.

(A.D. 33) Jesus is killed.

(A.D. 70) Jerusalem destroyed by the Romans.

BIBLE WHY READ IT?

T he Bible is a book that tells us about God and Jesus Christ. But many books do this. What's special about the Bible? Christians believe that the Bible is not just about God, but that God is speaking directly to us as we read his own words.

There are many books about God and Jesus

GOD-BREATHED

In the Bible, we see how God wants us to live. In a letter to his friend Timothy, Paul said, "All Scripture (the Bible) is God-breathed and is useful for teaching, rebuking, correcting and training…" The writers of the Bible were God's spokesmen. They were "inspired" by God to write the things God wanted them to write.

WORD PERFECT

In a letter to the Christians in Corinth, Paul wrote: "We speak not in words taught us by human wisdom, but in words taught by the Spirit." It wasn't just the ideas in the Bible that were inspired. Paul claimed that God enabled him to express those ideas in the clearest possible words.

HUMAN TYPEWRITERS?

Does this mean that the Bible writers were like God's robots? No! Each writer had his own way of writing and thinking, but all the ideas and words were true messages from God.

How do we know that the Bible is God's word to us? Turn to the pages on The Bible and Jesus, and How to Read the Bible.

Bible Search

- God-breathed: **2 Timothy 3:16**
- Words from the Holy Spirit: **1 Corinthians 2:13**
- Men guided by God: **Hebrews 1:1**
- Fishing: **Luke 5:4–7**
- The word of God: **1 Thessalonians 2:13**

FISHING

Jesus once told his friends to put out their fishing nets, and they would catch fish. Peter thought this was a silly thing to say, because he had fished all night in the same spot and caught nothing. But he did it, because Jesus had told him to. He hauled in a huge catch of fish.

In the same way, Christians should obey the teaching of the Bible because it comes from God himself. We can trust it and rely on it.

Fishing

BIBLE
AND JESUS

Many Christians believe that God's words in the Bible are still meant for us today. The Bible writers describe a God who never changes and whose laws and truths never change. Millions of Christians have discovered this for themselves. But the main reason for believing this is because Jesus himself taught that the Bible is God's word.

God is for the present as well as the past

OBEDIENCE

Jesus obeyed the teaching of the Old Testament. For example, after Jesus was baptized, he went into the wilderness. There the Devil tempted him to turn stones into bread. Jesus refused by quoting from the Old Testament, "Man does not live on bread alone, but on every word that comes from the mouth of God."

"Man does not live on bread alone."

PROPHECIES

Jesus' understanding of who he was came from the Old Testament. When Jesus was captured, a gang of men came to arrest him, carrying swords and clubs. Jesus said, "The Scriptures must be fulfilled."

After Jesus rose from the dead, he went to see his friends, and said, "Everything must be fulfilled that is written about me in the Law of Moses, the Prophets and the Psalms." (He referred to the whole Old Testament.)

Another time, Jesus said to his enemies, "The Scripture cannot be broken."

'The Scriptures must be fulfilled.'

NEW TESTAMENT

When Jesus was alive, the New Testament had not yet been written. So how did Jesus let us know that we could trust what is written in the New Testament? He did it by choosing twelve apostles.

APOSTLES

The Last Supper

Jesus chose twelve of his followers to be his apostles, to teach his message to the world. During his last supper with them, Jesus gave them a promise: 'The Holy Spirit will teach you all things and will remind you of everything I said…the Spirit of truth will guide you into all truth.'

Some parts of the Bible were written by apostles (including Paul), or by men who were close to them.

- In the wilderness:
Matthew 4:1–11
- Gethsemene:
Matthew 26:54
- Obeying the words of God:
Luke 24:44–47
- Eyewitness accounts:
1 John 1:1

Bible Search

BIBLE READING, PART ONE

Some Bibles are hard to understand

S ome Bibles are hard to read, because the language is old-fashioned. But today there are many new translations written in simple English. If you would like to read the Bible for yourself, try and get one of these Bibles. Choose a complete Bible, not a collection of Bible stories.

WHERE TO START?

There are sixty-six books in the Bible. Some are hard to understand. People who are learning to swim don't jump straight into the deep end of the swimming pool. They get in at the shallow end, and ask for help from a teacher.

In the same way, when you are starting to read the Bible, begin with a simple part. For example, start with the Gospel of Mark or Luke, and then go on to Paul's Letter to the Philippians.

Diving in at the deep end

TEACHERS

Struggling to understand

In the Book of Acts, there is a story about an important man from Ethiopia. He was struggling to understand the Book of Isaiah in the Old Testament.

A Christian man called Philip ran up to him. "Do you understand what you're reading?" Philip asked. "How can I understand, without a teacher?" the man replied. So Philip helped to explain it to him. We all need help when we read the Bible.

Philip helps the man to understand

READING

Many people find it helpful to use Bible reading notes. These notes give a short passage to read, and then explain what it means.

Some people like to read the Bible by themselves. Others would rather read it with their family or with other Christians. It doesn't matter which way you prefer to do it.

Reading the Bible with your family

GOD

Each time you read the Bible, and are thinking about what you've read, ask God to help you to understand it and to apply it to your life. Other people may help you to know what the Bible means, but God can speak through it to help us in our daily lives.

Bible Search

- The author: *2 Peter 1:21*
- God teaches his word: *Matthew 11:25–26*
- Teaching each other: *Colossians 3:16*
- Philip: *Acts 8:26–39*

BIBLE READING, PART TWO

The most important thing to remember when reading the Bible is that it is God's word, and God wants to speak to us through what we read. There are many different ways of reading the Bible. Here are some ideas.

We can pray to Jesus to ask for help in understanding the Bible

STEP 1

Pray. Ask Jesus to help you to understand the Bible.

Choose a book of the Bible to read (see the previous page). Usually it's better to start at the beginning of a Bible book, and read it through. It often helps in understanding a passage if you know what has come before it.

STEP 2

Most modern Bibles are split into sections with headings. Read one section and then stop. Read the next section another time.

Bible Search

- The seed: *Mark 4:1–20*
- A prayer for help: *Psalm 119:18*
- A person who loves to think about the Bible: *Psalm 1:2–3*

STEP 3

Ask yourself questions:
- *What is the point of this passage?*
- *Who or what is it about?*
- *Does it tell me anything about Jesus, God, the Bible or the Holy Spirit?*
- *Is there a promise to remember or a command to obey? Is there anything that will help me with a problem I have?*

PAUL IN CORINTH

Talk to God about what you have read, and ask him to help you remember it. You may want to tell God that you are sorry, or to thank him for something.

Is there anything you need to do, as a result of what you have read?

Is there anything I need to do?

A STORY

Jesus once told a story about the Bible. A farmer was sowing seed. Some fell on a path, and birds gobbled it up.

Some fell on rocky ground, where the roots couldn't grow and the sun dried up the young plants.

Some fell among weeds, which choked the growing plants.

And some fell on rich ground, where it grew and bore fruit.

The word of God is like that seed. The people who hear his word are like the different types of ground.

BIBLE
READING, PART THREE

Human nature doesn't change. God never changes. So it makes sense that the Bible should 'speak' to us today just as it did to people when it was written. But the Bible is not always easy to understand. Here are some points it's helpful to remember.

CUSTOMS

People's ways of living have changed since Bible times. For example, people wore sandals, and when they walked along dusty roads, their feet got very dirty. It was customary to wash a visitor's feet.

Jesus said, "You must wash one another's feet." Today, the message of these words is: "Don't be proud. Take care of your friends."

We should look after our friends

Bible Search

- A promise: *John 14:21*
- Foot-washing: *John 13:1–17*
- Meaningless: *Ecclesiastes 1:2*
- A jigsaw: *Matthew 7:7; John 14:14–15*

TYPES OF WRITING

There are many different types of writing in the Bible, which we read in different ways.

The first two chapters of Genesis are about the creation of the world, but they are more like poetry books than science books.

THE OLD TESTAMENT

We read the Old Testament because it teaches us about God, and helps us to understand why Jesus came. But there are many rules about food and behaviour that told the people of the time about God, but which don't apply to us today.

THE WHOLE BIBLE

A jigsaw puzzle

The teaching of the Bible fits together like a jigsaw puzzle. If you're stuck with something, keep going back to it. Something you read later on may give you a clue.

For example, Jesus said, "Ask and it will be given you." Does this mean we will get anything we want by asking, such as a hundred bars of chocolate? No! Jesus said in another place: "You may ask me for anything in my name and I will do it." He meant that we should ask in the way and for the reason that he would ask.

Asking for a hundred bars of chocolate

Pigs were considered unclean

ANY QUESTIONS

1 Name some Old Testament rules that we don't follow today?

2 How would you have welcomed a visitor to your house in Bible times?

BIBLE FACTS

T he Bible isn't like any other book in the world. This is because its writers were inspired by God. All the different writings give us a true picture of God, and of how he wants us to live. Without the Bible, we would know almost nothing about Jesus and his teaching.

The Bible isn't like any other book in the world

FACT FILE

- The Bible contains sixty-six books.
- It was written over a period of 1,500 years.
- Over thirty-five people wrote the books.
- The Old Testament was first written in Hebrew; the New Testament was first written in Greek.
- The Bible has sold more copies than any other book in the world.

The Bible was written by many different people

YEAST

One day, Jesus spoke about yeast. He said, "A woman took some yeast and mixed it with a lot of flour to make bread. All the flour rose."

God's word in the Bible is like that yeast. If we read it, think about it, and act on it, it changes our lives.

God's word is like yeast!

FINDING HELP

The Bible is not always easy to understand. But God has promised that the Holy Spirit will help us to understand it. A good place to begin is with the teaching and life of Jesus in the Gospels.

- Friends of Jesus: **John 15:14**
- Pray for enemies: **Matthew 5:44**
- Yeast: **Matthew 13:33**
- The Spirit as guide: **John 16:12–16**

HOW CAN THE BIBLE HELP ME?

Here's an example of how you can find help in the Bible. Suppose your best friend makes fun of you. You feel upset and lonely, and pray to Jesus. Then you remember:

- One of Jesus' best friends gave him away to his enemies. He knows how you feel.
- Jesus said, "You are my friends if you do what I say." You are not alone. Jesus is with you.
- Jesus said, "Pray for those who treat you badly." Pray for your friend, and decide not to gossip about it.

When your best friend makes fun of you

BIBLE
WHERE TO FIND HELP

Most people find that sometimes they feel scared, worried, lonely or ill. At times like these, God may seem far away. So Christians remember promises in the Bible, which help them to keep trusting God.

On this page are a few of the many verses or passages from the Bible that Christians have found helpful.

Needing guidance

ADVICE

When you need guidance, read:

Psalm 25:4–10: 'He guides the humble in what is right and teaches them his way.'

WRONG

When you've done something wrong, read:

• John 1:8–2:2: "If we confess our sins he is faithful and just and will forgive us our sins and cleanse us from all unrighteousness."

FEAR

When you are afraid, read:
• The story of Peter walking on the water. (Matthew 14:22–33)
• God's promise to Joshua: 'Be strong and courageous. Do not be terrified; do not be discouraged, for the Lord your God will be with you wherever you go.' (Joshua 1:9)

Peter walks on water

WORRY

When you are worried, read:
• Jesus' words to his friends in Matthew 6:25–34.
• Paul's words: "The Lord is near. Do not be anxious about anything, but in everything…with thanksgiving, present your requests to God." (Philippians 4:5–6)

Jesus used birds as an example in his sermon

ILLNESS

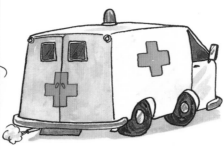

When you are ill, read:
Psalm 23: "The Lord is my shepherd…he makes me lie down in green pastures, he leads me beside still waters…even though I walk through the valley of the shadow of death I will fear no evil."

HAPPY OR SAD?

When you are happy, read:
Psalms 96 to 100.

When there is trouble, read:
Psalm 57 as a prayer.

Feeling happy

Bible Search

• Worried: *Psalm 55:22*
• Overworked: *Matthew 11:28–30*
• Something bad happens: *Romans 8:28*
• Bored: *Philippians 4:19*

BIBLE THE TRANSLATOR'S TASK

Hebrew

Aramaic

Greek

Speaking different languages

In Old Testament times, people spoke Hebrew. So the Old Testament was written in Hebrew. By the time of Jesus, everyone in Palestine spoke Aramaic. Palestine was part of the Roman empire, where most people understood Greek. So the New Testament was written in Greek.

THE TASK

Translating the Bible is very complex

The task of translating the Bible from Greek and Hebrew has four parts:
- To find out the exact meaning of the Hebrew and Greek used by the authors.
- To get as close as possible to the words of the authors.
- To put the original meaning into words which are easy to understand.
- To write in a way that is clear and pleasing to read.

AUTHOR'S WORDS

For hundreds of years, the Bible was copied out by hand. Great care was taken, but sometimes small mistakes were made. By comparing different old copies of Bible books, translators are almost always able to decide what the authors originally wrote.

EXAMPLE

We end the Lord's Prayer with the words: 'For thine is the kingdom, the power and the glory, for ever and ever. Amen'. These words are not in modern translations of the Bible, because they do not appear in the earliest copies of Matthew's Gospel. We think they were added at a later date by a monk. They were probably his comment in the margin, and got included by mistake!

A monk copies out the Bible

MEANINGS

Nobody speaks ancient Greek and ancient Hebrew now. To find out the meaning of the words, translators compare them with similar words elsewhere in the Bible and in non-biblical writings.

Here is an example. Paul sometimes uses the Greek word *ataktos*. About a hundred years ago, a large number of ancient scrolls were found, written in New Testament Greek. In these scrolls, *ataktos* meant 'playing truant from school'. So we know that Paul meant 'idle'. (See the next page to find out more about translations.)

Ataktos

- Idle: *1 Thessalonians 5:14*
- Jesus spoke Aramaic: *Mark 5:41*
- Lord's Prayer: *Matthew 6:9–13*

BIBLE
TRANSLATIONS

The Bible has been translated into more than 1,900 languages

Ninety years ago, parts of the Bible had been translated into 517 different languages. Today, the number stands at over 1,900 languages (with over 4,000 languages still waiting for translations!) Even when the Bible has already been translated into a language, new translations continue to be needed.

WORD INTO WORD

New words are continually being added to the English language, while old words die out or change their meaning. The way we write our sentences also changes. For these reasons, we keep on needing new translations of the Bible.

Translators have to make sure they don't change the meaning of the original. They must not leave anything out, or add any ideas.

AN EXAMPLE

In the Lord's Prayer we say, "Forgive us our trespasses..." This version of the Lord's Prayer is taken from the Authorised (King James) Version of the Bible written in 1611. In those days, 'to trespass' meant 'to do wrong things'. Today it usually means 'to go on land that doesn't belong to you'. So a modern Bible, such as the Good News Bible, has translated this as 'Forgive us the wrongs we have done'.

Bible Search

- The Lord's Prayer: *Matthew 6:9–13*
- Eternal life: *John 3:16*

An angry farmer

PRIVATE Keep out!

A NOSY TRANSLATION

In the Konkamba language of Ghana, the words "to have a nose" mean "to be alive." So how do you translate the Bible words "eternal life" into the Konkamba language?

The translators put "a nose which has no end!"

A nose which has no end!

TRANSLATIONS

Translations most suitable for children are:
- The Good News Bible, published by the Bible Society.
- The International Children's Bible, published by Nelson/Word.

Some Bible translations are especially for children

BIBLE DISCOVERIES
FROM OLD TESTAMENT TIMES

Egyptian paintings

Archaeology is the study of the past by digging up the remains of old civilizations. In the last two hundred years, amazing discoveries have been made. These help us to understand what it was like to live in Bible times, and sometimes also to help us to check the accuracy of Bible stories. (See also the pages on Digging and Dead Sea Scrolls.)

A SCHOOLBOY'S DISCOVERY

In the Book of Chronicles we read: "It was Hezekiah who blocked the upper outlet of the Gihon spring and channeled the water down to the west side of the City of David. He succeeded in everything he undertook." These words describe a remarkable piece of engineering.

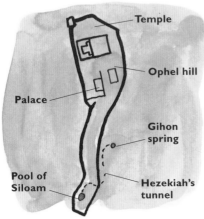

Temple
Ophel hill
Palace
Gihon spring
Pool of Siloam
Hezekiah's tunnel

The Gihon spring was outside the city of Jerusalem. Hezekiah's workmen built a 1680 foot tunnel from the spring to the Pool of Siloam, inside the city. In 1880 an Arab boy found this tunnel, by chance, when he was swimming in the Pool of Siloam.

On the wall of the tunnel are some Hebrew words written by the builders. They tell us how the tunnel was made. One gang of men worked from outside the city, and one gang worked from inside the city, hacking through solid rock with pickaxes. Amazingly, they met up in the middle.

Hezekiah's tunnel

Bible Search

- King Hezekiah:
  2 Chronicles 32:2–3, 30
- King Sennacherib:
  2 Kings 19:32–36

PAINTING AND WRITING

Paintings on the walls of tombs in Egypt show us how ancient Egyptians lived, worked and dressed.

From the writing on thousands of flat clay bricks (the libraries and records of ancient palaces), we know that the stories of Genesis are a remarkably accurate account of life three to four thousand years ago.

A CAGED BIRD

In the British Museum in London, you can see a hollow cylinder made from clay. It is covered with writing. It describes the victories of King Sennacherib of Assyria. He wrote: "I shut up Hezekiah in Jerusalem like a caged bird." Surprisingly, he does not add that he captured Jerusalem. The Bible tells us why. In answer to King Hezekiah's prayer, God sent a mysterious illness which killed 185,000 Assyrian soldiers outside the walls of Jerusalem. The rest went home!

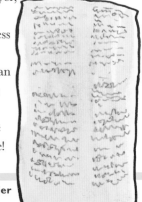

The hollow cylinder

BIBLE DISCOVERIES
FROM NEW TESTAMENT TIMES

We don't rely on archaeologists to prove that the Bible is true. Its most important teachings are spiritual. We find out from our own experience that Jesus is God, and that he rose from the dead. But by looking at archaeological evidence, it is interesting to see that the Bible writers recorded customs, names and dates accurately.

Archaeological discoveries

BURIALS

In the New Testament we read: "At the place where Jesus was crucified, there was a garden, and in the garden a new tomb in which no one had ever been laid." "Joseph placed it (the body of Jesus) in his own new tomb that he had cut out of the rock. He rolled a big stone in front of the entrance."

A tomb

ROCK TOMBS

Jerusalem was built on the top of a hill of limestone. There was very little soil, and few people were buried in the earth. So nearly all tombs were caves cut into the limestone rock by stonemasons. Luke said that Peter had to bend down before he could see into Jesus' tomb. The tombs discovered in Jerusalem have small, low entrances.

Tombs have been found with big boulders in front. These would have stopped wild animals getting into the tomb.

A GARDEN

Archaeologists have found that some of the tombs in Jerusalem have a flat area of ground outside. Rich people paid for a level area to be made in front of the tomb. This was turned into a garden for visiting relatives.

A RIOT

When Paul went to the Temple in Jerusalem, there was a riot. His enemies said, "He has brought Greeks into the Temple area." Archaeologists have found two notices carved in stone and written in Greek. They say: "No stranger may enter within the wall round the Temple enclosure. Whoever is caught is responsible for his death which will follow." The Roman soldiers saved Paul from being stoned to death.

Paul in the Temple

- Spiritual understanding: *I Corinthians 2:14*
- Peter bent down: *Luke 24:12*
- A big stone: *Matthew 27:60*
- A garden: *John 19:41–42*
- A riot: *Acts 21:28*

Bible Search

BIRDS
IN THE BIBLE

Israel has over 350 species of bird, although the Bible only mentions about fifty. People called many different types of bird by the same name, "sparrow."

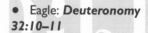

- Eagle: *Deuteronomy 32:10–11*
- Raven: *1 Kings 17:4*
- Holy Spirit like the dove: *John 1:32*
- Migrating birds: *Jeremiah 8:7*

Bible Search

Raven

SYMBOLIC BIRDS

In stories, the vulture often represented judgment. The powerful eagle swooping down to catch its young on its wings made people think of God's loving care. Owls were often used as a symbol of loneliness. Doves belong to the pigeon family. They are strong birds, able to fly long distances. They are gentle and loving, keeping one mate for life. Doves were the most important bird in the Bible. They were the only bird that could be offered as a sacrifice. A dove was God's symbol for the Holy Spirit.

WAITERS AND ALARM CLOCKS

The Hebrew word for raven means any large black bird. Ravens were once God's Elijah. bringing food to Elijah. Roosters were reliable alarm clocks in the morning.

Vulture

Owl

Cockerel

BIRDS ON HOLIDAY

Birds have highways in the air, just as we have highways on land. Israel lies under a busy air route for birds. Each autumn and spring, Israel is a resting place for many thousands of migrating birds.

BIRTH AND BABIES

Babies were thought of as a gift from God. The more you had the happier you were. But people thought that it was better to have baby boys than to have baby girls. When girls got married, they belonged to another family. But boys stayed with their parents and earned money. Parents felt they lived on through their sons.

A father and his son

BIRTH

Babies were born at home, with the help of a midwife. As soon as a baby was born it was washed, and rubbed with salt. The baby was wrapped in a cloth and then in strips of cloth. These were called swaddling clothes. Mothers thought that it made the baby's body grow strong and straight. When a baby boy was born, there was often a small party every night for a week. This was followed by a big party on the eighth day.

Salt

Party food

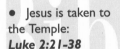

- Jesus is taken to the Temple: *Luke 2:21-38*
- John the Baptist is named: *Luke 1:59-66*
- Midwives who cared: *Exodus 1:15-21*

Bible Search

A party for a new baby

CIRCUMCISION

After eight days, every baby boy had a small piece of skin cut off from the end of his penis. This was a sign that he belonged to God and to God's people, the Jews. There was sometimes a small religious service to thank God for a baby girl.

NAMES

In Old Testament times, people thought your name had power over you. It was chosen carefully. By the time of the New Testament, a son was usually given his grandfather's name. He was also called "the son of" ("Ben" or "Bar") his father. There were no last names. Boys were probably named when they were circumcised.

PRESENTATION IN THE TEMPLE

The first boy to be born into a family was considered to belong to God. So when the baby was a month old, his parents went to the Temple to make an offering to God and 'buy back' the baby boy. They took two pigeons for a sacrifice, and paid five silver coins.

CAIN AND ABEL

The story of Adam and Eve shows how sin first came into the world, when they disobeyed God and ate the forbidden fruit. The story of their children, Cain and Abel, shows that sin was passed on. It became natural.

Cain was a farmer

Abel was a shepherd

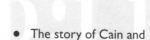

- The story of Cain and Abel: *Genesis 4:1–17*

- The way of Cain: *1 John 3:12*

- The way of Abel: *Hebrews 11:4*

MURDER: THE MOTIVE

Cain was a farmer, and his younger brother Abel was a shepherd. One day they both made offerings to God. Cain gave some of his crops, and Abel killed some of his finest lambs. God was pleased with Abel's offering, but took no notice of Cain's gift. Abel had given God the best, but Cain probably gave something he didn't really need. Cain was jealous.

Cain's offering

THE CRIME

Cain said to Abel, "Let's go out to the fields." While they were there, Cain attacked and murdered Abel. Cain did not murder his brother in a sudden fit of anger (which is bad enough) but commited premeditated murder!

Cain leaves home

ON TRIAL

When God asked Cain where Abel was, Cain lied and said he didn't know. He was insolent and said, "Am I my brother's keeper?" But God knew that Cain had murdered his brother. He told Cain his punishment was that he could no longer be a farmer. Nothing that he planted would grow. Instead, he had to leave home and live as a tramp.

Cain was filled with self-pity. He told God the punishment was heavier than he could bear, and that anyone who met him could kill him.

God put a "mark" on Cain to stop people from killing him. We are not told what this mark was.

CARPENTERS AND BUILDERS

Joseph teaches Jesus carpentry

Carpenters were important men in village life. They made and mended furniture, tools, stairs, chariots and door-posts. They also helped the local builder to put up the simple village houses. Before the Romans introduced benches, carpenters would sit on the ground to work outside their homes.

Jesus' father, Joseph, trained Jesus to be a carpenter.

A carpenter at work

TOOLS

Carpenters had a variety of tools. Axes were used for cutting down trees. Axe-heads were first made of bronze, and later of iron. The head was tied to a shaft. Trees were cut into logs with a saw.

To hammer things, a carpenter would probably use a stone. Nails were first made of bronze, and later of iron.

To bore a hole, a tool called an awl was used. Carpenters also had chisels and planes for shaping and smoothing wood. Builders used a plumbline to make sure a wall was straight.

Bible Search

- A carpenter at work: *Isaiah 44:13*
- A lost axe-head: *2 Kings 6:5–7*
- Foreign carpenters and stonemasons: *2 Samuel 5:11*
- Tearing up a roof to see Jesus: *Mark 2:4*

HOUSES

Village houses were usually made of mud bricks. To make a roof, a carpenter laid beams of wood across the top of a house, and filled the gaps with reeds or straw and mud.

Building a house

ANY QUESTIONS

1 How did a carpenter prepare wood for building a house?
2 What type of buildings were made from stone?

STONE BUILDINGS

Workers in stone made city walls, storage silos, wells, cisterns (pits for holding rainwater), arches, tunnels, and important buildings. It was hard, skilled work.

Splitting limestone

BUILDING WITH LIMESTONE

Large blocks of limestone were broken into smaller blocks. This is how it was done. A line of holes was chipped out with a chisel and hammer. Wooden pegs were stuck in the holes, and water was poured over the stone and wood. The wood soaked up the water, got larger, and broke the stone. The blocks of stone were then smoothed with a plane, so that they would fit together without mortar.

CHILDREN
IN THE BIBLE

In the Bible, children sometimes have important work to do to help God in his plan to rescue the world. Jesus showed children were as important to God as anyone else. He still welcomed them when his older followers wanted them to go off and play.

Jesus loved children

SAMUEL

Hannah and her husband Elkanah were sad. "Please, Lord, let me have a baby," Hannah prayed. "He can work full-time for you when he grows up."

Hannah prays

Samuel's birth was the happiest day of Hannah's life. When Samuel was old enough, Hannah took him to live with old Eli the priest, to help him in his work. One night, Samuel was woken by a voice. He thought it was Eli, but Eli said he'd been asleep. This happened three more times.

At last, Eli understood that the voice was God, calling Samuel. Eli said, "If you hear the voice again say, 'Speak, Lord, your servant is listening.'" Later that night, God gave Samuel a message for Eli. Samuel later became a great leader.

Samuel is woken by a voice

A SLAVE GIRL

Naaman and the slave girl

A young Israelite girl who was captured in battle was given to Naaman, the great Syrian general, as a slave. Naaman suffered from leprosy. When the girl saw this, she said, 'In my country there is a prophet called Elisha, who could heal Naaman.'

So Naaman set off for Israel, and went to Elisha's house. The prophet sent out a messenger to tell Naaman: "Wash seven times in the River Jordan." Naaman was annoyed that Elisha hadn't spoken to him in person, but he swallowed his pride and went to the river. There he ducked into the water seven times. And God healed him!

After that, Naaman worshiped God.

PAUL'S NEPHEW

When Paul was a prisoner, more than forty Jews swore that they would kill him. Paul's nephew, who was about twelve, heard of their plot. He told Paul, who sent him to see the governor. He was a brave boy, because Paul's enemies were dangerous men.

Paul's nephew overhears the plot

- Children welcomed: *Matthew 19:13–15*
- Samuel: *1 Samuel 1 and 3:1–21*
- Naaman: *2 Kings 5*
- Paul's nephew: *Acts 23:12–22*

Bible Search

CHRISTIAN LIFE: STARTING

The New Testament writers make it clear that there has to be a start to Christian life. No one is born a Christian. A human being can be very good. But a human being is not automatically a child of God. For that to happen, a new type of life is needed. And that new life is given, as a gift, when someone trusts Jesus.

No one is born a Christian

BORN AGAIN

John wrote: "To all who receive him (Jesus), to those who believed in his name, he gave the right to become children of God…" And Jesus said, "No one can enter the kingdom of God unless he is born again…the Spirit gives birth to the Spirit."

FINDING THE WAY

It may happen in this way. Let's look at what happens to a boy called Michael.
- Michael believes Jesus is the son of God, who died to set him free.
- Michael sees that compared with Jesus, things in his life are wrong, pointless, empty, or second-rate.
- Michael tells Jesus he is sorry. He asks Jesus to be his friend, and to take charge of his life. From now on he is "under new management."

Bible Search

- A promise: *John 6:37*
- New birth: *John 1:12; 3:3–6*
- Life at its best: *John 10:10*
- Zacchaeus: *Luke 19:8–9*
- Trusting: *Ephesians 2:8–9*

Michael

A TURN-AROUND

Sometimes when people become Christians, we say they have converted to Christianity. It happens in different ways:

- Paul saw Jesus in a blinding light on the road to Damascus, and stopped attacking Christians.
- Zacchaeus had a meal with Jesus, and stopped stealing money.

Zacchaeus and Jesus

- Timothy learned about Jesus when he was little.

Some people will tell you the exact hour they became Christians. Some people cannot remember when or how the change came. This doesn't matter. What is important is that they can say, "Now I trust Jesus." Jesus said, "Whoever comes to me I will never turn away."

47

CHRISTIAN LIFE: LIVING

Religion was a burden to most people in the time of Jesus. It was made up of hundreds of rules. That's why Jesus said, "Come to me, all you who are weary… and I will give you rest… for my burden is light."

The way of life Jesus offers is not an easy option. But Jesus helps us. "The load with my help is light," he said.

With Jesus your load is lightened

WHAT JESUS WANTS

Jesus said to his followers, "If anyone would follow me, he must deny himself and take up his cross and follow me." This means doing what Jesus wants, not what we want.

Jesus said, "Suppose a man wants to build a watchtower. First of all he works out the cost. If he starts to build, but has to give up because he runs out of money, everyone will make fun of him. In the same way, think before you decide to follow me. It's all or nothing. Are you ready for that?"

A man plans to build a watchtower

LIVING

How should a Christian live? Here are some pointers:

- Praying. This is how we keep in touch with Jesus.

- Bible reading. This is how we find out more about Jesus.

- Loving. Christians are meant to live in the love of God, wanting God's best for other people.

- Do not quit. Sometimes, we fail Jesus. We have to pick ourselves up, repent and keep on going (see the page on Temptation).

- Witnessing. (See next page.)

JESUS WITH ME

Question: How can Jesus be with me? I can't see him!

Answer: The Holy Spirit is the power, love and presence of Jesus with us.

BELONGING

Christians belong to God's family. They can help each other. Above all, God has promised to take care of his children, who belong to his kingdom. (See the pages on Kingdom of God and Church.)

Bible Search

- Rest: *Matthew 11:28–29*

- A death blow: *Mark 8:34–35*

- A watchtower: *Luke 14:28–33*

- The Spirit of Jesus: *Galatians 5:25; John 16:7*

CHRISTIAN LIFE:
WITNESSING

O ne of the last things Jesus said to his friends was this: "You will receive power when the Holy Spirit comes on you; and you will be my witnesses in Jerusalem… and to the ends of the Earth." Jesus still wants Christians to be his witnesses. With the help of the Spirit of Jesus, we can let our friends see the love of Jesus.

We can stand up for Jesus

THE REASON WHY...

This is how Peter put it: "But you are…a people belonging to God that you may declare the praises of him who called you out of darkness into his marvelous light."

A LAMP

Jesus said, "You are the light of the world." No one lights a lamp and then hides it. "In the same way," Jesus said, 'let your light shine before men, that they may see your good deeds and praise your father in heaven."

- Witnesses: *Acts 1:8*
- Praising: *1 Peter 2:9*
- A lamp: *Matthew 5:14–16*
- Don't be ashamed: *Luke 9:26*
- Caring: *Luke 10:25–37*
- Forgiving: *Matthew 6:12*

Bible Search

WITNESSING

How do Christians give witness to Jesus? Here are some ideas:
- By speaking

This doesn't mean we have to go around preaching to people! But sometimes our friends may ask us questions about God, and we can try to answer them. Or we can talk to other Christians about the way Jesus has helped us. Sometimes, it might mean standing up for Jesus when he is laughed at. Jesus said, "Don't be ashamed of me."

We can say how Jesus has helped us

- **By caring**

- **By fighting wrong things**

- **By forgiving**

CHRISTIANS THE FIRST

The apostles tell everyone about Jesus

I t was exciting to be one of the first Christians, for you never knew what was going to happen next. In the Book of Acts, Luke described some of the events of those early days.

The apostles wanted everyone in Jerusalem to believe in Jesus. Every day, they went to the great outer courtyard of the Temple, where they told everyone who would listen that Jesus was alive.

HOMES

The Christians met in each other's homes. They prayed together and prepared meals, and the special 'Lord's Supper' which Jesus had told them to eat. The Christians shared everything: food, homes and money. Some of the richer people sold houses and land, and the money was given out to Christians with no money.

The people of Jerusalem liked and respected the early Christians, and more and more people became believers.

Bible Search

- Healing a beggar:
  Acts 3:1–10
- Sharing:
  Acts 2:42–47; 4:32–36
- Prison:
  Acts 5:17–42

MIRACLES

Some amazing healing miracles took place. Sick people were brought into the streets on mats, just so that Peter's shadow could fall on them.

Peter heals the sick

Peter healed a lame man outside the Temple, and then preached about Jesus. The Temple police put him in jail. The next day, the Temple leaders held an emergency meeting. "You must stop this preaching!" they said. But Peter insisted, "We cannot help speaking about what we have seen and heard."

The Temple leaders were worried

ESCAPE FROM PRISON

One night all the apostles were thrown in prison, but an angel set them free! The next morning, they went straight back to the Temple to see the Temple leaders. "We must obey God, not you!" Peter said. "You killed Jesus and God raised him from the dead. We saw it ourselves."

The leaders were horrified and said, "We must kill these men." But a Pharisee called Gamaliel said, "Leave the men alone. You might find yourselves fighting God." So Peter and the others were flogged and set free. The flogging was nasty, but the apostles were glad to suffer for Jesus.

Peter is flogged

CHRONICLES
THE FIRST AND
SECOND BOOKS

A Persian

The two books of Chronicles were at first one book. They were written during the time the country was ruled by the Persians. The Israelites no longer had a king, but they had been allowed to rebuild their Temple. The books cover the same period of time as the First and Second Books of Kings (plus a bit of 2 Samuel), but they were written with a different purpose.

The Israelites' ancestors

UNDERSTANDING CHRONICLES

The people were having a hard time as they tried to rebuild their lives in Judah. They wondered whether God still cared about them. The writer of Chronicles wanted to show that God still had a plan for his people.

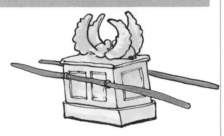

Hard times

He described how Temple worship had been set up by King David. He showed that God wanted his people to keep his laws, and would punish those who disobeyed. (The Babylonian army had captured Jerusalem because the people did not obey God.)

Chronicles looks mostly at events in the southern kingdom of Judah. But because many people from Israel settled in Judah at different times, Judah represented all God's people, and not just the two tribes of Benjamin and Judah.

THE ARK OF THE COVENANT

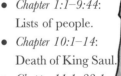

The Ark of the Covenant

The Ark of the Covenant was a special golden box which held the Ten Commandments. When David became the new king of the Israelites, the covenant box was brought into Jerusalem. David led the procession, singing with joy.

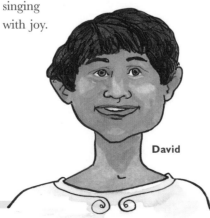

David

LISTS

The First Book of Chronicles begins with long lists of the Israelites' ancestors. This showed the people their links with the past. It also showed that the priests serving in Jerusalem were descended from Aaron, the first priest. These lists were written out by scribes. Scribes wrote down God's laws.

READING CHRONICLES

1 Chronicles
- *Chapter 1:1–9:44*: Lists of people.
- *Chapter 10:1–14*: Death of King Saul.
- *Chapter 11:1–22:1*: King David.
- *Chapter 22:2–29:30*: David's work for the Temple.

2 Chronicles
- *Chapter 1:1–9:31*: King Solomon.
- *Chapter 10:1–19*: The northern kingdom.
- *Chapter 11:1–36:14*: Kings of Judah.
- *Chapter 36:15–23*: Fall of Jerusalem.

CHURCH A FAMILY

'The Church" means all the people, all over the world, who are followers of Jesus Christ. The word *church* today also describes the building where Christians meet. In the New Testament, the word "church" means either a group of Christians in one place, or the complete number of believers.

A FAMILY

The Church is often called "a family". John wrote that each person who believes in Jesus becomes a child of God. God is their father, and other Christians are brothers and sisters. This stresses the loving care all Christians should have for each other.

DOCTRINE

Paul (then called Saul) was attacking Christians. Then he saw a great light in the sky and he heard Jesus say, "Why do you attack me?" So Paul understood that Jesus and Christians are closely united.

Paul compared Christianity to a body. Jesus was the head, and each Christian was a part of the body. Every single Christian has a different job to do in the Church, just as a hand, a foot and an eye have different jobs to do in a body.

If you catch flu, your whole body aches. When Christians are in trouble, Jesus (the head) and fellow Christians (the rest of the body) often feel the pain too and try to help.

Feeling ill

Bible Search

● The body, and its gifts:
Romans 12:1–8;
I Corinthians 12;
I Peter 4:10–11;
Ephesians 4:1–16

GIFTS

The Holy Spirit gives abilities to Christians so that they can help one another to know God better, and to show God's love in the world. In your church group, for example, you might find that each person is good at different things:

● Thinking up new ideas.

Thinking up new ideas

● Helping others to understand the Bible.
● Getting things done.
● Listening.
● Talking about Jesus.
All these, and more, are gifts of the Holy Spirit. No one has every gift! Each one is important.

Getting things done

God
made
us all
different

CHURCH ONE AND MANY

T he poet R. L. Stevenson once wrote:

'The world is so full of a number of things
I'm sure we should all be as happy as kings.'

God has made us all different. We should be glad about this.

Bible Search

- Love:
1 Corinthians 8:1–2

- Fan clubs:
1 Corinthians 1:10–17; 3:1–16

- Jesus' prayer:
John 17:20–23

DIFFERENCES

Some Christians like to worship God in a majestic cathedral. Others prefer a small, friendly group in someone's house. Such differences only become a problem when Christians start criticising each other, and saying their group is better than another.

Paul wrote that a Christian should not claim to know better than another Christian. He said, "Knowledge puffs up, but love builds up. The man who thinks he knows something does not yet…But the man who loves God is known by God."

People worship God in different places

PEOPLE

Christians should not be rivals

Some Christians are very impressed by a certain preacher, and start saying that preacher is better than the others.

This happened in Corinth. Paul wrote: "I appeal to you, brothers, that there may be no divisions among you…One of you says, 'I follow Paul', another, 'I follow Apollos', another, 'I follow Cephas'…" Paul said this was wrong, as all the men were servants of God, each with his own gifts and work. They were not rivals.

DOCTRINE

'Doctrine' means Christian teaching. Some Christians break away from other Christians, because they disagree about the way they understand the teaching of the Bible.

After his last supper, Jesus prayed for all the people who would one day believe in him. He said, 'May they be brought to complete unity, that the world may know you have sent me…' When Christians fight and argue, it gives non-Christians a bad idea of Christianity.

Christians fighting and arguing

TAIZÉ

At Taizé, a little village in the hills of Burgundy in France, thousands of Christians from all over the world meet together to pray, talk and study the Bible. All kinds of people, from bishops and nuns, to students and old people, from every kind of church, find there are no barriers between them.

53

CLOTHES FOR WOMEN, PRAYER AND THE RICH

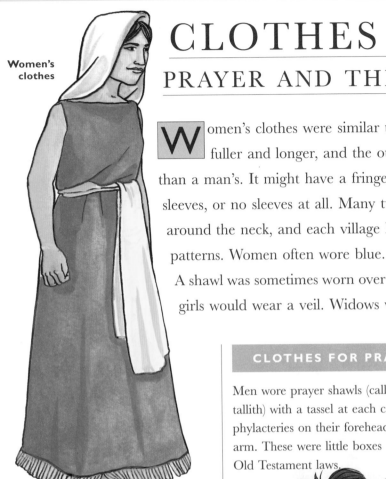

Women's clothes

Women's clothes were similar to men's. The inner garment was fuller and longer, and the outer tunic would be longer than a man's. It might have a fringe to cover the feet, pointed sleeves, or no sleeves at all. Many tunics had embroidery around the neck, and each village had its own special patterns. Women often wore blue.

A shawl was sometimes worn over the head. Unmarried girls would wear a veil. Widows wore a black veil.

An unmarried girl

RICH PEOPLE

The rich wore the same styles as the poor, but made of finer fabrics. Tunics might be made of linen or cotton, and cloaks out of silk. Cloaks often had tassels and blue ribbons at the corners, or fringes round the hem, to remind the wearer to obey God.

A rich person might wear leather shoes, instead of sandals, and a leather belt.

Headgear was elaborate, such as a turban with a fringe. Fine jewelry would be worn too.

CLOTHES FOR PRAYER

Men wore prayer shawls (called a tallith) with a tassel at each corner, and phylacteries on their forehead and left arm. These were little boxes containing Old Testament laws.

A phylactery

Some prophets, such as John the Baptist, wore one garment which was a cloak and tunic in one. It was made of woven camelhair, and was tied at the waist with a leather belt.

WASHING CLOTHES

Clothes were washed in running water in a stream. The water dislodged the dirt as it flowed through the material. Soap was made from sodium carbonate and fat or olive oil.

See also the pages on Soldiers, Priests, Pharisees, and Make-up.

Bible Search

- Fringes and tassels: *Numbers 15:38*
- John the Baptist's clothes: *Matthew 3:4*
- A runner: *2 Kings 4:29*
- A rich prize at a wedding: *Judges 14:12*

CLOTHES FOR MEN, CLOAKS AND ACCESSORIES

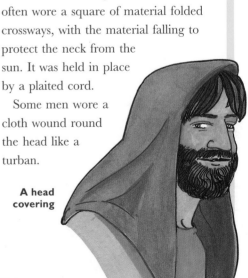

During the two thousand years covered by the Bible, the style of clothes changed very little.

The Jews loved nice clothes, dyed in bright colors. Vertical stripes were popular. Most people wore woolen clothes, or hair-cloth if they were poor, but rich people wore linen or silk. Many people had 'best clothes' as well as everyday clothes. The finest clothes were white.

MEN'S CLOTHES

New tunics were sold without an opening for the head

A man would wear an inner tunic, and another tunic on top. New tunics were sold without an opening for the head, to show that no one had worn them.

In Jesus' time, big looms were invented which allowed tunics to be made in one piece, without any seams.

Belts were made out of a long piece of cloth folded in half and wrapped two or three times round the waist. The folds made a good pocket. At work a man tucked his tunic into his belt, so he could move more easily.

Bible Search

- Jesus' tunic: *John 19:23–24*
- A runner tucks in his cloak: *2 Kings 4:29*
- Don't keep a man's cloak overnight: *Exodus 22:26–27*

CLOAKS

A cloak was used as an overcoat, blanket, and saddle cloth. For most people, a cloak lasted their lifetime. It was their most valuable piece of clothing: without it, people felt they weren't properly dressed.

A working man's cloak was made from two thick woolen blankets sewn at the shoulders, or it might be one large square of cloth with holes for his arms and head.

At night, people took off their belts and slept in their tunics, with their cloak for a blanket.

HEAD TO FOOT

People wore simple sandals, made of a leather base tied to the foot with a thong. These were taken off indoors.

For head coverings, men and women often wore a square of material folded crossways, with the material falling to protect the neck from the sun. It was held in place by a plaited cord.

Some men wore a cloth wound round the head like a turban.

A head covering

COLOSSIANS
THE LETTER TO

Paul's letters

T he apostle Paul wrote to the Christians at Colosse when he was in prison in Rome. Colosse was a town in Asia Minor (now called Turkey). The Christians at Colosse had only recently become Christians. It was difficult for them to get guidance on the Christian faith. At that time, the New Testament had not been written. Paul wrote to give advice.

THE FALSE TEACHERS

False teachers had arrived in Colosse. They had very odd ideas about how to be a good Christian. They told the Christians to worship angels, keep Jewish laws, and follow strict rules about eating and which days were kept as holy. The false teachers told the Christians that if they did all these things, they would be better than ordinary Christians.

But Paul told the Colossians: "In Christ are hidden all the treasures of wisdom and knowledge. You don't need to have special experiences or knowledge. Jesus is all you need."

False teachers spread wrong ideas

The false teachers followed strict rules about eating

UNDERSTANDING COLOSSIANS

Paul wrote to tell the Colossians about real Christian beliefs. He explained the incredible greatness of Jesus. Paul said Jesus was the visible image of the invisible God, who made everything in the universe, and who was the head of the Church.

READING COLOSSIANS

- *Chapter 1:1–14*: Paul's hello.
- *Chapter 1:15–23*: The importance of Jesus.
- *Chapter 1:24–2:7*: Paul's work.
- *Chapter 2:8–23*: Free from bad rules.
- *Chapter 3:1–4:6*: Living in God's way.
- *Chapter 4:7–18*: Paul's goodbye.

NEW LIVES

Paul told the Colossians to show by the way they lived that Jesus had changed their lives. He said, "Clothe yourselves with compassion, kindness, humility, gentleness and patience...Forgive as the Lord forgave you. And over all these virtues put on love."

Paul said, 'Clothe yourselves with compassion...'

Paul gave advice on how to deal with arguments. He said, "Let the peace of Christ rule in your hearts."

Paul also said, "Let the word of Christ dwell in you richly." He meant that once you knew the teachings of Jesus, these would guide you in your actions.

CORINTHIANS
THE FIRST LETTER TO

Paul's first letter to the Corinthians has been called "the problem letter," because he dealt with one problem after another. The answers he gives are also helpful for the Christian churches of today, and the problems they face.

PAUL IN CORINTH

Corinth was one of the main towns in Greece. It was a busy, rich seaport, and a center for business and arts. The people of Corinth followed many different religions.

Paul traveled to many countries to spread the news about Jesus. He went to Corinth on his second missionary journey. He stayed there for eighteen months.

While he was there, God said to him, "Do not be afraid; keep on speaking, do not be silent. For I am with you, and no one is going to attack and harm you."

Paul wrote his letter to the Christians in Corinth about five years later, from Ephesus.

Corinth

UNDERSTANDING I CORINTHIANS

The Christians in Corinth were very enthusiastic, but not very good at living a Christian life. Paul wrote to answer some of the problems they faced.

Paul said that rival groups should be united

PROBLEMS

• Some people were forming rival groups, following different apostles. Paul said this was wrong and that they should be united.

• Some people were showing off. They said things like "I can heal," "I can do miracles," "I'm better than you." Paul said that the Church was like a human body. In a body all the parts were important, had their own work to do, and needed each other.

Like a body, all parts of the church are important

• Some people didn't believe that they would live on after death. Paul said that God brought Jesus back to life, and if he lived again, Christians would too.

READING CORINTHIANS

• *Chapter 1–4*: Splits in the Church.
• *Chapter 5–10*: Problems about relationships and behavior.
• *Chapter 11–14*: Christian worship.
• *Chapter 13*: True love.
• *Chapter 15*: Life after death.
• *Chapter 16*: Paul's goodbye.

CORINTHIANS
THE SECOND LETTER TO

At the start of this letter to the Christians in Corinth, Paul wrote: "Let us give thanks to God… he helps us in all our troubles." This letter shows that Paul knew all about dealing with troubles, and the help God gives.

UNDERSTANDING 2 CORINTHIANS

After Paul had written his first letter to Corinth, false teachers had come to the town. They told people that Paul was proud, a thief, and not to be trusted. They said he had broken his promise to visit Corinth again.

Paul wrote to make sure that the Christians kept their faith in Jesus. He wanted them to know that they could trust what he said.

False teachers said bad things about Paul

SUFFERING

Paul said, "In everything we do, we show we are God's servants by patiently enduring troubles…" Paul himself endured prison, floggings, beatings and shipwrecks. He was mobbed, overworked, and often went without food and sleep. In his letter, Paul asked whether any of the false teachers could say they had experienced as many problems.

Flogging

Prison

Beatings

Shipwreck

Bible Search

- Sufferings:
2 Corinthians 6:3–10; 11:23–27
- Escape in a basket:
2 Corinthians 11:32–33
- A vision of heaven:
2 Corinthians 12:1–7

CLAY POTS

Clay pots are easily broken

The false teachers said Paul could not be trusted, but he refused to let it get him down. "We're like clay pots which can easily be broken," Paul said. "But we have God's treasure inside us, so we don't give up." God's power could be seen shining through Paul's weakness.

GIVE IT AWAY

The Christians in Jerusalem were poor. To help them, Paul collected money from rich Christians in other parts of the world. Paul's letter contains a lot of teaching about giving money. Paul said:
- "Give generously."
- "Give cheerfully."
- "Give because of the example of Jesus. He was rich but became poor for you."

Paul collects money to help poorer Christians

READING 2 CORINTHIANS

- *Chapter 1–7*: Paul's work for Jesus.
- *Chapter 8–9*: Giving.
- *Chapter 10–13*: Paul defends himself.

CORNELIUS
SHOWS CHRIST IS FOR ALL PEOPLE

Cornelius was a Roman officer living in Caesarea, where he was in charge of a hundred soldiers. He was a good man, who prayed regularly and helped anybody in need. One day, an angel came to Cornelius and said, "God has heard your prayers and seen your good deeds. Now, send some men to Joppa to find Peter."

Cornelius

THE HOLY SPIRIT

The next day, Peter went to Cornelius' house. He began to preach to Cornelius, his family and friends, about Jesus. Then the Holy Spirit filled the house, and all the Romans began to praise Jesus. The Jews with Peter were amazed, because the Holy Spirit had come to people who weren't Jewish. Peter baptized Cornelius and all his family.

The Romans praise Jesus

DOUBLE VISION

Peter was praying when he saw a large sheet, tied at the four corners, coming down from the sky. Inside were all sorts of animals, reptiles and birds.

A voice said, "Kill them and eat." "But I can't," protested Peter. "Some are unclean." (Foods forbidden to the Jews were known as "unclean.") The voice replied, "Do not call something unclean when God calls it clean."

Peter saw the vision twice more, before Cornelius' men arrived.

VISITORS

The Holy Spirit said to Peter, "These men are looking for you. I've sent them." Then Peter understood the vision. Until then, like all Jews, Peter had thought that non-Jews were 'unclean'. A Jew wouldn't even go into the house of a non-Jew. Now God was changing all that. Peter welcomed the men into his house.

A TURNING POINT

That was a turning point in the life of the Church. Later on, Christians held a meeting in Jerusalem to talk about whether Gentiles (non-Jews) could be Christians. Peter said, 'God has shown me that all people, Jews and Gentiles, may be saved. All they need to do is believe in Jesus.'
(See also the pages on Stephen and Paul.)

Peter's vision

Bible Search

- The angel: *Acts 10:1–7*
- Peter's vision: *Acts 10:9–23*
- Peter visits Cornelius: *Acts 10:23–48*
- The council of Jerusalem: *Acts 15:1–35*

59

CREATION

Everything we make is made out of something else. But God made planet Earth, space, the stars and time out of nothing – just by speaking.

He made the Earth as a home for men and women and he put them in charge. At every stage God said that everything was good. It was all exactly as he wanted it. It was like watching plants grow.

God created every plant and creature

Looking at the planets

IN THE BEGINNING

How we think the world began affects everything else we think and do. In the Bible it explains this. It says God is very powerful. He knows what is best for us and we must obey and trust him. Earth is the home God gave us, and we must look after our planet.

The Bible also tells us that we need to respect one another as we are all made and loved by God. God sent Jesus to save the world he loves. We should be hopeful about the future.

WHAT HAPPENED WHEN

In the beginning of the story of the creation, there was a shapeless mass of energy called chaos. Then God created the world day by day:

Day One. God created light, and made day and night.

Day Two. God created the sky and air.

Day Three. God created land, sea, grass, plants and trees.

Day Four. God created the sun, moon and stars, and the seasons.

Day Five. God created birds and fish.

Day Six. God created animals, insects, reptiles and people.

Day Seven. God rested.

In one of the psalms it says that when we look at God's world, we want to worship him because it is so beautiful. 'Look at the sea, so big and wide, its creatures large and small cannot be counted.' (Psalm 95:5–6)

ANY QUESTIONS
1 What do scientists say about creation?
To find out more, look at the opposite page.
2 What difference does this make?

- The story of creation: **Genesis 1 and 2**

- God, the great creator: **Psalm 33:6–9; Isaiah 40:26; Nehemiah 9:6; Hebrews 11:3**

- What Jesus said: **John 3:16**

Bible Search

CREATION AND EVOLUTION

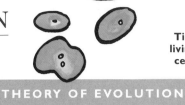

Tiny living cells

Christians discuss how the world was created

E volution is another way of looking at how the world was created. It is an idea that means that over billions of years we have evolved from tiny cells into human beings. Over the centuries, there have been many theories about how people were created.

The theory of evolution was developed in the last century by a man called Charles Darwin. Some Christians accept this idea and say that God used evolution to make the world, but others disagree. So Christians have many discussions about their different views.

THEORY OF EVOLUTION

The theory of evolution says that this is how living creatures developed. The first life on Earth was tiny living cells in the sea. As these cells reproduced, small changes appeared. All plants, animals and people came from these first cells. Over billions of years, they developed in different ways into different things.

FINDING OUT

If you pulled a TV to pieces, you might be able to find out how it works, but you will not find the man who made the TV inside it! This is a little like the way in which a scientist examines the world.

The scientist can try to find out how the world works. But he or she won't meet God by doing this. So the theory of evolution does not prove or disprove anything about God. You find God in a different way.

DIFFERENT VIEWS

● View One.
Some Christians say the theory of evolution goes against the teaching of the book of Genesis. They say that as the Bible does not tell lies, evolution must be a lie.
● View Two.
Other people say evolution proves that there is no God. It shows that the world came about by chance and that people are just like animals.

●View Three.
Some Christians believe that people have misunderstood Genesis chapter one. They say that Genesis is not a science textbook. It is more like a poetry book. Science can explain how the world was made. Genesis says who made the world. These Christians say that the seven days in which God created the world were not like our kind of days – they were very long periods of time, lasting billions of years.

How does a TV work?

CREED
WHAT A CHRISTIAN BELIEVES

Christians meet to work out a creed

A creed is a statement of what someone believes. One of the earliest Christian creeds was: "Jesus is Lord". Sometimes false teachers spread strange ideas about Jesus. So Christians met together to work out creeds, or statements of the Christian faith.

THE APOSTLES' CREED

This probably wasn't written by the apostles, but it does date back to the very early days of the Church, perhaps to the year A.D. 150. It is likely that the Apostles' Creed is a statement of the first Christians' beliefs.

The creed begins, "I believe in…" It is about the facts that Christians believe, but also about the trust they feel in God.

The Apostles' Creed

I believe in God, the Father almighty,
creator of heaven and Earth,

I believe in Jesus Christ, his only Son,
our Lord
He was conceived by the power of
the Holy Spirit
and born of the Virgin Mary.
He suffered under Pontius Pilate,
was crucified, died, and was buried.
He descended to the dead.
On the third day he rose again.
He ascended into heaven,
and is seated at the right hand of the Father.
He will come again to judge the living and
the dead.´

I believe in the Holy Spirit;
the holy Catholic Church,
the communion of saints,
the forgiveness of sins,
the resurrection of
the body,
and the life
everlasting.

Bible Search

- Paul: **Romans 10:9**
- Passing on what you know: **2 Timothy 1:13; 2:2**
- Jesus is Lord: **Acts 2:36**

WORD FOR WORD

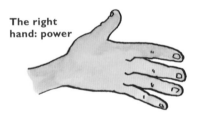

The right hand: power

These are the meanings of some of the words in the Apostles' Creed.
- Right hand: power
- Catholic: world-wide
- Communion: sharing in friendship
- Saints: all Christians

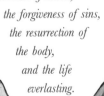

A creed unites Christians

CRIME AND PUNISHMENT

To commit a crime is to purposely act in a harmful way. There is crime against God, against people and against property. But for the Jews, all crime was a crime against God, because it broke his command: "Be holy, for I am holy."

The Old Testament gave all the laws that had to be kept. The Jews made rules to make sure justice was done. For example, when someone was accused of a crime, there had to be two eyewitnesses.

A stoning

PUNISHMENT

• Death penalty.
This was given for crimes including blasphemy (saying bad things about God), making idols, and adultery. The Jews usually stoned the guilty person to death.

Crucifixion was introduced by the Romans. In the time of Jesus, a death sentence could only be passed by the Romans.

• "An eye for an eye."
In Old Testament times, this meant that you could not do more to another person than he had done to you.

By the time of the New Testament, people normally made up for some offences by paying money to the victim. For example, if you left your well uncovered, and a donkey fell in it, you paid the animal's owner.

If a donkey fell in your well, you had to pay its owner

• Flogging.
The Jewish punishment of flogging, or whipping, was not as severe as a Roman flogging. The Romans' whips had lumps of lead or bone on them.

• Prisons.

In Old Testament times, prisons were not really used until after the Jews' exile in Babylonia (although enemies of the king were kept locked up). In New Testament times, prisons were common. People who got into debt were often sent to prison.

? **ANY QUESTIONS**
1 Why did the Jews believe all crimes were crimes against God?
2 Was 'an eye for an eye' a fair rule?

Bible Search

• Justice: *Exodus 23:6–8*
• Fines and payments: *Exodus 22:1–15*
• Stocks: *Jeremiah 20:2*
• Prison: *Jeremiah 32:2, Matthew 5:25, Acts 5:18*
• Flogging and stocks: *Acts 16:22–24*

COURTS

In Old Testament times, a court of law would be held outside, by the city gates. Cases were judged by the city elders.

In New Testament times, the Sanhedrin (a council of religious leaders in Jerusalem) was the main law court. Serious crimes against God were tried here. Smaller courts of law judged less important cases.

A court of law

DANIEL THE BOOK OF

Daniel

D aniel was probably a teenager when the armies of King Nebuchadnezzar marched into Jerusalem. He and his friends were taken as hostages to Babylon. There he was enrolled in a three-year training course to enter the service of the king. The book tells of some of his experiences and visions.

Bible Search

- A dream: *Daniel 2*
- Death by fire: *Daniel 3*
- Lions' den: *Daniel 6*
- Daniel's prayer: *Daniel 9*

UNDERSTANDING DANIEL

The Book of Daniel was written at a time when many Jews felt that evil was winning in the world, and that God had left them. The book shows that God triumphs over evil, and he never fails people who stand up for him.

READING DANIEL

- *Chapter 1–6*: Daniel at the Babylonian court.
- *Chapter 7–12*: Visions of future events. Some have come true; some will come true in the future.

A DREAM

"What does my dream mean?" King Nebuchadnezzar roared at his wise men. "Tell us the dream, and we'll tell you what it means" they said.

The king lost his temper. "Tell me both what the dream was, and what it means, or you'll be killed!" he bellowed.

Daniel prayed, and the next day he called out, "God has told me your dream." Daniel described the king's dream, and then told him its meaning. The king was so impressed that he put Daniel in charge of all the wise men.

DEATH BY FIRE

Daniel's friends Shadrach, Meshach and Abednego would not worship the great golden statue which King Nebuchadnezzar had made. The king was furious, and ordered the men to be burned in a furnace. He sat down to watch, but suddenly cried, "I can see four men walking around! Their God has sent an angel to save them."

The men came out of the fire completely unharmed.

King Nebuchadnezzar's wise men

DANIEL AND THE LIONS

When Daniel was an old man, the country was ruled by King Darius. Daniel's enemies plotted against him, and Daniel was thrown into a den of lions to be killed. But the lions did not eat him. King Darius realized that God had protected Daniel, so he made a law: everyone had to worship Daniel's God.

ANY QUESTIONS
1 Why did God save Daniel's three friends?
2 How did God help Daniel?

While David was out in the fields, Samuel visited his seven brothers

DAVID THE FAMOUS KING

More stories have been written about David than about any other person in the Bible, except Jesus. David was the greatest king his country had. He made the army strong, and beat the Philistines. He reorganized the government of the country. He also organized the worship of God.

AT THE PALACE

David joined King Saul's staff as an armour carrier. Sometimes he played the harp for Saul, to calm him when he was in a bad mood. David became close friends with Saul's son Jonathan, and married Michal, Saul's daughter. David was the best fighter in Saul's army. Saul began to grow jealous.

MICHAL

Michal realized David's life was in danger. She helped David to escape through a window. Then she put a statue in the bed, covered it with a sheet, and put goat's hair over its head.

That night, Saul sent his men to fetch David. Michal told them that David was ill. When the men saw what they thought was David, in bed, they went away.

Michal put a statue in David's bed

OUTLAW

David hid in the rocky desert with his men. Once, Saul and his soldiers stopped at the cave where David was hiding. They did not see David, and David had the chance to kill Saul.

When Saul left the cave, David shouted after him that he had just spared Saul, when he could have killed him. Saul realized that David was a great man.

Read more about David on the pages on Children and Queens.

- David's song of praise: *1 Chronicles 29:10–13*
- Kindness to Saul's son: *2 Samuel 9*
- David anointed king: *1 Samuel 16:1–13*
- A good king: *2 Samuel 8:15*

A SHEPHERD

David had seven elder brothers. God told Samuel that he had chosen one boy in the family to be the next king. So, one day Samuel went to Bethlehem to visit the brothers. David was still out in the fields with the sheep. Nobody thought he was important enough to meet Samuel.

God told Samuel that none of the brothers he had met was to be king. So Samuel asked to see David.

David was God's choice. Samuel anointed him and told the family that David would be the next king of Israel after Saul.

DEAD SEA SCROLLS

In Bible times, books were long rolls (called scrolls) of leather, parchment, or even thin copper. The Dead Sea Scrolls were found by chance in caves to the west of the Dead Sea. Over 500 scrolls and fragments of scrolls were discovered in eleven caves.

CAVES AND JARS

In 1946, a shepherd boy fell through a hole in the rocky cliffs by the Dead Sea. He found himself in a cave. All around him were clay jars, many broken by falling rocks. He looked inside them, hoping for gold. Instead he found a roll of leather, and two bundles wrapped in cloth. These turned out to be more precious than a hoard of gold. The bundles were the first of the Dead Sea Scrolls.

AN AMAZING FIND

Since then, archaeologists have found over 500 scrolls and fragments of scrolls in eleven caves.

The scrolls were written between 250 B.C. and A.D. 68. They were hidden in the caves when the Romans attacked Palestine in A.D. 68. These precious scrolls did not perish because the dry air of the caves, and the specially made pottery jars, kept them safe.

THE BIBLE

A hundred of the scrolls are books or parts of books of our Old Testament, all written in Hebrew. The most spectacular find was a huge leather scroll, 23 feet long, of the whole of the Book of Isaiah.

QUMRAN

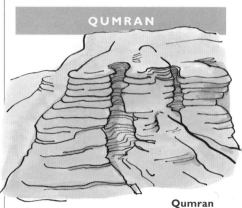

Qumran

Archaeologists have excavated a group of buildings at a place called Qumran, near to the caves where the scrolls were found. They found the room where the scrolls were written, and the place where the jars were made. They discovered that the scrolls were the library of a group of very religious Jews, probably called Essenes, who lived together at Qumran.

IMPORTANCE

The scrolls show us that our Old Testament books of the Bible have almost certainly not been changed since the days they were first written. The Isaiah scroll is a thousand years older than any other copy we have of the Book of Isaiah.

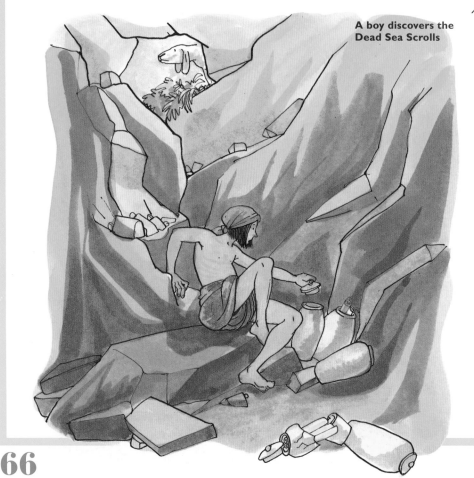

A boy discovers the Dead Sea Scrolls

A mummy

DEATH AND BURIAL

What happens to us when we die? The Egyptians believed that when kings, priests and rich people died, they traveled to a land ruled over by the god Osiris. In many tombs, a boat was laid by the coffin, for the journey. The Egyptians believed that the soul needed a body. So bodies were embalmed, or turned into mummies, to stop them rotting.

PALESTINE

A dead person was washed, and rubbed with sweet-smelling oils. Then the body was wrapped in white cloths. Jewish law said that burial had to take place within eight hours.

Relatives carried the body on a wooden frame to the place of burial. The procession was led by the women. People cried, put ash on their hair, and walked with bare feet. Sometimes they tore their clothes as a sign of grief. Even the poorest families paid for mourners to weep and wail, and had at least two flute players.

A funeral procession

Bible Search

- A family tomb: *Genesis 50:12–13*
- Burial of Jesus: *John 19:38–42*
- Dorcas dies: *Acts 9:36–39*

GRAVES

Only the poorest people were buried in public cemeteries. Most ordinary people had graves on their own land. Graves were quite shallow, and covered with a stone slab. This was whitewashed to remind people not to walk on it.

TOMBS

Some people were buried in caves, and rich families had tombs cut in rock. All the members of a family would be buried in the same tomb.

The entrance was small and low, and closed off with a large stone which was rolled into place. Inside, passages and stone stairs led from one cave to another. Each cave had stone ledges, or alcoves cut into the wall, where the bodies were placed. In some underground tombs, each small cave had its own door.

When a body had rotted away, the bones were put in a stone box called an ossuary, and placed in an alcove.

AFTER THE FUNERAL

There was a funeral meal, and up to thirty days of mourning. No work was done for the first three days. Very religious people didn't wash during this time.

67

DEATH AND KILLING

When, if ever, is it right to kill another person? This is an age-old question, but medical technology also raises some new problems. It is possible to find guidelines in the Bible, but Christians sometimes reach opposite conclusions from these. In that case, Christians must respect another person's sincerely-held opinion.

SOME PROBLEMS

- Should murderers be killed?

The death sentence?

- Do I have the right to end my own life?

Suicide?

- Should a fetus be aborted?
- If someone is kept alive in a hospital by a machine, when should that machine be turned off?

Should a machine be turned off?

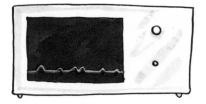

- Is war ever right?
- Should a dying person be helped to die?

BIBLE GUIDELINES

- Life is a gift from God, and should be treated with reverence.
- God is in control of life. Human beings should obey God's laws.
- Jesus gave us a deeper understanding of many Old Testament laws. He taught that love is the rule in life, not revenge.
- Weak people are to be protected.
- Death is part of someone's life; it is not the end.
- Jesus said to Peter, 'Put your sword back in its place. All who draw the sword will die by the sword.'

'Put your sword away.'

- People reflect God's nature: *Genesis 1:27*
- Do not murder: *Matthew 5:21*
- Strength from God: *Philippians 4:13*
- Put back your sword: *Matthew 26:52*

ABORTION

Abortion is an operation to terminate a woman's pregnancy at a very early stage, when the baby is still a tiny fetus. Abortion is always a very difficult decision.

Some Christians think that the Biblical guideline of protecting the weak, should always be applied here. Others believe that abortion is sometimes necessary, for example if the mother's life is in danger, or if the baby would be severely handicapped.

THE HOSPICE MOVEMENT

In recent years, the hospice movement has grown. In a hospice, people who are terminally ill spend their last days being cared for in gentle and loving way.

Care in a hospice

THE SAMARITANS

In 1953, Chad Varah, a clergyman, invited anyone who was considering suicide to phone him. This idea grew into an organization called the Samaritans. Today the Samaritans receive over two million calls a year.

Calling the Samaritans

DEUTERONOMY
THE BOOK OF

The Book of Deuteronomy takes the form of a series of talks by Moses, just before the Israelites set out to invade the Promised Land of Canaan. Moses went over the lessons they had all learned since leaving Egypt, and summed up the laws God had given them.

UNDERSTANDING DEUTERONOMY

Moses told the Israelites that if they kept all God's laws, everything would go well in the new land. If they forgot God's laws, they would suffer.

A thousand years later, when the people were taken off as prisoners into exile in Babylonia, they thought about these words, and were cheered. Although God had punished them by the exile, he would forgive them if they turned back to him.

PHYLACTERIES AND MEZUZAHS

Through Moses, God told the people not to forget his laws. He said, 'Tie them on your arms. Wear them on your foreheads. Write them on your doorposts.'

When they are praying, Jewish men wear two small black leather boxes, called phylacteries. One is strapped to the forehead, and one to the left arm. Inside the boxes are very small rolls of parchment with parts of God's laws written on them in special ink. The passages are: Exodus 13:1–10; 13:11–16; and Deuteronomy 6:4–9; 11:13–21.

On the doorposts of many Jewish homes today you can see a small box called a mezuzah. In this there is a rolled-up parchment, containing passages from the Book of Deuteronomy.

A mezuzah

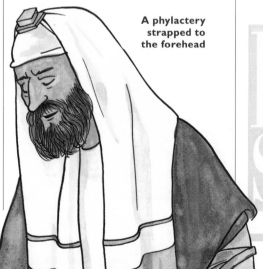

A phylactery strapped to the forehead

READING DEUTERONOMY

- *Chapter 1*: 1–4:43: Moses' first speech.
- *Chapter 4*: 44–26:19: Moses' second speech.
- *Chapter 27*: 1–30:20: Moses' third speech.
- *Chapter 31*: 1–29: Joshua is made leader.
- *Chapter 31*: 30–32:47: The song of Moses.
- *Chapter 32*: 48–34:12: Moses dies.

MOSES

Just before Moses died, God showed him the Promised Land of Canaan, and Moses knew that his work was done. Soon the Israelites would live in Canaan.

Moses told the Israelites not to worship false gods, but when they went into Canaan they were constantly tempted to worship the Canaanite gods.

A Canaanite temple

Bible Search

- A song of God's love: 32:10–14
- Chiseled in stone: 10:1–2

69

DEVIL THE ENEMY OF CHRISTIANITY

The Devil, or Satan, is the center point of evil in the world. After Jesus was baptized, he went off by himself into the desert. There he was tempted by the Devil. But Jesus didn't give in. The Devil doesn't have God's power. When Jesus was alive, he always conquered the Devil.

Jesus is tempted by the Devil

A BAD ANGEL

No one knows where the Devil came from. But the Bible seems to suggest that he was an angel who became jealous of God. He was thrown out of heaven, and now tries to get revenge.

A DEADLY ENEMY

The Devil is the enemy of Christianity:
• The Devil masterminded the death of Jesus.
• The Devil stops people believing in Jesus. "The god of this age has blinded the minds of unbelievers," said Paul.
• The Devil wants to destroy Christians. Peter wrote: "Your enemy the Devil prowls around like a roaring lion looking for someone to devour."

Bible Search

• The world: *John 15:18–19; 17:15*

• Armor: *Ephesians 6:10–18*

• Resist: *James 4:7*

• Jesus with us: *1 John 4:4*

• The Devil has many disguises. Jesus called the Devil "the father of lies". Paul tells us that the Devil could change himself to look like an angel of light!

One of the Devil's main tricks is to tempt people to do wrong, by making it seem right

Peter compared the Devil to a prowling lion

THE WORLD

The word *world* had another meaning in the Bible: it described all the people and organizations that didn't obey God. Jesus called the Devil the "prince of the world".

One day on the far shore of the Sea of Galilee, Jesus met a madman. The madman was so strong that he smashed the chains people put on him. He felt he had been taken over by evil spirits. Jesus healed him and said, "The prince of this world has no hold on me."

The madman broke the chains that were holding him

The Devil thought he had won when Jesus died. He didn't expect Jesus to rise again! Paul wrote that Jesus triumphed over the Devil by the cross.

Jesus rose from the dead

DIGGING UP THE PAST

Archaeology is the science of studying the remains of earlier times. By digging down into the remains of old cities, we can find out about the people who lived there. People made their settlements by water, and the same site often continued to be used for thousands of years. Gradually, layers of buildings and objects, called strata, built up on top of each other.

A dig

STRATA

Strata tell archaeologists about different periods; for example a layer of ash shows that a city burned down.

Each layer will contain the foundations of buildings, perhaps part of a wall, and sometimes also pottery, jewelry, idols, coins, tools, and weapons. These are all mixed up with soil and rocks. There will be no clothing, leather, paper or wood, as these rot away.

When a wall is found, archaeologists look for the floor that goes with it. A floor shows where one layer ends: anything below the floor belongs to another layer.

STARTING A DIG

Sometimes strata build up to form a hill, or tell. This is often a promising site for digging.

First, a section is dug downwards, to find a good place to start. Then a trench may be dug in steps along the sloping side of the tell. The different strata show up like layers in a cake.

The site is divided into fields measuring 65 square feet. Each field is divided into even smaller squares. In this way, a plan can be drawn of the site, and each object is marked down exactly where it is found.

A FIND

Groups of archaeologists work in teams in different places on the site. Sieves are used to make sure no tiny objects are missed.

Every single thing found in a square is carefully cleaned, photographed, drawn, described, labeled and put in a bag. Items are then taken away to a museum for further study.

Read about some of the finds that teach us about Bible times on the pages on Bible Discoveries.

Sieving earth

DRUGS AND ADDICTIONS

A drug is a substance which alters the chemistry of the body. Some drugs take away pain; others give a feeling of happiness. The word drug has come to be used for anything that gives people a 'high'. People who can't live without a drug are addicted to it.

Tea, coffee and cigarettes are all legal drugs

FOOD

Eating problems

These days many people can't control their eating. Some people eat far too much; other people starve themselves.

The Devil tempted Jesus to use his powers to get food when he was in the wilderness. Jesus said to the Devil: "Man should not live on bread alone, but on every word that comes from the mouth of God." He meant that food should not control our lives.

HOPE

People can be cured from addictions with the help of doctors and friends. Many find they are helped by prayer and the friendship of Jesus. Jesus said, "I have come that they may have life, and have it to the full."

Paul described our bodies as a temple which we should take care of. He wrote: "Don't you know that you yourselves are God's temple, and that God's Spirit lives in you."

- Paul's advice: *Timothy 5:23*
- Temple: *1 Corinthians 3:16,17*
- Jesus: *Matthew 4:4; John 10:10*
- Setting an example: *1 Corinthians 8:13*

DRUGS

Some drugs are legal, such as alcohol, coffee and cigarettes.

Alcohol is not harmful if we don't drink too much of it. Even Jesus drank wine. However, some people can't control their drinking and become alcoholics. Some Christians don't drink at all, to show that life can be lived without alcohol!

Cigarettes are another common drug, but they are dangerous to health.

The government has banned many harmful drugs. Some people still take them, perhaps to act big or to escape problems. But when the drug wears off, the problem is still there.

After the drug has worn off

GAMBLING

Cards and dice are used for gambling

Some people are addicted to the excitement of gambling. Many Christians say that money is a gift from God and should be put to good use, not gambled in the hope of getting more back.

ECCLESIASTES
THE BOOK OF

What's life all about? What's the point of living? These are the questions asked by the man who wrote the Book of Ecclesiastes. Most of the time he decides that there's no meaning in life. "Useless! Useless! Completely useless! All things are useless!" he says.

What is life about?

THE WRITER

The writer was a rich and powerful old man. He called himself "son of David", and he may have been King Solomon. He said, "I am wiser than anyone who ruled Jerusalem before me." But "son" could also mean he was a descendant of Solomon, or like Solomon. The writer used Hebrew words that were not known in the time of Solomon. The book was probably written at the end of the Old Testament period.

UNDERSTANDING ECCLESIASTES

The Book of Ecclesiastes shows how empty Jewish religion had become in the years leading up to the birth of Jesus. The fact that this book is included in the Bible, shows that God doesn't write off people who find life meaningless.

READING ECCLESIASTES

The book is rather like a vast picture of a busy scene, showing various things happening to people. Some became rich and famous, some had fun, some achieved understanding, some were oppressed, and some became jealous. The writer saw it all as a waste of time, for death came to everyone.

Some people became rich and famous

Some people had fun

Some people were oppressed

Some people became jealous

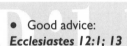
Bible Search

- Good advice:
Ecclesiastes 12:1; 13

- A time for everything:
Ecclesiastes 3:1–8

- A poem about old age:
Ecclesiastes 12:1–8

- About eavesdropping:
Ecclesiastes 7:21

THE SECRET OF HAPPINESS

Sometimes the writer saw happy people, and wondered what the secret of their happiness was. He realized that they didn't spend time trying to get things for themselves, and said, "I have seen what is best for a person to do on Earth. He should eat and drink and enjoy his work... This is a gift from God... God keeps him occupied with gladness of heart."

A happy person

ELIJAH A GREAT PROPHET

Jezebel sent a slave to kill Elijah

Elijah was one of the great prophets of Israel. He saved his country from a takeover by the priests of the Canaanite god Baal. Elijah came from Tishbe, on the edge of the desert.

Queen Jezebel, wife of King Ahab of Israel, wanted to make Baal the only god in Israel. She decided to kill every prophet of God that she could find.

A SHOWDOWN

"There will be no rain until I say so," Elijah told Ahab. Slowly, the grass turned brown. The harvest failed.

Three years passed. Elijah told Ahab to summon the leaders of Israel, and 850 priests of Baal and Asherah, to Mount Carmel.

The harvest failed

Elijah told the people they couldn't worship both God and Baal. He said, "Let the priests of Baal sacrifice a bull. I will do the same. The God who sends fire to his sacrifice is the true God."

- Ravens feed Elijah:
  1 Kings 17:1–6
- A widow:
  1 Kings 17:10–24
- A showdown:
  1 Kings 18
- God speaks to Elijah:
  1 Kings 19

FIRE

From morning to night, the priests of Baal pranced round their altar. They cut themselves with knives. "O Baal, answer us," they shouted. There was no reply.

At the end of the day, Elijah prayed to God. Lightning flashed and burnt up Elijah's sacrifice. "The Lord is God," the people cried. The priests of Baal were killed. Then God sent rain to end the drought.

Elijah prepares to sacrifice a bull

MOUNT SINAI

Jezebel was furious when she heard what had happened. "I will kill Elijah," she vowed. Elijah had to run for his life. He went to Mount Sinai in the desert.

God sent a mighty wind, and an earthquake followed by fire. Then silence fell. God asked Elijah why he was there. "The people of Israel have killed all the other prophets. Now they are after me," said Elijah.

God sent Elijah back to stir up rebellion and to overthrow Ahab. "Find Elisha, to be your friend and to help you," God said.

Read more about King Ahab and Queen Jezebel on the pages on Gardens and Queens.

74

Elisha watches as Elijah is carried up to heaven

ELISHA THE SUCCESSOR

Elijah was a prophet. He was getting old, and one day God told him that he had chosen someone to take over from him. God instructed Elijah to find a man called Elisha, and take him on as an assistant and future successor.

Elijah found Elisha at work plowing a field. He gladly agreed to work with Elijah.

ELIJAH VANISHES

Elijah knew that soon God would take him into heaven. He asked Elisha if there was anything he could do for him beforehand.

'Give me a double share of your spirit,' Elisha said. He meant 'May I carry on your work as a prophet after you?'

Suddenly a chariot of fire, drawn by horses, appeared. Elijah was swept into the chariot, and he was carried up to heaven.

A POOR WIDOW

A widow came to Elisha for help. "My sons are going to be sold as slaves to pay off the money I owe," she said. "All I have left is a little olive oil."

Elisha replied, "Ask your friends to lend you all their empty jars. Pour your oil into the jars."

The woman started pouring her oil, and it didn't run out. When the jars were full, the oil stopped flowing. The woman sold the oil and paid off her debts.

A WAR STORY

The king of Aram was at war with the king of Israel. But every time he tried to set up an ambush, the king of Israel found out.

The king of Aram's men told him that Elisha was able to forsee the planned attacks, and warned the king of Israel. So the king of Aram sent his army to capture Elisha.

But Elisha prayed, and the enemy army couldn't recognize him or work out what he was doing. Elisha led them into the city of Samaria. When the men realized what he had done, they found they were trapped.

Elisha told the king of Israel to prepare a feast for the enemy army. When the king of Aram found out what had happened, he never tried to fight the king of Israel again!

Bible Search

- Plowing:
  1 Kings 19:19–21

- The widow's oil:
  2 Kings 4:1–7

- The blind army:
  2 Kings 6:8–23

The poor widow

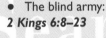

EMPIRES
SUPERPOWERS IN BIBLE TIMES

When one country becomes powerful, and attacks and conquers many other countries, these become part of its empire. Like a great sea wave, an empire would rise up and control much of the known world for a time: perhaps fifty, a hundred, or maybe a thousand years. Then it would lose its power and another empire would take its place.

BABYLONIA

Babylonia was in the southern part of what is now Iraq. Abraham came from the city of Ur in this area (often called Mesopotamia).

Fifteen hundred years after Abraham's time, the Babylonians conquered Assyria. Later they destroyed Jerusalem. Babylonia was very strong about 1850 B.C. under King Hammurabi, and also between 612 B.C. and 539 B.C.

EGYPT

Egypt is one of the world's oldest civilizations. Its people were great artists and craftsmen. Egypt was at its most powerful between 3000 B.C. and 1000 B.C.

Moses, the leader of the Israelites, was adopted by an Egyptian princess and grew up in Egypt.

ASSYRIA

Assyria was the northern part of modern Iraq (the land between the Tigris and Euphrates Rivers). Its capital was Nineveh. The people were fierce warriors, and conquered Israel. Assyrian kings also built beautiful palaces and temples.

The Assyrian empire was greatest from 1400 B.C. to 1100 B.C., and between 911 B.C. and 609 B.C.

PERSIA

Persia is now northwest Iran. King Cyrus II of Persia captured Babylon in 539 B.C. He told the Jews they could go back home to Judah. The Persians held their enormous empire for nearly 200 years between 549 B.C. and 331 B.C., until they were conquered by a Greek, King Alexander the Great.

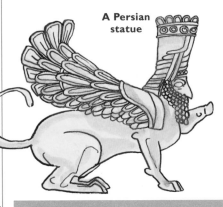

A Persian statue

Bible Search

- God in control:
  Isaiah 45

- The end of Babylon:
  Isaiah 14:22–23

CANAAN

Canaan was not an empire. It was a small country, but it was important because all trade routes passed through it. The Canaanites became wealthy from trading. Canaan linked three continents: Europe, Asia and Africa, so all the great countries wanted to control it.

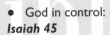

The people of Assyria were fierce warriors

END OF THE WORLD

How will the world end? A large meteor could come crashing into our planet. Or we could blow ourselves up. But Christian teaching is that it will not happen by chance: the end of the world is in God's control.

Jesus said the end of the world would be unexpected, like a thief in the night. "Be ready for my coming at any time!" Jesus said.

WHEN?

The Old Testament teachers promised that God would put an end to the evil in the world. The first step was Jesus' birth in Bethlehem, and the final step will be the end of the world. Bible teaching on this subject is often difficult to understand.

Jesus said that only God knew when the end of the world would be. It could be tomorrow, or in thousands of years' time. We should not waste our time trying to work out when it will be.

Working out when the end of the world will come

The end of the world will be like a thief in the night

SECOND COMING

The Bible says that when the world ends, Jesus will come again, and this time the whole world will know about him. He will come as a great king, with all his angels.

Dead people are in eternity with Jesus. But when the world ends, they will come back to life, with new bodies. The Bible does not say what these new bodies will be like. Paul compared them to a plant and a seed. A plant, although it comes from a seed, does not look like a seed.

JUDGMENT DAY

The Bible says that at the end of the world, everybody will be judged.

Then God will make a new Earth. There will be no more suffering of any kind.

Everybody will be judged

- Be ready:
  Mark 13:32–36

- Judgment:
  Matthew 25:31–46

- New world:
  Revelation 21:1–5

- Jesus speaks to everyone:
  Romans 2:12–16

Bible Search

EPHESIANS LETTER TO

A Roman soldier

P aul wrote to the Christians in Ephesus in about A.D. 61 when he was a prisoner, probably in Rome. He did not address the letter to anyone in particular. So he probably hoped it would be passed on to all the Christian groups in and around Ephesus.

EPHESUS

Ephesus was a beautiful and important Roman city, the chief city in Asia. It had streets paved with marble, public baths, temples and libraries.

Ephesus had a famous temple to the goddess Diana (also called Artemis). It was one of the Seven Wonders of the ancient world.

The silversmiths of Ephesus made a lot of money selling little models of Diana to visitors.

A statue of the Roman goddess Diana

Christians read Paul's letter

ARMOR

Paul was under house arrest, probably in Rome, and was guarded day and night by a soldier. Roman soldiers were protected by their armor. In his letter to the Ephesians, Paul wrote that Christians needed to wear God's invisible armor to fight evil. This armor was truth, honesty, peace, faith, and salvation. For a weapon, he added, Christians could use God's words.

UNDERSTANDING EPHESIANS

How should Christians live together? The answer Paul gives is "united": united in love for Jesus, and united in love for one another.

Paul wrote: "The Church is Christ's body…We will grow up in every way to be like Christ, who is the head. The whole body depends on Christ".

Bible Search

- God's armor: *Ephesians 6:10–20*
- Paul's visit to Ephesus: *Acts 19*
- Darkness and light: *Ephesians 5:8*

A united people

READING EPHESIANS

- *Chapter 1:2–2*: Paul's hello
- *Chapter 1:3–2:21*: Jesus and the Church.
- *Chapter 4:1–32*: United we stand.
- *Chapter 5:1–6:24*: Following Jesus and facing the enemy.

ESAU

Esau and Jacob were the twin sons of Rebekah and Isaac, and the grandsons of Abraham. Abraham and his family had settled in Canaan. But when Abraham's son, Isaac, was old enough to get married, Abraham decided that his wife should come from the country where Abraham was born: Mesopotamia.

Esau the hunter

ELIEZER'S CAMELS

Abraham sent his servant, Eliezer, to Mesopotamia. He took with him ten camels loaded with presents. Eliezer arrived at the city of Nahor and sat down to watch women drawing water from a well. He prayed: "I'll ask one of the girls for water. If she gives me a drink and also offers to water my camels, let this be a sign that she is the wife for Isaac."

REBEKAH

Eliezer saw Rebekah approaching the well. When Eliezer asked her for a drink, she offered to water the camels too. She was the one!

Eliezer explained why he had come to Rebekah and her family. Rebekah was brave, and agreed to go to Canaan and marry Isaac.

ESAU AND JACOB

Rebekah and Isaac had twin sons: Esau and Jacob. As the elder son, Esau had special rights called his birthright. A birthright was the right to be the head of the family when the father died. In this case, it also meant the right to inherit God's promises to Abraham and Isaac. In time, Esau would take over as the leader of the people.

One day, Esau was hungry, and asked Jacob for some soup. Jacob said he would give him some – for a price. The price was that Esau should give up his birthright to Jacob. Esau agreed.

Brave Rebekah

Rebekah's stew

A BLESSING BY DISGUISE

Isaac was old, blind and close to death. He sent Esau out to kill a deer and make his favorite meal. Isaac planned to bless Esau after he had eaten. Rebekah overheard. She wanted Jacob to receive his father's blessing, not Esau. She quickly cooked a stew. Then she dressed Jacob in his brother's clothes and put goatskins on his hands and neck so that he felt hairy like Esau. The trick worked. Jacob got Esau's dying blessing. Giving a blessing before you died was like making a will.

Isaac and Jacob

- Eliezer finds Rebekah: *Genesis 24*
- Daddy's pet: *Genesis 25:24–29*
- The birthright: *Genesis 25:29–34*
- The trick: *Genesis 27*

Bible Search

ESTHER THE BOOK OF

In the entire Book of Esther, the word "God" never appears. But the book shows God at work in things that happen. He guided Esther, arranged coincidences, and saved the Jews from being murdered by the king.

The story begins in 483 B.C. The events took place at the same time as the events described by Ezra and Nehemiah.

A beauty contest

XERXES AND VASHTI

Xerxes was the powerful king of Persia. He was fabulously rich. His palace was a marvelous place, with gold and silver chairs, floors of marble inlaid with shells and jewels, and cups and plates of gold.

One night, Xerxes held a party. He sent for his beautiful wife, Vashti, because he wanted to show her off to his guests. But Vashti refused to let herself be paraded about in front of Xerxes' drunken friends. Xerxes was furious and declared that Vashti was no longer his wife, and he would choose a new queen.

Vashti refused to go to the party

THE NEW QUEEN

A nationwide beauty contest was held to find a new queen. The winner was Esther, a very beautiful Jewish girl. Esther was an orphan. Her uncle Mordecai, who worked for the king, had brought her up.

HAMAN

Haman was King Xerxes' pompous chief minister. Everyone was supposed to bow down before him. But Mordecai would not worship a human being. To get his revenge, Haman persuaded Xerxes to order the killing of all the Jews in the empire.

Haman

ESTHER SAVES THE JEWS

When Esther heard of the threat to her people, she fasted and prayed for three days. The book shows how she acted with great bravery to save her people.

Today, Jews still celebrate this escape from mass death with a feast and a holiday. This is the feast of Purim.

UNDERSTANDING ESTHER

The story of Esther shows that even in the middle of a foreign land, God saves his people when they cry to him for help.

READING ESTHER

- *Chapter 1–2*: Esther becomes queen.
- *Chapter 3*: Haman's plot.
- *Chapter 4–7*: Esther outwits Haman.
- *Chapter 8–10*: The Jews are saved from death.

EXILE
THE FALL OF JERUSALEM

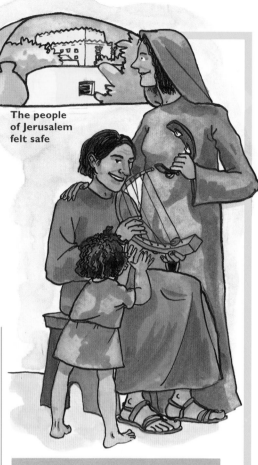

The people of Jerusalem felt safe

We're safe," said the people in Jerusalem. "The Temple is here. God won't let anything happen to his house." But the prophet Jeremiah wasn't happy with the way people lived. "Clean up your lives!" Jeremiah warned. "If you don't, God will bring disaster on you." Hardly anyone believed him. But Jeremiah was right. In 586 B.C., King Nebuchadnezzar burnt Jerusalem to the ground.

Jeremiah

COUNTDOWN TO COLLAPSE

627 BC Jeremiah began preaching.
612 BC Babylon became the new world super-power instead of Assyria.
609 BC Jehoiakim became king of Judah. He tried to silence Jeremiah.
605 BC Jehoiakim fought Babylon.
604 BC Nebuchadnezzar, king of Babylon, attacked Jerusalem. He took many people as hostages, to make sure Jehoiakim did what he said.
598 BC Jehoiakim rebelled again.
597 BC King Nebuchadnezzar captured Jerusalem. He made Zedekiah king. All the important people were taken prisoner.
588 BC King Zedekiah rebelled.
587 BC King Nebuchadnezzar surrounded Jerusalem.
586 BC Jerusalem was destroyed.

A BLIND KING

King Zedekiah tried to escape when the Babylonians took over Jerusalem. But he was caught as he was running away. He was blinded and taken prisoner.

The Babylonians took many of the people of Jerusalem back to Babylon as prisoners. Only the lazy, poor and old were left behind in Jerusalem. But even they rebelled! They killed the Babylonian governor and ran away to Egypt, dragging Jeremiah with them.

To find out what happened next, see the page on Exile.

King Zedekiah

DON'T FIGHT

Jeremiah told the people, "Don't fight the Babylonians. They're sent by God to teach you a lesson." His enemies called him a traitor and threw him into prison.

But a man called Ebed-Melech pleaded with King Zedekiah for Jeremiah's release, and the king agreed.

To find out more about Jeremiah, see the page on the Book of Jeremiah.

Bible Search

- Jeremiah warns the people: *Jeremiah 7:1–15*
- Attempted murder of Jeremiah: *Jeremiah 38:1–13*

EXILE OF THE JEWS

King Nebuchadnezzar

Exile means not being allowed to live in your own country. When Judah was captured by the Babylonian king, Nebuchadnezzar, many of the people were forced to go and live in Babylonia. At first, their exile was a nightmare come true. Yet some good did come of it, as the people learned important lessons during this time.

BABYLONIA

Babylonia was the low, flat land between the Tigris and Euphrates rivers, which is modern Iraq.

The Jews must have missed their own country. One of the lines of their songs said, "By the waters of Babylon we sat down and wept… There on the poplars we hung our harps."

The Jews weren't kept in prison in Babylonia. They settled down in houses near the Kebar canal, in an area called Tel Abib. The Jews probably worked as builders for King Nebuchadnezzar, and had their own land to farm.

King Nebuchadnezzar ruled for forty-three years. He made Babylon into a magnificent city. The Book of Daniel tells the story about how Nebuchadnezzar came to worship God.

A Babylonian building

The exiles meet together

SYNAGOGUES

Led by the prophet Ezekiel, the exiles began to meet together each Sabbath to study their scriptures, to pray and worship God. This was how the first synagogues began. The word 'synagogue' means 'meeting together'.

Ezekiel taught that God was using the exile to teach the people to obey him. The Jews were never again tempted to worship idols.

A LETTER

The prophet Jeremiah sent a letter to the exiles from Jerusalem. He wrote, "Build houses and settle down…plant gardens. In seventy years' time, God will bring you back. He has plans to prosper you and not to harm you."

SCRIBES

A group of men made up their minds to study the law of Moses and to obey God in every way. These men carefully copied down the scriptures and collected together many of the old stories and writings. The men were called scribes.

Bible Search

- A letter: *Jeremiah 29:1–24*
- King Nebuchadnezzar: *Daniel 4*
- A meeting: *Ezekiel 8:1*
- A sad song: *Psalm 137*

EXILE
RETURN TO JERUSALEM

Nehemiah returns

During the time the Jews were forced to live in Babylonia, they became settled. Some of them became wealthy. The years went by, and then King Nebuchadnezzar died. After his death, Persia, under King Cyrus, became the new world power. In 539 B.C., Persia invaded Babylonia. Cyrus sent all the exiles back to their own countries.

THE CYRUS CYLINDER

The Cyrus cylinder

In the British Museum in London, you can see a clay cylinder. There is writing all round it. It tells what happened when King Cyrus entered Babylon.

Zerubbabel and Joshua lead the exiles

HOME

You would have thought the Jews would have been delighted to return to their own country, but not everybody was. Those who did begin the journey back had many problems.

Bible scholars have different ideas about the order of events when the Jews returned home, but this is what may have happened.

● 537 B.C. Sheshbazzar was made governor of Jerusalem and started rebuilding the Temple.

● 525 B.C. Zerubbabel (the grandson of the last king) and Joshua the priest returned to Jerusalem with 50,000 of the exiled Jews. They planned to rebuild the Temple. In 516 B.C., the Temple was finished. The prophets Haggai and Zechariah encouraged the rebuilding.

● 458 B.C. Ezra, the scribe, went back to Jerusalem with more exiles and large sums of money. Ezra's job was to teach God's laws.

● 445 B.C. Nehemiah led a group back to Jerusalem. He started rebuilding the city walls, and fifty-two days later, the walls were finished.

● 445 B.C. The people made a covenant, or agreement, with God. They promised that they would be God's holy people.

● 433 B.C. Nehemiah went back to Babylon. The people began to break their promise to God. The prophet Malachi told them to keep their word to God, but they didn't.

Nehemiah returned to Jerusalem. He was furious, and set about putting everything right.

That's where the Old Testament ends. But it is over 400 years before Jesus comes. What happened in the meantime? See the page on Exile: Waiting for the Messiah.

Ezra returns

EXILE

WAITING FOR THE MESSIAH

When the Jews came back from exile in Babylonia, they made up their minds to live according to God's laws. This decision was to be tested in the years ahead. The time between the ending of the Old Testament and the birth of Jesus is often called 'between the Testaments'. It lasted over 400 years, and during that time, the Jews were ruled by the Persians, the Greeks, themselves, and the Romans.

Bible Search

- Brave people:
Hebrews 11:32–38
- The King will come:
Zechariah 2:10–13; 9:9–11

Judas Maccabeus

WAITING

The new Temple was not very splendid. The country of Judah was tiny and poor. Yet the Old Testament prophets had promised a golden age, and a splendid kingdom. Where was it? Still to come! Many people longed for the Messiah who would lead them to victory and glory.

A Persian

400 YEARS OF RULERS

- *Persian rule.*
Judah was part of the Persian empire. For a while Esther, who was a Jew, was a queen of Persia (see the page on Esther).

Alexander the Great

- *Greek rule.*
In 331 BC, Alexander the Great conquered Persia. Ten years later he died, and his vast empire was split between his generals.

   Many Jews liked Greek rule. But in 168 BC the Greek ruler, Antiochus IV Epiphanes, tried to force the Jews to become Greek and worship Greek gods. He put the statue of Zeus in the Temple and made the people work on the Sabbath. There was a revolt led by Judas Maccabeus, and after bitter fighting, Antiochus gave in.

- *Self-rule.*
Four years later, Judas' family, the Hasmoneans, began to rule the country. The Jews divided into religious groups. Some wanted worldly power; some only wanted to serve God. (See the pages on Zealots and Pharisees.)

- *Roman rule.*
In 63 B.C. the Roman general, Pompey, captured Jerusalem.
From 37 B.C. to 4 B.C., the Romans let King Herod rule the country as their puppet king. He built many magnificent buildings, and started to rebuild the Temple. But Herod was an evil man.
   Eventually, the Romans destroyed Jerusalem in A.D. 70.

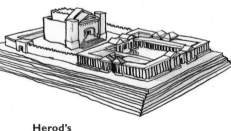

Herod's Temple

The Egyptian pharaoh

EXODUS THE GREAT ESCAPE

Exodus is the name we give to the Israelites' escape from Egypt, and their long journey to the Promised Land. If there had been no Exodus, there would have been no nation of Israel.

FLIGHT IN THE NIGHT

The Israelites were slaves in Egypt. Moses was their leader. Many times, he asked the pharaoh (king) to set his people free, but the pharaoh refused. So God sent terrible plagues to the Egyptian people. The final, most terrible plague, forced the pharaoh to let the Israelites go free. (See the pages on Plagues and Passover.)

WITHOUT A MAP

God himself led the people; by a pillar of fire during the day, and a pillar of cloud at night. For the first few days, they traveled quickly. Then they came to a sea.

Back in Egypt, building sites and brickyards were silent. There were no longer any Israelite slaves to work in them. The pharaoh changed his mind. "They're not going to walk out on me!" he shouted. He called up his army, including his war chariots, and they set off in pursuit.

The Exodus

MIRACLE BY THE SEA

The sea that the Israelites had reached is usually said to be the Red Sea. But the Hebrew words in the Bible actually translate as the 'Sea of Reeds'. It may refer to a large stretch of water where the Bitter Lakes are now.

The Israelites looked back and saw clouds of dust: the Egyptian army. They were terrified.

Moses lifted his rod over the water. And an east wind sprang up, driving back the waves, so there was a corridor across the sea bed. Then the people walked across.

STUCK IN THE MUD

The pharaoh and his army raced towards the gap in the water, and on to the muddy sea bed. They tried to catch up with the Israelites, but the chariot wheels kept getting stuck. When the last Israelite had reached the opposite shore, Moses stretched out his hand, and the water flowed back. The pharaoh's army was drowned.

ANY QUESTIONS
1 Why did the pharaoh decide to chase after the Israelites?
2 How did God help the Israelites to escape?

The Israelites cross the sea

85

EXODUS THE BOOK OF

The Book of Exodus tells the story of the Israelites' escape from Egypt and the laws God gave them. It introduces us to Moses, the Israelites' great leader. It is an important book because it shows how the people became a nation.

UNDERSTANDING EXODUS

The book shows God's amazing power and love. The Israelites were just a bunch of slaves, yet God rescued them, and made them his people.

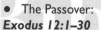

- The Passover:
  Exodus 12:1–30
- The Ten Commandments:
  Exodus 20:1–17
- A victory song:
  Psalm 78:12–14

THE PASSOVER

The Israelites were slaves in Egypt. The ruler of Egypt, the pharaoh, refused to let them leave. So God sent plagues to Egypt. In the final, most terrible plague, the eldest son in every Egyptian family died.

Israelite children were unharmed. Moses had warned the Israelites to smear lamb's blood on their doors, so the angel of death would pass over their houses.

Jews today still celebrate the night their children were saved, at the feast of Passover.

The eldest son in every Egyptian family died

THE RED SEA

The pharaoh let the Israelites go free after the final plague.

Moses led the people out of Egypt. When they came to the sea, God parted the waters so they could walk across the sea bed. The Book of Exodus calls the sea the 'Sea of Reeds'. This may have been the Red Sea.

THE TEN COMMANDMENTS

Moses

On Mount Sinai, God gave Moses the Ten Commandments, written out on two stone slabs. These were laws telling the people how to live. Now the people knew how to please God: by keeping his laws.

A WORSHIP TENT

The Book of Exodus describes the making of God's beautiful worship tent, the Tabernacle, and the golden covenant box where the Ten Commandments were kept, the Ark of the Covenant.

READING EXODUS

- *Chapter 1–4*: Moses, the leader.
- *Chapter 5–14*: Escape from Egypt.
- *Chapter 15–18*: Life in the desert.
- *Chapter 19–24*: God gives his laws.
- *Chapter 25–40*: How to worship God.

The Israelites leave Egypt

Ezekiel's vision

When Jerusalem was destroyed, the future looked black for the people. But one day, God gave Ezekiel a vision. He saw a valley full of dry bones. When he spoke to the bones, they rose up into the air, and with much rattling, joined together. Flesh and hair grew on the bones, and turned into people. Now the valley was full of people, but they were lifeless. Then, at God's command, the people began to breathe. They stood up, alive.

So Ezekiel told the people of Jerusalem, 'God will bring you back to your own country. You will have a Temple again. You will be God's people.' This amazing promise gave the people hope.

EZEKIEL THE BOOK OF

One day, Ezekiel was standing by the Kebar River in Babylonia. Suddenly he saw a great cloud, and flashing lights. He saw creatures with four faces and four wings. He saw wheels, with eyes on the rims. It was a vision: a sight of non-earthly things. Ezekiel described this vision and others in the Book of Ezekiel.

UNDERSTANDING EZEKIEL

Ezekiel saw the power, glory and holiness of God. Fifty times, he quoted God's words: 'You shall know that I am the Lord.' He meant that God wanted each man, woman and child to know him.

EZEKIEL

Ezekiel was a twenty-five-year-old trainee priest, at the time King Nebuchadnezzar of Babylonia attacked Jerusalem. Along with all the leading people of Judah, he was taken away to Babylon as a prisoner. In Babylonia, the captured people settled down to a new life. They found houses and work. When Ezekiel was thirty, God called him to be a prophet.

Bible Search

- Vision of God's throne: *Ezekiel 1:4–28*
- Street theatre: *Ezekiel 12*
- Dry bones: *Ezekiel 37*

READING EZEKIEL

- *Chapter 1–3*: Called to be a prophet.
- *Chapter 4–12*: Doom for Jerusalem.
- *Chapter 13–32*: Messages to the people of the world.
- *Chapter 33–39*: Hope for the future.
- *Chapter 40–48*: Plans for a new Temple and a new life.

Ezekiel saw dry bones

87

EZRA THE BOOK OF

King Cyrus

Israel (the northern kingdom) had been destroyed by the Assyrians. The people of Judah (the southern kingdom) were defeated by the Babylonians in 597 BC. The Babylonians forced many of the Jews to live in exile in Babylonia.

EZRA

The Book of Ezra starts when the Persians had just defeated the Babylonians to become the new world superpower. King Cyrus told the Jews that they were free to go back home to Jerusalem and Judah. It was the miracle that the prophet Jeremiah had promised. The book tells the story of two occasions when the people returned home. The first return was led by Zerubbabel, the second, eighty years later, was led by Ezra.

Ezra was a priest who grew up in Babylonia. The new king asked Ezra to lead the people back to their homeland. Ezra agreed and they set out on the long trek back home.

- Ezra appears:
  Ezra 7

- Lists of animals:
  Ezra 2:66–67

- Ezra's sad prayer:
  Ezra 9:6–15

UNDERSTANDING EZRA

Ezra's job, when they reached Jerusalem, was to make God's law the law of the land.

Ezra and Nehemiah, the governor of Jerusalem, worked together to bring the people back to God.

The Book of Ezra is Ezra's view of what happened, and includes papers, documents and letters by other people.

Ezra

Ezra held a meeting in the rain

REVIVAL IN THE RAIN

Ezra was horrified to find that many of the Jews had married foreigners who led them away from God. He held a long open-air meeting. It was pouring rain, but that didn't stop him. The Jews promised they would only worship God.

READING EZRA

- *Chapter 1–2*: The first return to the homeland.
- *Chapter 3*: Restarting the worship.
- *Chapter 4:1–23*: Trouble.
- *Chapter 4:24–6:22*: The Temple is finished.
- *Chapter 7–8*: Ezra in Jerusalem.
- *Chapter 9–10*: Return to God's laws.

See also the pages on Nehemiah and Exile.

FAITH A STRONG BELIEF

A Roman soldier
asks Jesus for help

Faith is deciding that Jesus is God and that he is as real as you are, and then relying on God's promises and living his way. Believing in God, but not showing it by your actions, is not faith. "Even the demons believe," said James. Faith means keeping going when everything is difficult.

**Three strangers
visit Abraham**

ABRAHAM

One day in the desert, three strangers came to Abraham. They were angels. "You will have a son," God said. Abraham and his wife were very old, but that didn't keep Abraham from trusting God's promise. It was a great example of faith.

A WAY OF LIFE

God gave Jesus to be our friend. He asks us to trust Jesus.

• By trusting Jesus we become God's true children.

• By trusting that Jesus died on the cross to take the punishment for our sins, we receive forgiveness.

• In daily life, trusting that Jesus keeps his promises, helps us to see his power at work.

Faith is deciding to trust and obey Jesus without proof that he loves us and that he is able to help us. Sometimes faith means keeping going when there seems no reason, and everything is black and difficult.

**Jesus and
his friends**

A SOLDIER

"Please heal my servant," said a soldier to Jesus. "I'll come with you," said Jesus. The soldier said, "I'm not good enough for you to come to my house. I know that if you give the command, my servant will be healed." "This Roman soldier has more faith than anyone I've found," said Jesus. And he healed the servant.

FAITH WORKS

"We've seen Jesus. He's alive again!" said Jesus' friends to Thomas. "It's impossible. I don't believe you," said Thomas. "I'll only believe if I can see him and touch him for myself."

Jesus came to Thomas. "Look at me," he said. "Stop doubting and believe. Those who believe without seeing me will be truly happy."

On another occasion, a sick woman touched Jesus' cloak. "Daughter, your faith has healed you. Go in peace and be freed from your suffering," said Jesus.

Bible Search

• Abraham: *Romans 4:18–25*

• God's promise: *John 3:16–19*

• Heroes and heroines of faith: *Hebrews 11*

• A sick woman: *Mark 5:24–34*

FAME
AND AMBITION

If someone asks you, "What do you want to be when you're grown up?", you might reply, "I want to be famous and have lots of money."

We should always try and make the most of our abilities. But if our only aim in life is to get to the top, and if we look down on people who don't do so well, then we've lost sight of Jesus.

Wanting to be rich and famous

WELL DONE

Jesus told a story about three servants who were given sums of money by their master. Two of the men increased the money by buying and selling. Their master was very pleased with them. But the third servant buried his money in the ground. The master was angry at the servant's stupidity. Jesus was saying that the most important thing is to do what God wants. That makes us "famous." in his eyes, whatever our position in the world.

The servant who buried the money

DON'T SHOW OFF

Trying to sit next to the host

At parties, guests often tried to show how important or famous they were by choosing the best seats either side of the host.

Jesus said, "Don't sit down in the place of honor, somebody more important than you may have been invited. Sit lower down the table, and your host may ask you to move further up. Then everyone will see the respect in which you're held."

ANY QUESTIONS
1 What sort of ambitions is it good to have?
2 Is it right to want to be famous?

JAMES AND JOHN

Jesus told the disciples that he would be killed and then rise again. James and John asked if they could sit on his right and left (the best seats) when Jesus was brought back to life. Jesus said, "Rulers love to show their power over people… but if one of you wants to become great, then he must serve the others like a servant…"

AMBITION

It is wrong to be ambitious if our aim is just to increase our fame or wealth. Jeremiah said to his servant: "Should you seek great things for yourself? Seek them not." But Paul's ambitions were good: to preach the gospel of Jesus in new places, and to know Jesus.

Bible Search

- James and John:
Mark 10:35–45

- The best seats:
Luke 14:7–10

- Using ability:
Luke 19:11–28

- Good ambition:
Romans 15:20;
Philippians 3:10–11

FAMILIES IN BIBLE TIMES

In the Book of Genesis, Laban said to his nephew Jacob, "You are my own flesh and blood." Even distant relatives were regarded as equally part of the whole family (or "clan"). If one person was in trouble, the others came to help. Nothing was more important than your family.

HUSBANDS

A man was the head of the family. His wife called him 'Master'. A man could have more than one wife, especially if his first wife had no children. But most men could not afford more than two wives.

In New Testament times, it was not common to have more than one wife.

WIVES

In Bible times, a wife was the property of her husband. (Today, most people believe that a wife is not the property of her husband, but an equal partner in the marriage.) But she was loved and respected by her husband, and she was responsible for creating a happy home for her family.

Bible Search

- Laban to Jacob:
  Genesis 29:14

- Two wives:
  I Samuel 1:1–8

- Peter's mother-in-law:
  Mark 1:29–31

A husband with two wives and children

DIVORCE

Divorce was not approved of, and was probably not very common. To divorce his wife, a man had only to write a letter and give it her. He had to return her dowry (the money or property brought by a woman to her husband when she married).

Divorce

RELIGION IN THE FAMILY

One of the chief religious festivals of the year, the Passover, took place at home with the family, not in the synagogue.

On his thirteenth birthday, a boy was considered to be a man. A religious service called Bar Mitzvah was held in the synagogue, followed by a party. The boy now had to obey the religious laws.

OLD PEOPLE

There were no old people's homes, and elderly people were always looked after by their children. The Gospels tell us that Peter's mother-in-law lived with him.

Old people lived with their family

FAMILIES TODAY

The traditional idea of a family is two parents and a child or children, plus other relations such as grandparents, aunts, uncles and cousins. But every family is different. There are many families with just one parent; other families have grown to include half-sisters, half-brothers and stepmother or stepfather. These large families remind us of the large families of Bible times.

Every family is different

Some families have one parent

A GIFT

Family problems

Families are God's gift, but there are often problems within families.

There were family problems in Bible times too; for example Joseph's brothers sold him to be a slave, and King David's son, Absalom, plotted to drive his father from the palace.

PARENTS AND CHILDREN

The apostle Paul wrote: "Do not make your children angry. But raise them with the training and teaching of the Lord."

Parents who love their children try to make sure they grow up in the right way. The Book of Proverbs says: "The Lord corrects those he loves, just as a father corrects the child that he likes."

The fifth commandment says, "Honor (respect) your father and mother." Paul wrote: "Children obey your parents the way the Lord wants. This is the right thing to do."

Paul said, "A believer should take care of his own relatives, especially his own family." When Jesus was dying on the cross, he told his friend John to look after Mary, his mother.

Children should obey their parents

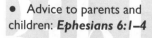

- Advice to parents and children: *Ephesians 6:1–4*
- Jesus: *Matthew 12:46–49*
- Caring for the elderly: *1 Timothy 5:4; 8*
- Punishing children: *Proverbs 3:12*

JESUS

Jesus said, "Whoever does the will of my father in heaven is my brother and sister and mother."

The term *family* also describes a group of people who live together because they love God and obey him. Many nuns and monks consider themselves to be a family.

Waiting for the rain

FARMERS
AND GRAIN CROPS

When the Israelites settled in Canaan, they became farmers. Each family was given their own plot of land. All work was done by hand, with the help of working animals.

Farmers waited for the October rains to soften up the rock-hard earth, before starting to plow.

Bible Search

- A sowing story:
Matthew 13:1–9
- A harvest story:
Matthew 13:24–30
- Harvest festival:
Exodus 23:16

SOWING THE SEED

Fields were plowed with a simple plow (a stick with a fork at one end) pulled by an ox. Then the farmer walked up and down, throwing handfuls of seed from a basket into the furrows. Next, the field was plowed again to bury the seed.

A farmer ploughing

HARVESTING

Harvesting

Harvesting started in April, after the March rains. Most farmers used a semi-circular sickle to cut the crops. The crops were tied into sheaves, and loaded on to a cart. A donkey pulled the cart to a level piece of ground known as a threshing floor.

THRESHING

The crops had to be threshed to separate the grain from the stalks. To do this, farmers beat the sheaves with sticks, or an ox trampled over them. Another way of threshing was for an ox to pull a flat, wooden threshing-sledge over the sheaves; the underside of the sledge was studded with stones or iron.

Threshing

WINNOWING

The grain had to be collected from among the broken stalks. In the evening, when a breeze sprang up, the threshed corn was tossed into the air with a long-handled wooden winnowing fork. The grain fell to the ground, but the stalks, or chaff, were lighter and blew away in the breeze. Stalks were collected to burn on fires.

GRAIN

The grain was separated to get rid of bits of stick and stone, and put into sacks to be sold or stored. Flour was made by grinding the grain between two flat stones.

FESTIVALS

A festival, or feast, was held to remember God's goodness, or to ask for his help, or perhaps to renew the promise to serve him. All public holidays were religious festivals. Everyone enjoyed festivals, and often there was a party. The main festivals are described below.

Celebrating Purim

PASSOVER

Passover, in March or April, celebrated the time that the Israelite families escaped the plague which killed the eldest son in every Egyptian family. This was during the time the Israelites were slaves in Egypt.

On the first evening of Passover, a meal of roast lamb and bitter herbs, with unleavened bread (bread made without yeast), was eaten. Unleavened bread was eaten all the following week.

WEEKS

Weeks, later called Pentecost, was the main harvest festival. It was held fifty days after Passover, in June, when the grain had been harvested.

Shelters

DAY OF ATONEMENT

The Day of Atonement was held near the end of September. On this day, no one ate any food. The people asked God to forgive them for their sins. At the Temple, a goat was killed, and a second goat was driven into the desert. This was to show that God had taken away the sins of the people.

SHELTERS OR INGATHERING

In the autumn, a seven-day party was held to celebrate the end of the olive and grape harvests. The people made shelters out of branches, where they slept in memory of the years the Israelites spent in the wilderness after escaping from Egypt. Prayers were held for rain for the new crops.

PURIM

Feasting, drinking, games and fancy-dress parades were held to celebrate the day when God saved the people from their enemies (see the page on Esther).

DEDICATION

The festival of Dedication, or Lights, took place in December. Each evening, lamps were lit in houses and synagogues to mark the year 165 B.C., when the Temple was rebuilt.

Bible Search

- Festivals: *Leviticus 23*
- Day of Atonement: *Leviticus 16*
- Purim: *Esther 3; 9*
- Shelters: *John 7:37–38*
- Dedication: *John 10:22*

FISHING,
FISH AND FISHERMEN

Most fishing in Palestine was done in the Sea of Galilee, which was a large inland lake. On a calm day, over three hundred fishing boats might have fished for the twenty or so different kinds of fish that lived there. At least seven of Jesus' twelve apostles were fishermen.

Bible Search

- A coin: *Matthew 17:24–27*
- Jesus preaches from a fishing boat: *Matthew 13:1–23*
- Fish for lunch: *John 9:9*

MONEY FISH

When Jesus had to pay his Temple tax, he told Peter to go fishing! The first fish Peter caught was holding a silver coin.

(There is a type of fish which carries its young in its mouth. When the young are old enough to look after themselves, the mother picks up an object to stop them gliding back into her mouth. She usually chooses something brightly colored or shiny.)

FISH TO EAT

Jews did not eat much meat, so fish was a very important everyday food. Fish from the Sea of Galilee was salted, pickled or dried. It was also sold to many other countries.

FISHING BOATS

The fishing boats on the Sea of Galilee were wide, solid and slow. Usually, they had a crew of about six. Often, fishermen went together to buy a boat and some nets. The boats had oars and probably one central sail in the shape of a triangle.

Fishing was very tiring work. Fishermen had to be strong. They had various ways to try and catch fish:
- A line with a bone hook on the end.
- Spearing fish with harpoons.
- Attracting fish to the surface at night with a light.
- Pulling a large drag-net behind a boat.
- Using a throwing net.

A throwing-net's catch

Spearing fish

THROWING-NETS

When Jesus called Peter and Andrew to follow him, they were 'casting their nets' in the water. These circular nets had weights round the edges. They were thrown over shoals of fish in shallow water. As the net sank, the fish were trapped.

95

FLOWERS,
HERBS AND SPICES

In the Bible, just as all small birds were called "sparrow", so many flowers were called "lilies". Flowers were not grown in gardens, so the flowers we read about were wild flowers.

Jesus said, "See how the lilies of the field grow. They do not labor or spin, yet I tell you that not even Solomon in all his splendor was dressed like one of these."

Lilies

A garlic bulb

Garlic was common in Egypt and was used to flavour bread. When the Israelites were in the wilderness, after escaping from Egypt, they longed for the garlic of Egypt.

Myrrh was a sweet-smelling resin collected from the branches of a small thorny tree that grew in Arabia and Africa. It was used to make medicine and an oil. Myrrh was put on Jesus' body when he died.

Frankincense was a whitish gum, collected from cuts made in branches of a large tree that grew in Arabia and Africa. It was burned to make a scented smoke. It was very expensive. The wise men who visited the baby Jesus, brought him gifts of frankincense and myrrh.

Gall was a name used for the poisonous hemlock plant or pain-killing opium plant. Jesus was offered wine mixed with gall when he was dying on the cross.

Spikenard was a small spiky plant that grew in India. Oil (nard) collected from the spikes was used as a perfume.

FLOWERS

In spring and summer, the hills and valleys of Galilee were bright with wild flowers: blue anemones, purple pea blossom, scarlet tulips, yellow narcissi and irises, red poppies and anemones, white daisies and lilies, and different coloured crocuses and hyacinths.

A valley in Gallilee

HERBS AND SPICES

Herbs and spices were used to stop food going bad, to make it taste better, and as a perfume for the body or the air.

The herbs that were used in Bible times are still used today. They include cumin, dill, mint, coriander, cinnammon, rue and saffron.

Myrrh

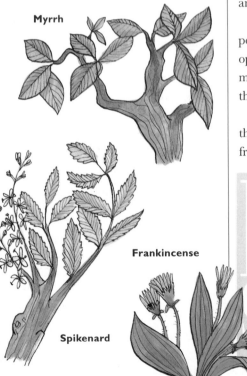

Frankincense

Spikenard

Bible Search

- Solomon and wild flowers: *Luke 12:27–28*
- Spikenard: *John 12:1–8*

96

FOOD AND COOKING

Jewish laws included certain rules that had to be followed when cooking. For example, meat and milk dishes could not be cooked or eaten together.

On special occasions, such as a wedding, or when a baby was born, there would be a party. Parties went on for many hours, or even days. All sorts of special food would be prepared for a party.

Corn is being roasted on this metal plate. Sometimes corn is ground and mixed with water to make a porridge.

Wine is kept in tall bottles or animal skins, and drunk out of metal cups. Wide cups made of metal, or flat hard rounds of bread, are used for plates.

Grinding grain between two stones to make flour.

Often, the only seasoning used is salt. Sometimes herbs and spices are added too.

Goats' milk is mixed with salt, and left to harden into cheese. It's delicious with fresh bread.

Locusts boiled in salt water have a shrimp-like taste.

To make bread, water is poured into some flour and mixed. Then yeast, or uncooked bread dough left over from the last batch, is added and mixed well. The dough is left to rise, then formed into round shapes. Some dough is put aside for the next day. The bread is baked in an oven, or on an upturned pot over the fire.

Cakes are made with wheat flour, mixed with water and sweetened with honey. Eggs are not used. Cakes may be flavoured with mint or cinnamon. Honey doughnuts are made into animal shapes and fried in olive oil.

Grasshoppers are often fried in olive oil.

Flat pieces of dough are pressed on the inside of a chimney-shaped oven, and left to cook.

To make locust biscuits, locusts are dried in the sun, ground into a paste, mixed with honey and wheat flour, and baked over a fire.

Food is cooked on fires outside, or near the door in the living room. Only large houses have kitchens. A lamb and a calf have been killed, and are being roasted on a spit.

Turkish delight is made from starch (from corn), mixed with honey, and with pistachio nuts or almonds added.

This boy is hungry. He's dipped a piece of bread in honey.

This skin bag, hung between three sticks, contains goat's milk. It's shaken and squeezed until butter is formed.

FOOD AND DRINK

Making a stew

Jewish meals were fairly simple. Bread was the main food. There were usually two meals a day, but not at set times. People ate when they were hungry. The evening meal was the only time the family sat down together to eat (apart from on the Sabbath).

BREAD

Poor people ate bread made from barley, and rich people ate bread made from wheat. It was shaped into round, flat buns. It quickly went dry and mouldy, and fresh bread had to be baked every two or three days. Bread was broken and not cut.

VEGETABLES AND SEEDS

Leek

Garlic

A soup made of vegetables and sometimes edible seeds (peas, beans, lentils), was eaten every evening with bread. Lentils, beans, onions, garlic, and leeks were all common. There were no potatoes, carrots, parsnips or cabbage.

Pulses

Lettuce

FRUIT

Figs, grapes, apricots and dates were eaten fresh from the tree. These fruits were also dried and pressed together to make "cakes". Olives were pickled or eaten fresh. People also enjoyed other fruits, such as pomegranates and melons, and nuts such as pistachios, walnuts and almonds. There may have been apples, but there were no oranges or bananas.

Bible Search

- A boy's lunch: *John 6:8*
- Esau's meal: *Genesis 25:34*
- Breakfast: *John 21:9*
- Emergency rations: *2 Samuel 17:28–29*

MEAT AND FISH

Meat was a luxury. If a guest was expected, mutton, lamb or goat might be added to the evening stew. Roast meat was a great treat. Jewish laws said that only meat from animals which ate grass and had cloven hoofs could be eaten. Pork was forbidden.

Neither chicken nor eggs were eaten in Palestine.

Fish was an important everyday food, which was salted or dried. Jewish laws only allowed fish with scales and fins to be eaten.

DRINKS

People drank milk, but it was usually goat's milk, rather than cow's milk. Yogurt drinks were also made from milk. Grapes and pomegranates were boiled down to make a rich, sweet drink. Grape juice and red wine were very popular.

HONEY

Cane sugar was not known, so honey was very important for sweetening food. For children, it was a great treat to be given part of a honeycomb to eat.

FORGIVENESS
FROM GOD

Feeling guilty

Many people feel guilty because of wrong things they've done. For these people, the Christian message is good news. God accepts people exactly as they are. He loves them, forgives them, and then gives them the power to change.

Forgiveness is God's gift, but we have to want it and accept it.

Bible Search

- Falling short: *Romans 3:23*
- Wiping out debts: *Colossians 2:13–14*
- The gift: *Ephesians 2:4; 5; 8*
- Jesus: *1 Peter 2:24*

SIN

When we do something wrong, we are doing wrong against God. The word for this is sin. Sin is a rebellion against God, when we have not followed his laws and gone our own way. The story of Adam and Eve is the story of the first sin.

An archer may shoot an arrow which falls short of the target. In the Bible, sin is sometimes described as "missing the mark", falling short of God's standard.

Missing the mark

FORGIVENESS

Sometimes sin is pictured as a list of wrong things, rather like an "I Owe You", that we need to pay up. Paul said, "He forgives us all our sins, and has canceled the written code (wiped out the list of debts)."

Forgiveness is not easy. God is completely good, right and fair. He can't just excuse wrong. The Bible says that the punishment for sin is "death", meaning being cut off from God.

Wiping out debts

JESUS

Jesus died on the cross as punishment for our sins. Peter wrote: "He himself bore our sins in his body on the tree... by his wounds you have been healed."

A RUNAWAY SON

Jesus told a story about a son who took his share of his father's money and left home. He had a great time, until he ran out of money, and had to take a job feeding pigs. Then he saw what a fool he'd been, and returned home. His father rushed to meet him. The son said, "Dad, I've sinned against God and against you..." His father threw a party to celebrate his return. It is a picture of how God accepts people who are sorry for their sins.

The son enjoys himself

The son returns

FORGIVENESS
FORGIVING ONE ANOTHER

Sometimes we want revenge

When someone upsets or hurts us we want to hit back. Sometimes, if we can't hurt the person who hurt us, we hurt someone else. Some people hold on to their grudges for years. They want to get their revenge. For many people, forgiveness only begins to be possible when they think about Jesus.

JESUS

Jesus did no wrong at all. Yet his enemies made him suffer death by slow torture. He took the pain, horror and hatred into himself, and changed it into love. On the cross he said, "Father, forgive them, they don't know what they are doing."

Jesus suffered death by slow torture

LAW-BREAKERS

Two of God's commandments are, "Love God with your whole self" and "Love your neighbour as you love yourself." We often break these laws, yet God forgives us. So we should forgive other people. Paul wrote: "Be kind and compassionate to one another, forgiving each other, just as in Christ, God forgave you."

A STORY

Jesus told a story about a servant who owed his king a huge amount of money. "Sell him, his family, and his house," said the king.

The servant begged the king to give him chance to pay back the money, and the king felt sorry for him and wiped out the debt.

The servant went away and found someone to whom he had lent a little money. "Pay up or else," said the servant. "I'm sorry, I can't," the man said. So the servant had the man thrown into prison.

The king was furious when he found out. The servant was punished until he had paid every last penny.

The servant is punished

FORGIVE AND FORGET

Jesus said, 'If you forgive men when they sin against you, your heavenly Father will also forgive you. But if you do not forgive men their sins, your Father will not forgive you.' Forgiving doesn't just mean saying, 'I forgive you.' It means forgetting all about the wrong, and wiping it out of your mind.

Forgiving each other

Bible Search

- Wages of sin: *Romans 3:20*
- Unforgiving servant: *Matthew 18:21–35*
- Forgiving others: *Matthew 6:12, 14–15*

FREEDOM
THROUGH JESUS

"**I** am with you and I will rescue you," said God to Jeremiah. God sets his people free. This is seen throughout the Bible, starting with God's rescue of the Israelite slaves from Egypt. When Jesus began his work, he said, "The Spirit of the Lord… has sent me to proclaim freedom for the captives."

FREEDOM

There are different sorts of freedom. There is the freedom to choose one thing instead of another. Children may often have a more limited freedom to choose, because parents decide for them!

There is also inner freedom: being free from fear, worry, guilt, bad habits, and wrong thoughts. This is the freedom which Jesus came to give to everyone through Christianity.

A CRIPPLED WOMAN

In the synagogue one Sabbath, Jesus saw a woman who couldn't stand up straight. Jesus said to her, "You are set free from your illness." The Pharisees grumbled that Jesus was working on the Sabbath. But Jesus said, "Satan has tied up this woman for eighteen years. Shouldn't I set her free?"

Jesus heals a crippled woman

Parents often make choices for their children

- The Spirit: *2 Corinthians 3:17; Galatians 5:16–18*
- Bad habits: *Romans 7:18–19; 8:2–4*
- What freedom is for: *Galatians 5:13*
- Slave to sin: *John 8:31–36*

Burdened by rules

The Jews thought that if they worked very hard to keep all God's laws, they would go to heaven. They felt they had to earn God's love. But Jesus showed that going to heaven was a gift, because no one lives perfectly and deserves heaven.

Paul said, "It is for freedom Christ has set us free…do not be burdened again by a yoke of slavery." By "yoke" he meant religious laws and rules devised by people.

WHAT FREEDOM IS FOR

Does Jesus set us free to do whatever we like? The answer is 'no'. People are made to serve, just as birds are made to fly. Jesus set us free to serve God and each another.

Paul wrote that the Holy Spirit helped Christians to live in freedom.

Read about free will on the page on Looking for God.

We are all lonely sometimes

FRIENDSHIP
CARING AND SHARING

Human beings need friends. This is how God made us. Adam, the first man, was alone and lonely. But then God made Eve so that she could be a friend for Adam.

The Book of Proverbs has some wise words about friends: "A friend loves at all times." Most people find that at some time in their life they are lonely. Whatever the reason, this is a chance to find out that Jesus is a friend.

JONATHAN AND DAVID

David was a shepherd when he helped the Israelite army to beat the Philistines by killing Goliath. Saul, the Israelite king, was delighted with David's victory and took him to live in his palace. David became great friends with Saul's son Jonathan. They made a pact to be friends forever. Jonathan sealed the pact by giving David his clothes, his sword, and bow and arrows.

Jonathan and David became great friends

JESUS

In Jesus we can see that true friendship is a two-way bond. Jesus loved and helped his friends; he also wanted their friendship. These are examples.

● Sharing knowledge: Jesus said, "I've called you friends, for everything that I learned from my father I've made known to you."

● Loyalty: Jesus stuck by his friends, even when they let him down. After Jesus' arrest, Peter denied knowing him three times. When Jesus was brought back to life after being crucified, he went to find Peter and forgave him.

● Support: Just before he was arrested, Jesus asked his friends to be with him and pray with him.

Jesus prays with his friends

● Protection: When the soldiers arrested Jesus, he said, "I'm the one you want. Let these men go." The disciples were allowed to go.

● Love: Jesus said, "Greater love has no one than this, that he lay down his life for his friends." And that's what Jesus did.

Bible Search

● A friend loves: *Proverbs 17:17*

● Jesus: *John 15:12–15*

● A friendship meal: *Revelation 3:20*

● Jonathan and David: *1 Samuel 18:1–4; 20:1–42; 23:16–18*

FURNITURE IN RICH
AND POOR HOMES

I f we looked into a typical house in Palestine in Jesus' time, we would think that it was almost empty, because there would be so little furniture.

When the Israelites lived as nomads in tents in the desert, their furniture had to be easy to pack and carry on camels or donkeys. So people only owned basic, essential items. Things did not change greatly later on, when the Israelites settled down and lived in houses.

Nomads carried their furniture on camels

TABLES AND CHAIRS

Poor people ate on the floor

Rich people's houses often had very low benches running along two or three sides of the room. Sometimes these were covered with beautiful cushions.

Poor people didn't have any chairs. The only type of seat would have been a stool, but most people sat on mats on the floor.

An animal skin spread out on the floor was used as a table.

ROMAN SEATING

The Romans used dining couches when they ate. These couches were arranged in a horseshoe shape around a table. Servants came through the gap to bring the food. The guests lay stretched out on the couches, while they enjoyed their meal.

The Romans ate whilst lying on couches

BEDS

The poorer you were, the closer you slept to the ground! Kings and wealthy people slept in bronze or wooden beds with legs.

Most people slept on the floor on mats. These were sometimes stuffed with wool. There were no blankets. People wrapped themselves in their cloaks or covered themselves with a goatskin. If you were lucky, you might have a stuffed goatskin for a pillow. More often, people had wooden, or even stone pillows. Babies slept in woolen cradles slung from the roof, or sometimes even in an animal's feeding trough, as Jesus did.

LIGHT AND STORAGE

Food and clothes were stored in wooden chests.

Lamps would be placed on a metal lampstand, or in a hollow in the wall. Big earthenware pots held water. There were pottery jars for flour and olive oil, and bowls for cooking and eating.

Bible Search

- A stone pillow:
Genesis 28:11

- Rich living:
Amos 6:4

- Luxury bedroom furniture:
2 Kings 4:10

GALATIANS THE LETTER TO

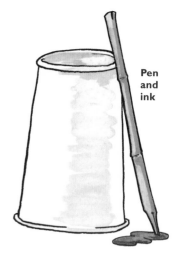

Pen and ink

Paul's letter to the Christians in Galatia was probably written about A.D. 48, about fourteen years after Jesus died. It was Paul's first letter, and probably the first of our New Testament books to be written.

Galatia was a large Roman province in what is now central Turkey.

GALATIA

Paul went to Galatia to preach about Jesus. It was his first missionary journey. You can read about Paul's adventures in Galatia, and the towns he visited, in Acts 13 and 14. In Lystra, Paul's enemies stoned him until they thought he was dead.

Paul

UNDERSTANDING GALATIANS

Paul wrote this letter in white-hot anger. He had just heard that false teachers had come to the new Christian churches of Galatia. These teachers were saying that in order to be a true Christian, it was not enough to rely on Jesus. You had to keep the Jewish laws as well. If these teachers had their way, the Christian faith would be destroyed.

ANGRY WORDS

"Let these teachers be condemned to hell!" Paul wrote. "You foolish Galatians, who has bewitched you?" he asked. "I'm astonished that you are deserting Christ so quickly."

Paul emphasized that a person's Christian faith began with that person trusting Jesus to forgive them. Their faith, or trust, was to be the mark of Christian life. "You can't earn your way into heaven by keeping laws," Paul said.

READING GALATIANS

- *Chapter 1:1–10*: Paul's hello.
- *Chapter 1:11–2:21*: Paul's experiences.
- *Chapter 3:1–20*: An example of faith.
- *Chapter 3:21–4:31*: The purpose of the law.
- *Chapter 5:1–26*: Go on in freedom.
- *Chapter 6:1–10*: Help one another.
- *Chapter 6:10–18*: Paul's goodbye.

A false teacher preaches

AN ARGUMENT

Peter came to see Paul in Antioch. The two of them ate meals with non-Jews. This was against Jewish laws. As soon as some false teachers turned up, Peter became afraid. He stopped eating with non-Jews. "That's terrible!" said Paul to Peter. "Jesus makes all Christians equal."

Bible Search

- Equal rights for all Christians: *Galatians 3: 26–29*
- How to be right with God: *Galatians 2:16*
- Angry words: *Galatians 1:6; 3:1*

GARDENS
IN CITIES AND VILLAGES

In cities, houses were crowded together. Only very rich people could afford gardens. Their big houses had courtyards with fountains, ornamental pools and flowering trees. Sometimes they had gardens outside the city walls. These were often shady orchards. In villages, some people had gardens by their houses. But water was limited, and gardening was work. Vegetables and herbs were grown to eat and sell in the markets.

GARDEN OF GETHSEMANE

Jesus often went to the Garden of Gethsemane outside Jerusalem. The word *Gethsemane* means "olive press". The garden was a grove of olive trees. It was one of many private gardens on the slopes of the Mount of Olives. Here, Jesus could escape from the crowds. It was here that he spent his last night.

THE KING OF PERSIA

The Book of Esther describes the king's garden at his palace in Susa. There were white and blue drapes, tied with white and purple cords to silver rings on marble pillars. The floor was made from marble, inlaid with mother-of-pearl, shells and jewels.

KING AHAB'S GREED

King Ahab wanted to buy Naboth's vineyard, but Naboth refused to sell it. King Ahab's wife, Jezebel, didn't understand Ahab's problem. In her view, the people and the land all belonged to the king. She arranged for Naboth to be stoned to death. Then she took over his vineyard.

The prophet Elijah told Ahab how wicked he had been, and Ahab was very ashamed and sorry for what he had done. God forgave him, but because Ahab's crime was so serious, God said he would punish Ahab's descendants.

A TOMB IN THE GARDEN

Wealthy people were sometimes buried in caves in the hillside. Often, a garden was planted in front of the tomb. Jesus was buried in a garden tomb like this. When Mary first saw Jesus, after he had risen from the dead, she thought he was the gardener.

A king's garden

Bible Search

- A bride: *Song of Songs 4:12*
- Ahab's greed: *1 Kings 21*
- A king's garden: *Esther 1:5–6*
- Gethsemane: *Mark 14:32–42*

GENESIS THE BOOK OF

The word *Genesis* comes from the Greek translation of the first words of the Bible: "In the beginning." The Book of Genesis tells us about the making of the world, the first marriage, the first sin, and the first murder. And it tells us of the beginning of God's plan to rescue the world from evil, and the start of the Jewish nation.

READING GENESIS

Chapter 1–3: The world, Adam and Eve, and sin.

Adam and Eve

Chapter 4–10: Cain, Abel and Noah.

Cain and Abel

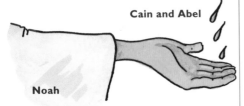

Noah

Chapter 11: The Tower of Babel.
Chapter 12–26: Abraham and Isaac.

Abraham

Chapter 27–50: Jacob and Joseph.

UNDERSTANDING GENESIS

In Genesis, we are shown the greatness, goodness and love of God. He did not give up on the world he had made. He asked for loving obedience from men and women. Here are some well-known passages in Genesis:

- 1:1–2:4: The story of creation.
- 9:12–17: The rainbow.
- 27: Jacob tricks his father.
- 28:10–22: Jacob's ladder.
- 37:1–11: Joseph's special coat.

Joseph

AUTHOR

Jews have always said that Moses wrote Genesis. Moses was an Israelite, but was adopted by an Egyptian princess. He was brought up to learn "all the wisdom of Egypt". He made it his job to collect together and write down the stories of the Israelites.

FATHER ABRAHAM

Abraham was the father, or founder, of the Jewish nation. He followed God's command to leave his own city of Ur to live in Canaan. Two thousand years later, Paul wrote: "Abraham believed God and God accepted Abraham's faith, and that faith made him right with God. So you should know that true children of Abraham are those who have faith."

THE FIERY MESSAGE

Jacob was Abraham's grandson. One night, a stranger appeared and began to fight with him. Jacob could not win, but he said, "I will not let go unless you bless me." The man said, "You shall not be called Jacob any longer, but Israel," and disappeared. "Israel" meant "the man who struggles with God". Jacob realized that the stranger had been God. Israel became the name of Jacob's descendants, and the name of their country.

Moses probably wrote on papyrus scrolls

GHOSTS
AND DEMONS

There is a great deal of interest today in the occult. Occult means supernatural, mystical, perhaps evil, forces which are beyond our understanding. The Bible speaks very strongly on this subject. It says: "Let no one be found among you who…is a medium or spiritist or who consults the dead. Anyone who does these things is detestable to the Lord."

A medium

GHOSTS

Many people tell weird stories about ghosts. Ghosts are supposed to be the spirits of dead people who haunt the Earth. There's no hint at all in the Bible that dead people come back to this world. (See the page on Heaven.)

A ghost

Demons may control people

DEMONS

In the Gospel stories, demons (evil spirits) are very active, causing illness and madness, and controlling people. The stories show that Jesus came to the world to destroy the power of evil.

EXORCISM

Exorcism means driving away demons, ghosts or spirits with the power of Jesus. Special religious services and blessings are carried out to do this.

STEER CLEAR

God protects people from demons. But people who go out of their way to get in touch with evil spirits risk being taken over by them. This is one reason why the Bible forbids seances (meetings where people attempt to receive messages from the spirits of the dead).

Isaiah wrote: "When men tell you to consult mediums and spiritists, who whisper and mutter, should not a people enquire of their God? Why consult the dead on behalf of the living?"

Paul said, "Whatever is true, whatever is noble, whatever is right, whatever is pure, whatever is lovely… think about such things." And Jesus said, "I am the way, the truth and the life."

Paul told people to think of what is pure and lovely

See also the page on Superstition and Magic.

Bible Search

- Detestable things: *Deuteronomy 18:9–13*
- Wise words: *Philippians 4:8*
- A waste of time: *Isaiah 8:19*
- Jesus: *Matthew 12:22–29; John 14:6*

GIDEON
BEATS THE ENEMY

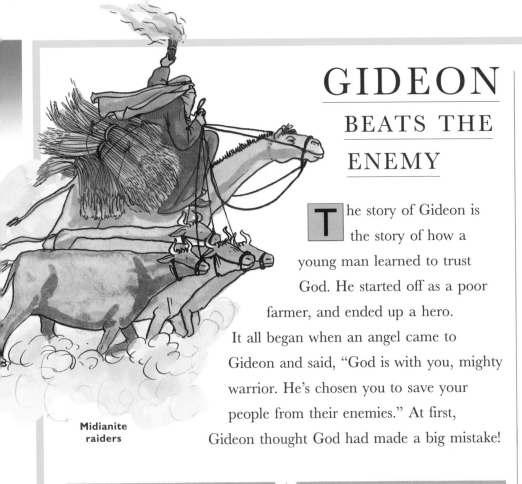

Midianite raiders

T he story of Gideon is the story of how a young man learned to trust God. He started off as a poor farmer, and ended up a hero. It all began when an angel came to Gideon and said, "God is with you, mighty warrior. He's chosen you to save your people from their enemies." At first, Gideon thought God had made a big mistake!

A MISSION

For seven years, the Israelites were bullied by Midianite raiders from the desert. The Midianites would attack on camels and steal crops and cattle, while the Israelites were forced to hide in caves.

The Israelites had begun to worship the Canaanite god Baal, but in the end they prayed to God to come to their rescue.

- Gideon's story: *Judges 6 and 7*
- The beginning: *Judges 6:11–24*
- Wet wool: *Judges 6:36–40*
- A smashing success: *Judges 7*

GOD CALLS GIDEON

One day, an angel came to Gideon and told him that God wanted him to save the Israelites from the Midianites. The first thing Gideon had to do was to get rid of the idol of Baal which the people had been worshipping. He did it in the night when no one could see him!

Gideon's second mission was to fight the Midianite army and drive them away. There were thousands of Midianites, and Gideon had only 300 men on his side. How could Gideon win?

Gideon gets rid of Baal

A SMASHING SUCCESS

Gideon gave each of his soldiers a sword, a trumpet and a smouldering torch hidden in a pottery jar. In the dead of night, they surrounded the enemy. When Gideon blew his trumpet, his men blew their trumpets, broke the jars and waved the flaming torches in the air. They yelled out, 'For the Lord and for Gideon!'

Gideon blows his trumpet

The Midianites were terrified and ran for their lives. They thought they were surrounded by a great army!

Now the Israelites no longer had to live in fear. For the next forty years, Gideon ruled over the people in peace.

GIVING AND TAKING

Life is a gift given to us by God. And God "richly provides us with everything for our enjoyment." But his best gift was Jesus. John wrote: "God so loved the world that he gave his only Son, that whoever believes in him should not perish but have everlasting life."

Peter and John help a lame man

GREED

Humans are greedy. We want to take the best things for ourselves, or we take more than we need. We are greedy for all kinds of things: food, money, power, medals, fame, toys, and information. Our greed can get us into a lot of trouble.

Greedy for food

ADAM AND EVE

Adam and Eve, the first man and woman, were greedy for the fruit which God had forbidden them to eat, because the Devil had promised it would give them power. When they disobeyed God and ate the fruit, their action was the start of all the trouble in the world.

ZACCHAEUS

Zacchaeus was a tax-collector. He was a bad man who cheated and robbed the taxpayers. But then he met Jesus, and he changed. He gave half his things away, and he paid back four times the money he had stolen.

A LAME MAN

Peter and John met a lame man begging for money. Peter said, "Silver and gold I do not have, but what I have, I give you. In the name of Jesus Christ of Nazareth, walk." We too should help people when we can.

THE GOOD GIVING GUIDE

In Paul's letter to the Corinthians, he said that people should give cheerfully and generously. In Matthew, Jesus told people not to make a big thing of giving, just so that other people would admire them. He told them that they should give generously, but keep quiet about it instead.

For more about giving, turn to the pages on Money and People in Need.

Bible Search

- A cheerful giver:
  2 Corinthians 9:7–11

- God's gifts:
  1 Timothy 6:17; John 3:16

- A lame man:
  Acts 3:1–10

GOD WHO IS HE?

David and Goliath

I n the Old Testament, names were important. A person's name described what he or she was like. God called his son "Jesus", because the word meant "the Lord saves".

It is impossible for one word to sum up everything about God. But some of the names used to describe God tell us a little about him.

YAHWEH

"Yahweh" is often translated as "Lord" in our Bibles. It used to be translated as "Jehovah", but that was incorrect.

One day, Moses was looking after sheep in the mountain land called Midian. Suddenly, he saw a bush on fire. He went closer, and there God told him to rescue the Israelites from Egypt. "Who are you?" asked Moses. God replied, "YHWH". The Hebrew language had no vowels, and these are consonants. The word probably means "the God who is always present".

ABBA

Abba

The Jews had always known that God was their father. But Jesus showed them the full meaning of the word. He called God "Abba", a word meaning "Daddy".

God is the strong, loving father who is an example to all parents. Through faith in Jesus, we are all God's children.

JUDGE

God judges and punishes wrong. In the end, no one gets away with evil. Jesus will come at the end of the world to judge evil. God forgives those who trust Jesus.

Moses and the burning bush

GOD OF ARMIES

David walked out by himself towards the great giant, Goliath. "I'll make mincemeat of you," sneered Goliath. "You have your sword, spear and javelin," David said. "But I come to you in the name (the power) of the God of armies…"

The name "God of armies" shows that God is all-powerful and fights for his people.

- God of armies:
  I Samuel 17:15
- Judge:
  Genesis 18:25
- Yahweh:
  Exodus 3:1–14
- Today's battles:
  Ephesians 6:10–20

Bible Search

GOD AND HIS ACTIONS

Who is God? What is he like? In the Bible, we see that God controlled the events which are described. God made our planet and everything in it. From this we see his incredible power. By looking at what people do, we can tell what sort of people they are. Here are some of the things we know about God from his actions.

THE EXILE AND RETURN

God wanted his people to love and trust him. When the people worshiped other gods, King Nebuchadnezzar destroyed the Temple and took the people as prisoners to Babylonia. God used King Nebuchadnezzar as his agent to teach the people a lesson.

King Nebuchadnezzar destroys the Temple

THE ISRAELITES' ESCAPE

When the Jews wanted to describe God, they looked back to when he led them out of Egypt in the Exodus. Here we see:

● God's love. He saved people who were weak and miserable, because he loved them.

● God's power. God sent plagues to Egypt. He led the slaves to freedom through the sea. In miracle after miracle, he gave them water and food. Nothing was too hard for God.

● God's holiness. God came to Mount Sinai in darkness, storm and lightning. The whole mountain smoked and quaked. But the people never saw God. He doesn't have a physical body.

The parting of the sea

Mount Sinai

● God's goodness. On Mount Sinai, God gave the people his laws. He wanted his people to keep his laws, and live good lives.

Bible Search

● God's love and power: *Psalm 136*

● God on Mount Sinai: *Deuteronomy 4:15–16; Hebrews 12:18–20*

● God's love: *John 3:16*

● The cross: *1 Peter 2:24*

JESUS

In Jesus, we see God's forgiving love in action, in a human life. John wrote: "God so loved the world that he gave his one and only son, that whoever believes in him shall not perish but have everlasting life."

Jesus

(Turn also to the page headed Trinity.)

111

GOD LOOKING FOR

The fool says there is no God

God is beyond our understanding. If we knew everything about God, he would no longer be God. The Bible never sets out to "prove" God exists, but takes it for granted. The opening words of Genesis are: "In the beginning…God…"

A psalmist said that atheists (people who don't believe in God) are fools: "The fool says in his heart, 'There is no God.' "

DON'T KNOWS

Some people take pride in saying they're not sure if God exists. The Bible's answer to these people (agnostics) is: "You will seek me and find me when you seek me with all your heart. I will be found by you."

Instead of saying, "I'm not sure if God exists," agnostics should ask themselves, "Do I want to find God?"

Agnostics should ask themselves 'Do I want to find God?'

Bible Search

- Finding God: *Jeremiah 29:13*
- Thomas: *John 20:24–29*
- Taste and see: *Psalm 34:8*
- Jesus' story of the lost sheep: *Luke 15:1–7*

GOD SEEKS US

There is a big difference between the Christian faith and all other religions. Christianity teaches that God came to find us. Jesus said, "I have come to seek and search for the lost."
The prophet Ezekiel said God was like a shepherd looking for his lost sheep. He would "search for the lost and bring back the strays… bind up the injured and strengthen the weak."

DOUBTING THOMAS

When Thomas saw Jesus after the resurrection, Jesus said, "Look at my hands…stop doubting and believe… Because you have seen me, you believe; blessed (happy) are those who have not seen me and yet believe."

TASTE AND SEE

In the end, we cannot prove or disprove the existence of God. The first step to knowing God is a step of faith. This means believing in him, praying to him and obeying Jesus, without proof he exists. Christian teaching is that as time goes on, we will come to know God for ourselves, from our own experience. This is what the psalmist means when he says, "Taste and see that the Lord is good."

GOSSIP
AND FINDING FAULT

Gossiping

It sometimes seems as though everybody talks behind other people's backs, and enjoys nasty gossip. Jesus had some tough words to say about gossip: "People will have to explain every careless thing they have said. This will happen on the Day of Judgment."

Bible Search

- Judged by what you say:
  Matthew 12:36–37
- Gossip:
  Proverbs 10:8; 18:8; 26:20
- Plank versus speck:
  Matthew 7:1–5

GOSSIP

The writer of The Book of Proverbs had wise words on gossip:
- "The words of a gossip are like tasty bits of food. People take them all in."
- "Foolish talk will lead to your ruin." (People don't trust a gossip.)
- "Without wood, a fire will go out. Without gossip, quarreling will stop."

People take in gossip like crows pecking for tasty morsels

FINDING FAULT

We find it all too easy to find fault with other people. We might describe them as stupid or crazy. But Jesus warned: "Don't judge other people, and you will not be judged. You will be judged in the same way that you judge others."

Sometimes we decide that someone else has acted wrongly. But we do not have to make nasty remarks about him because of it.

PLANK VERSUS SPECK

A carpenter

Jesus told people not to be hypocrites. He said, "Why do you look at the speck of sawdust in your brother's eye and pay no attention to the plank (of wood) in your own eye? How can you say to your brother, 'Let me take the speck out of your eye,' when all the time there is a plank in your own eye?'"

Finding fault

In the busy markets of Jesus' day, carpenters were often seen carrying long planks of wood over their shoulders. Everyone would have known what Jesus meant by having a plank of wood in your eye!

HOPE

Paul said, "When you talk, do not say harmful things. But say what people need: words that will help others become stronger."

Jesus said that the Holy Spirit would help Christians know the right words to say.

Say things to help others

GOVERNMENT
IN OLD TESTAMENT TIMES

T he Jewish nation grew from the descendants of one man: Abraham. Abraham's grandson, Jacob, had twelve sons. Their families became the twelve clans, or tribes, of Israel. Jacob, his sons and their families, went to live in Egypt to escape famine in Canaan. Over many years, their numbers grew. In Egypt we first hear of 'elders', who were leaders among the Israelite people.

MOSES

Hundreds of years later, the Egyptian rulers made the Israelites into slaves. But eventually Moses, one of the Israelite leaders, led the slaves out of Egypt. To deal with arguments and difficulties, he split the people into groups, led by elders.

An Egyptian ruler

JUDGES

Joshua took over from Moses. When the Israelites reached the Promised Land, he divided it into twelve areas, one for each tribal group. There was no central government. A judge, who was rather like a cross between a sherrif, a warrior chief and a preacher, ruled over one tribe or group of tribes. In each village, elders led the people.

Bible Search

- Elders: *Exodus 3:16; Ruth 4:9–11; Jeremiah 29:1*
- God rules: *Exodus 19:5–8*
- Give us a king: *1 Samuel 8:5*
- Taxes: *1 Kings 4:7; 27–28*

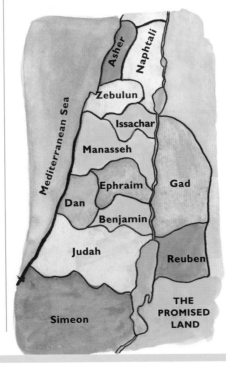

The kingdoms of the twelve tribes of Israel

Mediterranean Sea

Asher
Naphtali
Zebulun
Issachar
Manasseh
Ephraim
Dan
Benjamin
Gad
Judah
Reuben
Simeon
THE PROMISED LAND

KINGS

As time went on, the Israelites felt they wanted a king. God chose Saul to be the first king; he was followed by David.

David had a full-time army, and needed money to pay for it. That meant that people had to start paying taxes.

Money to pay taxes

When David's son Solomon became king, he divided the country into twelve districts with a governor in charge of collecting taxes in each district. Solomon ruled from Jerusalem with the help of a full-time staff. Each village had its own council of elders.

OCCUPYING ARMIES

When the country was invaded by foreign armies, the Israelites were ruled by governors chosen by the invaders.

Under Greek rule, a Council of Jewish elders, led by the High Priest, was in charge of religious affairs. In 143 B.C, the people broke free from Greek rule. The High Priest now ruled the country. This lasted until the Romans captured Jerusalem in 63 B.C.

The High Priest

GOVERNMENT
IN NEW TESTAMENT TIMES

A Roman coin

T here was civil war, yet again, in Palestine. Many Jews were sick of the fighting. In 63 B.C., the Romans stepped in to bring some peace and order to the land. That was the start of the Roman occupation.

In 37 B.C., the Romans put the half-Jewish Herod in power.

KING HEROD THE GREAT

In many ways, Herod was a clever ruler. The golden and ivory Temple in Jerusalem was built on his orders.

But the Jews hated Herod, and he was so terrified of losing his throne that he turned into a crazed killer. When news reached Herod that a baby had been born in Bethlehem who would become king of the Jews, he ordered all baby boys in Bethlehem to be put to death.

Herod orders the killing of baby boys

HEROD'S SONS

When Herod died, the Romans divided the country into three, and put three of his sons in charge: Archelaus, Herod Antipas, and Philip.

Archelaus was made ruler of Judea and Samaria in the south. He was cruel and stupid. After ten years, the Jews begged the Romans to get rid of him. Then Judea was made a Roman province and a Roman governor, called a procurator, was put in charge. Pontius Pilate was procurator during Jesus' time.

Herod Antipas was made ruler of Galilee. The third son, Philip, ruled Iturea in the far northeast. He was a gentle and clever man.

THE SANHEDRIN

The Sanhedrin

As long as the Jews paid the Roman taxes, and didn't rebel, the Romans allowed them to rule themselves. A council of religious leaders, called the Sanhedrin, was made up of seventy specially chosen men. They were priests, teachers of the law, elders (men from the most important families), Sadducees and Pharisees (the two opposing religious parties). The High Priest was in charge. The Sanhedrin had the power to judge, punish and imprison people brought before it.

Showing kindness

Bible Search

- Saved by grace: **Ephesians 2:8**
- Throne of grace: **Hebrews 4:16**
- Jesus: **John 1:16–17**
- Grace for a problem: **2 Corinthians 12:9**

GRACE GOD'S LOVE

G od is love. This idea is the basis of all Christian belief. God's love is active and powerful. Grace means God's loving kindness to people who do not deserve it.

The word *grace* is not used in the Old Testament, but the idea is there. Words like *mercy* and *kindness* reflect it.

JESUS

The New Testament writers took the Greek word for grace, and gave it a new meaning. It stood for the love God showed when he sent Jesus to die on the cross. Paul wrote: "By grace you are saved through faith."

Showing love

Saying grace before a meal

SAYING GRACE

Grace is also the short prayer we say to give thanks or ask for blessing. The words "The grace of the Lord Jesus be with you" mean "May you go on knowing Jesus' love, care and forgiveness."

GRACE TO BE STRONG

Paul had a problem. He prayed, but it didn't go away. But he was able to live with it because God gave him grace. "My grace is all you need," God said.

This gift of God's love and strength is given to people who know they need Jesus.

Paul prays for help

THE THRONE OF GRACE

The writer of Hebrews calls God's throne a "throne of grace". By "throne" he meant the central point of God's power. "Let us approach the throne of grace with confidence," the writer says, "so that we may…find grace to help us in our time of need." He meant God listens to our prayers and answers them.

GREEKS AND ROMANS

Jesus was born in Judea in about 6 B.C. By then, Judea (the new name for Judah) was a tiny part of the mighty Roman empire. Roman engineers had built well-paved roads between all the main cities. In this new world there were no language problems: every educated person spoke Greek. (This helped with the spread of the Christian message.)

Educated people spoke Greek

THE GREEKS

About 800 years before the birth of Jesus, self-governing Greek cities grew up along the coast of Greece. From 500–320 B.C. many brilliant writers, artists and thinkers lived in these cities. Their ideas about science, medicine, architecture, politics, law and freedom, are still important today.

The thinkers Socrates (470–399 B.C.) and Plato (428–348 B.C.) lived in Athens. In Athens every citizen had a say in the government of the city: democracy was invented in Greece.

In 334 B.C., Alexander the Great set out to conquer the world. His aim was to spread the Greek way of living and thinking.

Plato

Socrates

ROME

Rome was at first a single, powerful city in Italy. By war and treaties it grew stronger, until Rome ruled Italy. By 156 B.C., the Roman armies had made Rome the new world power, conquering other countries to make the Roman empire even bigger than the Greek empire. It contained 54 million people.

The Romans made good rulers. As long as people paid their (often heavy) taxes, and did not rebel, the Romans let them rule themselves and keep their own religions and customs.

GODS

The Greeks worshiped a large number of gods. The Romans took over the Greek gods and gave them Roman names. The chief Greek god, Zeus, was given the Roman name Jupiter.

Zeus

AQUEDUCTS

To bring water to a town, the Romans built bridges that carried water, called aqueducts. Over one million cubic metres (35 million cubic feet) of water a day flowed across the aqueduct outside Rome. It also flowed through underground pipes into thousands of city baths, troughs and fountains.

See also the pages on Exile: Waiting for the Messiah, Sports, Schools and Government (New Testament times).

The Pont du Gard aqueduct built by the Romans in France

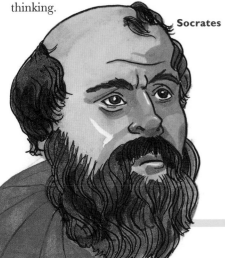

GREEN
ISSUES

The Earth is in crisis. From the television and newspapers, we hear terrible stories of the destruction of our planet. But there is also good news. Many hundreds of thousands of people all over the world are taking part in the the battle to save the Earth.

Rainforest

GOD'S EARTH

"The Earth is the Lord's," said a psalm writer. God wants us to look after the Earth and bring the best out of it.

We should not use up all the Earth's resources. When God gave the people manna to eat in the desert, he told them not to take more than they needed. People who were greedy and took too much found that it went rotten.

Jewish teachers taught that leftover food should be kept and not thrown away. When Jesus fed 5,000 people, he told his friends to collect all the leftover food. Jesus said, "Watch out and guard yourselves against every form of greed."

A FEW FACTS

- Rainforests: If present trends continue, the world's rainforests will be destroyed within fifty years.
- A layer of gas called the ozone layer, shields the Earth from the sun's harmful rays. But now it has a hole in it which is the size of the USA.
- Half of West Germany's trees are dying because of acid rain.
- Nuclear waste has polluted the seas. Plutonium from nuclear reactors remains lethal after 240,000 years.

This list could go on and on.

WHAT CAN WE DO?

The best ways for us to help look after the Earth are to:
- Educate ourselves, and find 'green' ways of living.
- Stand up against pollution and the wrong use of resources. Boycott the products of bad companies.
- Pray and support people who are working to save planet Earth.

Finding out how to look after the Earth

Bible Search

- God's world: *Psalm 8:6; 24:1–2*
- Greed: *Luke 12:15; 1 Timothy 6:10*
- Manna: *Exodus 16:14–20*

GUIDANCE
BY DREAMS AND SIGNS

- God guides: *Isaiah 63:14*
- Gideon: *Judges 6:36–40*
- A warning: *Deuteronomy 13:1–5; Matthew 12:38–39*

We see how God loves and guides his people over and over again in the Bible.

God's guidance was sometimes simple and clear. When the Israelite slaves escaped from Egypt and went into the desert, they were often led by a pillar of cloud during the day, and a pillar of fire at night.

Dreams

GIDEON

God told Gideon to fight the enemy invaders. Gideon was scared, and asked God for a sign that Israel would be saved. He put sheep's wool on the ground and prayed for it to be first wet, when the ground was dry, and then dry when the ground was wet. God did as he asked.

Gideon puts sheep's wool on the ground

DREAMS

God spoke to his people through dreams in times of particular danger and change, for example when Joseph was taken to Egypt and sold as a slave; when the Israelites were captured and taken off into exile; and when Jesus was born.

COWS

An Egyptian pharaoh dreamt that seven fat cows came out of the Nile. Seven thin, ugly cows followed them and ate up the fat cows. Nobody could tell him what his dreams meant until Joseph, who had been kept in prison, was brought before him. Joseph told the pharaoh that the dream meant there was going to be a famine. The pharaoh was impressed and made Joseph his chief minister. Joseph was able to save the people from starvation, by storing up lots of grain before famine struck.

Joseph orders grain to be stored

OUR DREAMS

Most of our dreams have no special meaning. But sometimes a powerful dream can help us, not because it's a message for other people, but because it tells us about ourselves. A bad dream may show us that we're scared or worried, and may need to talk to someone about a problem.

GUIDANCE
MAKING DECISIONS

In Old Testament times, God guided his people by dreams, voices, signs, visions, and prophecies. God used some of these methods in New Testament times, and still does today. But the chief way he guides us is by the example of Jesus, and by giving us the Holy Spirit. A psalmist said, "He guides the humble in what is right and teaches them his way."

Understanding from those who love us

● *Through people.*
God sometimes gives extra gifts of understanding to people in the Church or to people who love us. These people can often help us.

THE HOLY SPIRIT

Jesus said to his friends, "The Holy Spirit will guide you into all truth" Sometimes people talk of the Holy Spirit "speaking" to them. They don't mean they hear a human voice. They mean an idea has come into their mind, or everything has clicked into place. They know that this has come from God, partly because they now feel very peaceful. Paul said, "And the peace of God…will guard your hearts."

Everything clicks into place

THE BOOK OF ACTS

In Acts we see how the Holy Spirit guides Christians:
● *By prayer.*
When the Christians in Antioch were praying, the Holy Spirit told them to send out missionaries. Prayer doesn't always change things around us, but it can change the way we think and feel.

Praying

● *By the life and words of Jesus.*
Jewish leaders told Jesus' friends to stop preaching, but they said, "We must obey God rather than men." We can test our "guidance" by making sure it agrees with the teaching of Jesus, and the Bible.

Reading the Bible

Understanding from people in the Church

● *Through circumstances.*
God is in control of events. We can often tell what he wants by what happens.

For example, the early Christians had to decide whether to let non-Jews be part of the Church. After a lot of discussion, they finally decided that they would, when Paul told them what God was doing, and Peter told them what the Bible said.

Bible Search

- A big problem: **Acts 15**
- A promise: **Psalm 25:9**
- Putting God first: **Acts 5:29**
- Peace: **Philippians 4:7**
- Truth: **John 16:13**

ANY QUESTIONS
1 Why did the apostles disobey the Jewish leaders?
2 How do we know if the guidance other people give us is good?

HABAKKUK,
ZEPHANIAH, HAGGAI AND ZECHARIAH – THE BOOKS OF

H abakkuk, Zephaniah, Haggai and Zechariah were all prophets. Habakkuk and Zephaniah were preaching in Jerusalem before it fell to the armies of Babylon. Haggai and Zechariah were preaching when the Jews came back after their exile in Babylonia.

HABAKKUK

The book begins with a conversation between Habakkuk and God. Habakkuk asked, 'Why do evil people in Jerusalem get away with their actions?' God replied, 'I'm sending Babylonia to punish them.' Habakkuk protested, 'Jerusalem isn't that wicked! Babylonia is worse!' God answered, 'I'll punish Babylonia as well. But the righteous will live by their faith.' The book ends with Habakkuk's declaration of faith: 'Though the olive crop fails, and the fields produce no food…yet I will rejoice in the Lord.'

God punishes Jerusalem

ZEPHANIAH

Zephaniah was a nobleman and a descendant of King Hezekiah. He prophesied that terrible times would come, but that one day the people would change their ways and trust God. Then, said the prophet, "God will quiet you with his love, he will delight over you with singing."

Zephaniah

HAGGAI

Sixteen years after the Jews had returned from exile, the Temple still had not been rebuilt. Haggai said that everything would fail until this was done. The Book of Haggai tells us that the people set to work and built the Temple with God's words ringing in their ears: "Be strong and work, for I am with you."

ZECHARIAH

The priest Zechariah also urged Zerubbabel, the governor of Jerusalem, to rebuild the Temple. His book lists eight visions showing that God was in control of future events and would make his people happy. Zechariah's most famous words described Jesus' entry into Jerusalem on a donkey: "Rejoice greatly, O daughter of Zion! See your king comes to you, gentle and riding on a donkey."

Jesus rides into Jerusalem on a donkey

READING THE PROPHETS

Habakkuk
- *Chapter 1-2*: Habakkuk grumbles.
- *Chapter 3*: A prayer.

Zephaniah
- *Chapter 1-3*: Messages of doom and hope.

Haggai
- *Chapter 1-2*: Rebuild the Temple.

Zechariah
- *Chapter 1-7*: The visions.
- *Chapter 8-14*: A happy future.

Sixteen years after the Jews returned, the Temple still had not been rebuilt

121

HAPPINESS
THROUGH
CHRISTIAN FAITH

The Christian faith is not gloomy. When Jesus was born, the angel said, "I bring you good news of great joy." And not long before he died, Jesus said to his friends, "I have told you this so that my joy may be in you, and your joy may be complete."

THE SERMON ON THE MOUNT

One day, Jesus and his friends went up a mountain. He sat down and started to talk about how he wanted his friends to live in the world. Jesus began with a poem that we call "the Beatitudes."

Jesus recites the Beatitudes

Bible Search

- Beatitudes:
  Matthew 5:1–10
- Angels' news:
  Luke 2:10
- The joy of Jesus:
  John 15:11

THE BEATITUDES

The word comes from a Latin word meaning "happy". Many people reading the Beatitudes might say, 'That's not my idea of happiness!' But the poem describes an inner happiness that God gives as his gift to people who live in his way.

Beatitude
Meaning

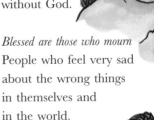

Blessed are the poor in spirit
People who can't cope without God.

Blessed are those who mourn
People who feel very sad about the wrong things in themselves and in the world.

Blessed are the meek
Those who give way to other people.

Blessed are those who hunger
People who long for right things to be done and thirst for righteousness.

Blessed are the merciful
People who are kind.

Blessed are the pure in heart
Those who are sincere when they pray, and help other people.

Blessed are the peacemakers
People who work to get rid of bitterness, anger and wrong.

Blessed are those who are persecuted because of righteousness
People are laughed at and treated badly because they are loyal to Jesus.

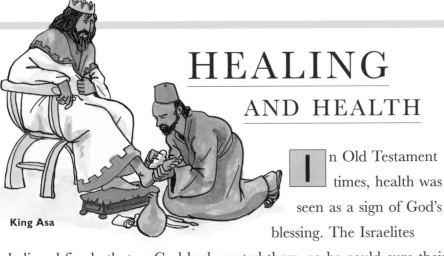

King Asa

HEALING
AND HEALTH

In Old Testament times, health was seen as a sign of God's blessing. The Israelites believed firmly that as God had created them, so he could cure their illnesses. The Old Testament criticized one king, Asa, because he had a bad foot disease and "did not seek help from the Lord, but only from doctors."

HEALTH AND WHOLENESS

To the Israelites, health meant being well in body, in spirit, and in mind. They had a proverb about this: "Being cheerful keeps you healthy. It is slow death to be gloomy all the time."

Being cheerful

Being gloomy

JESUS

Wherever Jesus went, he healed people who were ill. These healings were a sign that God had come to the Earth. As well as healing people's bodies, Jesus also healed their spirits, by forgiving their sins. This is what he meant when he said, "My peace I give you."

THE EARLY CHURCH

When Paul sailed to Rome, he was shipwrecked on the island of Malta. While he was there, he met a man in bed with a fever. Paul prayed, laid his hands on the man, and healed him. After that, other people on the island came to Paul to be healed. Paul later wrote that the Holy Spirit gave some Christians the gift of healing.

James wrote that when Christians were ill, they should ask their church leaders to pray for them to be healed.

Bible Search

- King Asa: *2 Chronicles 16:12*
- Being cheerful: *Proverbs 17:22*
- Forgiving sins: *Mark 2:1–12*
- On Malta: *Acts 28:7–9*
- God's power: *2 Corinthians 12:7–10*
- Healing gifts: *1 Corinthians 12:28*

STILL ILL?

God's healing often comes through doctors (one of the early disciples, Luke, was a doctor). But disease affects everyone, because it is part of an imperfect world. People who follow God can still suffer. Paul had an illness that would not go away. God promised to be with Paul and to give him strength to work for God despite his illness. Paul's illness made him rely more on God; it was not a punishment for his sins or lack of faith.

See also the page on Illness.

Paul had an illness that would not go away

ANY QUESTIONS
1 Why do you think God gave some of the early Christians the power to heal?
2 How would Paul's illness have made him rely more on God?

123

HEAVEN
AND HELL

The word "heaven" has two meanings in the Bible. First, it means everything that God has created beyond the Earth. Second, it means God's home, where God rules as king, and his wishes are always obeyed.

Just before he was killed, Jesus said to his friends, "Trust in God. Trust also in me. In my Father's house are many rooms. If it were not so, I would have told you. I am going there to prepare a place for you."

John described heaven as a sea of glass

IS HEAVEN A PLACE?

Heaven may not be an actual place, as we understand it. It's not another planet, for example. It's easier to think of heaven as another dimension. John said, "Everyone who believes in him will have eternal life." This is God's life of love and happiness, outside time.

It is easier to think of heaven as another dimension

A PICTURE

In the Book of Revelation, John tried to describe heaven. He talked about music, singing, light, a great sea of glass, and flashing lightning. God's throne looked as if it was made of shining jewels and a rainbow.

In heaven, John saw crowds of people praising God. He wrote: "Never again will they hunger. Never again will they thirst. …And God will wipe away every tear from their eyes."

Bible Search

- Many rooms: *John 14:1–4*
- A throne in heaven: *Revelation 4*
- A song in heaven: *Revelation 7:15–17*
- Hell: *Matthew 8:12; 25:41–46*

HELL

The Greek word *gehenna* is often translated as "hell". Gehenna was a garbage dump outside Jerusalem, where a fire was kept burning to destroy the rubbish.

Jesus talked of "the darkness". Hell is being cut off from God. Some people think hell goes on forever. Others say that those who don't go to heaven are wiped out forever.

WHO GOES TO HEAVEN?

Those people who trust Jesus to forgive them, and who obey him by living in loving ways, can go to heaven. John wrote: 'Whoever believes in him shall not perish but have eternal life.'

Gehenna, the rubbish dump outside Jerusalem

See also the pages on End of the World, and Ghosts.

HEBREWS
THE LETTER TO

A mystery letter

T he Letter to the Hebrews is a mystery letter. In Bible times, letters started with the name of the sender, and then gave the name of the person or people the letter was sent to. This letter does neither. But with a little detective work, we can discover many things about it.

WHO WAS IT WRITTEN TO?

Here are some clues:
• Over and over again, the letter quotes from the Old Testament, which is the Jewish Bible.
• It compares the work of Jesus with the work of priests, and says Jesus has done what they couldn't do: he has forgiven sin once and for all.
• The letter keeps saying, "Do not give up."

Our conclusion is that the letter was written to Christians, perhaps priests, who were in danger of returning to their old faith of Judaism.

The Old Testament

THE WRITER

The letter gives some clues about the writer:
• The writer was a man (certain words are written in masculine form).
• He knew his Old Testament very well.
• He was not an apostle.
• He was important in the Church (he seems to expect people to do what he says).

In the New Testament, one person fits this description: Apollos. Luke described Apollos as a "learned man with a thorough knowledge of the Scriptures" who "was a great help to those who had believed". He might be the writer.

UNDERSTANDING HEBREWS

The writer pictured Christian life as a race in a Roman arena. The great crowd of spectators were all the Old Testament men and women who trusted God. The goal of the race was Jesus. The competitors were Christians. The spectators were cheering on the Christians, so they did not lose heart.

READING HEBREWS

• *Chapter 1–7*: Jesus is greater than Old Testament leaders.
• *Chapter 8–10*: Sacrifices are no longer needed.
• *Chapter 11–13*: The life of faith.

Bible Search

• The sacrifice of Jesus: **Hebrews 10:1–10**
• People who lived by faith: **Hebrews 11:1–40**
• A race: **Hebrews 12:1–3**
• Apollos: **Acts 18:24–28; 1 Corinthians 1:12**

Christian life pictured as a race in a Roman arena

HOBBIES AND GAMES

T he prophet Zechariah wrote that the "city streets will be filled with boys and girls playing there." Bible writers did not describe the games children played. Instead, we learn about them from objects found by archaeologists, and from paintings on pottery and walls.

Bible Search

- Samson's riddle: *Judges 14:10–20*
- Children's games: *Matthew 11:16–17*
- Throwing dice: *Mark 15:24*

HOBBIES

People probably didn't have hobbies. The sort of things we may have as hobbies, such as sewing, or fishing, were skills that people put to good use to earn money. There were no bird-watchers or chariot-spotters!

GAMES

Jesus talked of children playing at weddings and funerals. The prophet Isaiah said, "Little ones dance about. They sing to the music of tambourine and harp."

We know that Roman children played ball games. For one game, everyone stood in a circle and threw a ball from one person to another. The winner was the person who dropped the ball least often.

Roman girls would play knucklebones, which was the same as our game of jacks or fives.

In many places, archaeologists have found squares scratched on the pavements, as if for hopscotch. Riddles and quizzes were popular at parties, and sometimes prizes were given.

TOYS

Archaeologists have found rattles and whistles, and also tiny clay pots and furniture. Little figures have also been found, but these may be idols, not dolls. Jewish children probably did not play with dolls, as the Jewish law did not allow people to make images of people.

Many playing boards for board games have been found, made out of wood, clay or even ivory. These were for chess, solitaire, ludo, and draughts.

DICE

Dice have also been discovered. Soldiers threw dice to decide who would get Jesus' cloak when he was killed. They probably carried dice around with them in their belts.

Dice were thrown and pieces of wood moved into squares, where they were robed, crowned or given a sceptre. This may be the game scratched on the floor of the Antonia Fortress in Jerusalem. Perhaps soldiers played this game on the night Jesus was caught, and used Jesus as the playing piece.

Jewish law forbade gambling.

HOLINESS

T hink of a blazing fire, white-hot in the center, so bright that you can't look at it. The prophet Ezekiel said God looked like glowing metal with fire inside it. And from his waist down he looked like fire. We know that God is not really a fire. The prophet Ezekiel used the description to help us understand the holiness of God.

Bible Search

● A holy person:
Colossians 3:12–14

● God as a fire:
Ezekiel 1:27; Hebrews 12:29

● In training:
1 Corinthians 9:24–27

● God's command:
1 Peter 1:13–16

A HOLY GOD

When we say God is holy, we mean:
● He is completely good. One day, he will get rid of everything that is bad.
● He is utterly different from us. God's holiness is the goodness and greatness which shines out of him. It is seen best in Jesus.

A BURNING BUSH

Moses

One day, Moses saw a bush on fire. A voice said, "Take off your sandals. You are standing on holy ground." God was in that bush, so the ordinary ground became holy.

In ways like this, God taught his people that any object he used, shared his holiness. So the word "holy" came to be applied to anything "set apart" for God.

Think of holiness as a blazing fire

A HOLY PEOPLE

In the Old Testament, God gave his people a command: "Be holy, because I, the Lord your God, am holy."

In the New Testament, Jesus showed that God's holy people were the people who followed him and obeyed him.

ANY QUESTIONS

1 Why did God tell Moses to take off his sandals?
2 How does a person become holy?

THE GIFT OF HOLINESS

We can't make ourselves holy. Holiness is a gift from God. First, God forgives us when we trust Jesus (this is called justification). Then he gives us his Holy Spirit, who helps us to become more and more like Jesus as we obey him (this is called sanctification).

IN TRAINING

Paul said that followers of Jesus were in training, and must not give in to wrong feelings and actions. "Without holiness no one will see the Lord," said the writer of the Letter to the Hebrews.

HOLY SPIRIT
WHO IS HE?

The Holy Spirit is God at work in our world. We cannot see him, just as we cannot see the wind. But we can see what the Holy Spirit does, just as we can see what the wind does. The Holy Spirit is not an 'it', but a person. He is what we call God as we experience him in daily life.

The Bible uses symbols, or pictures in words, to describe the Holy Spirit.

We cannot see the Holy Spirit

Bible Search

- Water: *John 4:14*
- Wind: *John 3:8, Acts 2:2*
- Fire: *Acts 2:3*
- A dove: *John 1:32*

WIND, FIRE AND WATER

Old and New Testament words for *spirit* mean "spirit", "wind", or 'breath'. Jesus said the Spirit is like the wind which you cannot see or control. On the Day of Pentecost (see the next page) the Spirit was actually felt like a rushing wind, and seen as fire. In a hot, dry land the most marvelous sight is a leaping spring of fresh, bubbling water. Jesus said the Holy Spirit is like that spring.

DOVE

When Jesus was baptized, the Holy Spirit came to him in the shape of a dove. The dove is a gentle, loving bird, keeping one mate for life.

THE GO-BETWEEN GOD

Jesus said that the Holy Spirit was truth, and Paul wrote that the Holy Spirit gave fellowship. The Holy Spirit helps us to understand and appreciate the world around us. Above all, he points us to Jesus.

The Holy Spirit gives fellowship

THE COUNSELLOR

Jesus called the Spirit a counselor. A counselor helped people in trouble with the law. The Holy Spirit helps us in our troubles.

A counsellor

ANY QUESTIONS
1 How did Jesus describe the Holy Spirit?
2 How do we see the Holy Spirit at work in the world?

A dove

The Holy Spirit made
Samson very strong

- Bezalel: *Exodus 31:3*
- Jesus works with the Spirit: *Matthew 12:25–32*
- A promise comes true: *Acts 2:14–21*
- Directing the first Christians: *Acts 13:2–4*

HOLY SPIRIT
IN THE BIBLE

We cannot see the Holy Spirit, he is invisible like the wind. But in the Bible we can read about some of the things he has done. The Holy Spirit first appears in the first chapter of Genesis.

GOD'S TASK FORCE

In the Old Testament, the Holy Spirit gave certain men and women the skill to carry out special jobs for God. To Bezalel he gave artistic skills to make God's worship tent, the Tabernacle. Saul was filled with great happiness, in order to praise God. Samson was made extremely strong, so he could fight the enemy. Ezekiel was sent visions and the power to tell people God's word.

The Tabernacle

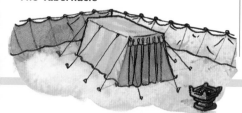

A dove

JESUS

We see the Holy Spirit at work most clearly in the life of Jesus. For example, Jesus did not have a human father. The Holy Spirit made him grow in Mary's womb. When Jesus was baptized, the Holy Spirit appeared in the form of a dove. The Holy Spirit led Jesus into the wilderness, where he was tempted by the Devil. The Holy Spirit gave Jesus the power to free people from evil. With God the Father, the Holy Spirit raised Jesus from the dead.

A PROMISE COMES TRUE

In the Old Testament, the Holy Spirit only came to a few people. When Jesus went back to heaven, the Holy Spirit came to everyone who trusted Jesus. This is what God had said would happen.

The Spirit guided the men who wrote the Bible so that they put down the things God wanted us to know.

THE FIRST CHRISTIANS

The Christian Church really began fifty days after the death of Jesus, on the day of the Jewish festival of Pentecost. On that day, Jesus sent the Holy Spirit to each of his followers. They were no longer sad and frightened, and began to speak out about Jesus.

The good news of Jesus spread like wildfire. The early Christians acted on the Holy Spirit's orders.

The good news of Jesus spread

HOLY SPIRIT AT WORK TODAY

The Holy Spirit carries out God's plans. He is at work today in the lives of Christians: in the Church, in the world, and in the universe.

He is working to bring about God's rule of peace and love. The prophet Isaiah said that one day the whole world would be full of the knowledge of God, and that would be the work of the Holy Spirit.

The Holy Spirit will guide us

JESUS AT THE WELL

One hot afternoon, when Jesus was resting by a well, he said, "Whoever drinks the water I give him will never thirst...it will become in him a spring of water." He meant that the Holy Spirit is the gift of Jesus to everyone who obeys him.

THE GIFTS OF THE SPIRIT

The Spirit gives gifts and skills to Christians. He helps us to pray and understand the Bible. He helps us to be brave and to know what to do. And he helps us to love one another.

Jesus said, "I am the vine...if you remain in me you will bear much fruit."

Paul wrote that the "fruit" of the Spirit was love, joy, peace, patience, kindness, goodness, faithfulness, gentleness and self-control.

Bible Search

- Future harmony:
  Isaiah 11:6–9

- Jesus at the well:
  John 3:4–15

- The vine and fruit:
  John 15:1–8; Galatians 5:22–23

The Holy Spirit helps us to be brave

NEW BIRTH

When we trust Jesus, we become God's children. This "second birth" is the work of God's Spirit. In the New Testament, the Spirit is called "Holy" ninety times. The Spirit makes people holy; that is, like Jesus.

ANY QUESTIONS
1 What does the Holy Spirit give to Christians?
2 How do we become God's children?

Jesus said, 'I am the vine...'

HOMES CAVES AND EARLY HOUSES

The earliest homes, in the Stone Age, were caves. Caves gave shelter from wind and rain, and protection from wild animals. By the time the Bible was written, some people still lived in caves.

The first houses looked rather like caves, and were built out of stone.

CAVES

Very poor people, who could not afford houses, lived in caves. And caves were a good place to live and hide for people who were on the run from their enemies. A cave was the headquarters and home of David and his outlaws, when he was hiding from Saul.

Caves also made good hideouts for gangs of robbers.

A home in a cave

WHAT WERE CAVE HOMES LIKE?

A natural cave could be made bigger with flint tools. Seats were cut out of stone, and a hollow might be made in the wall, where a lamp could be placed. Walls were sometimes decorated. A hearth would be made near the mouth of the cave, so that smoke from the fire could escape.

The family lived near the entrance of the cave, where it was lighter. Food would be stored at the back of the cave, or in a smaller cave leading off the main cave.

STABLES

Sometimes caves were turned into stables for animals. The story of Jesus' birth tells us he was born in a stable: this may have been a cave.

VERY EARLY HOUSES

By about 4000 B.C., New Stone Age men had left their caves. Some learned to be farmers. They built small, round, cave-like homes out of stone. Their houses were grouped close together for safety, and surrounded by a stone wall. Traces of these first houses have been found in Jericho, which is probably the oldest city in the world, founded about 8000 B.C.

Bible Search

- Israelites in caves: *Judges 6:2*

- David in hiding: *1 Samuel 22:1*

- Homes for poor people: *Hebrews 11:38*

HOMES LIVING IN TENTS

People who lived a traveling life were called nomads. They moved from one waterhole to another with their flocks. They lived in tents.

Abraham, Isaac and Jacob all lived in tents. Their descendants, the Israelites, never forgot that they came from wandering tent dwellers.

Seats were carpets or straw mats, and beds were mats. The table was a round piece of leather. It had rings round the edge so that a cord could be threaded through and drawn up into a bag to use when travelling. Water-bottles were made from goat's skin. There were baskets for storage, and the few cooking pots were made out of metal.

WHAT WERE TENTS MADE OF?

At first, tents were made from animal skins. Later, when people learned how to weave, they were made from goat or camel hair.

The skins were held up by wooden poles measuring up to 7 feet high. The more important you were, the more poles you had. Usually there were nine. The center pole was slightly taller than the rest. Wooden pegs and ropes kept the tent steady. The tent's entrance faced the direction from which visitors were most likely to come, and was kept open during the day. This was so it looked welcoming.

Animal skin

Richer families might have a group of tents, with separate tents for the women and children, and for servants. The main tent was put up in the middle with the servants' tents surrounding it.

INSIDE A TENT

Inside were two rooms divided by a curtain. The back room was for women and children, and was where the cooking was done. There was very little furniture, because everything had to be carried on donkeys when people moved on to their next camp.

SETTING UP CAMP

Campsites were set up near water, and close to trees which could give shelter. There was always a danger from wild animals, and from other nomads too. Sometimes there were fights over wells and the use of precious water.

- Quarrels over water: *Genesis 26:19–22*
- Abraham's tent: *Genesis 18:1–2*

Rope and pegs   **Tent poles**

HOMES VILLAGE HOUSES

T he simplest village houses were like a square box, with a flat roof. The whole family and their animals slept in one room. Other houses had a wall outside, enclosing a yard, where the animals could be kept. Richer families might have an extra story.

Bible Search

- Roof of clay and branches on wooden beams: *Mark 2:4*
- Safety first: *Deuteronomy 28:8*
- Extra bedroom: *2 Kings 4:10*

UP ON THE ROOF

Houses had a flat roof with a slight curve to allow rain to flow into a gutter. There was a low wall round the roof to stop people falling off.

The roof was used like an extra room. Grapes and figs were spread out to dry along with wet clothes. People would go out there to pray and think. They sat out talking to their friends, or even held parties there. On warm nights, the family slept on the roof.

WALLS

Walls were made of stone (in rocky areas), or built from mud and straw bricks which had been baked in an oven. Bricks were stuck together by a mortar made from lime. Foundations were important because Palestine was in an earthquake area. If a house was not built on rock, foundations were dug to be as deep as the walls were high.

Walls were often whitewashed.

WINDOWS AND DOORS

There were only one or two small high windows, with no glass. In winter, these might be covered by an animal skin.

Small windows kept the house cool in summer and warmer in winter.

The doorposts were made of wood or stone. Doors were only closed at night, or when there was no one at home. Doorways were low, and grownups had to stoop to go in.

INSIDE A HOUSE

Inside the house was a raised platform made from stone, or mud and stone chippings, where the family lived. Next to it was a floor of stamped-down earth, where the animals slept at night. There was a manger for the animals' food. People lived outdoors and on the roof as much as possible. Food and pots were stored in a hollow in the wall.

A fire would be lit in a hollow. There was no chimney, and the room was smoky when the fire was lit. The walls were black from smoke. Lots of insects lived in cracks and holes in the walls. There was a store area where food for winter and tools were kept. Houses were only about 6 feet high.

Doorways were low

HOMES

T he people of Israel were not especially good builders or architects, but the house design below seems to have been invented by them, and was common. This type of house would have been lived in by a family with an average income.

PAUL IN CORINTH

In Jerusalem, archaeologists have found the remains of a town home that was burnt down by the Romans in A.D. 70. It had a basement with a kitchen, bathroom, courtyard and three other small rooms. There were about twenty rooms on the ground floor, and another floor as well. There were large stone basins for storing water.

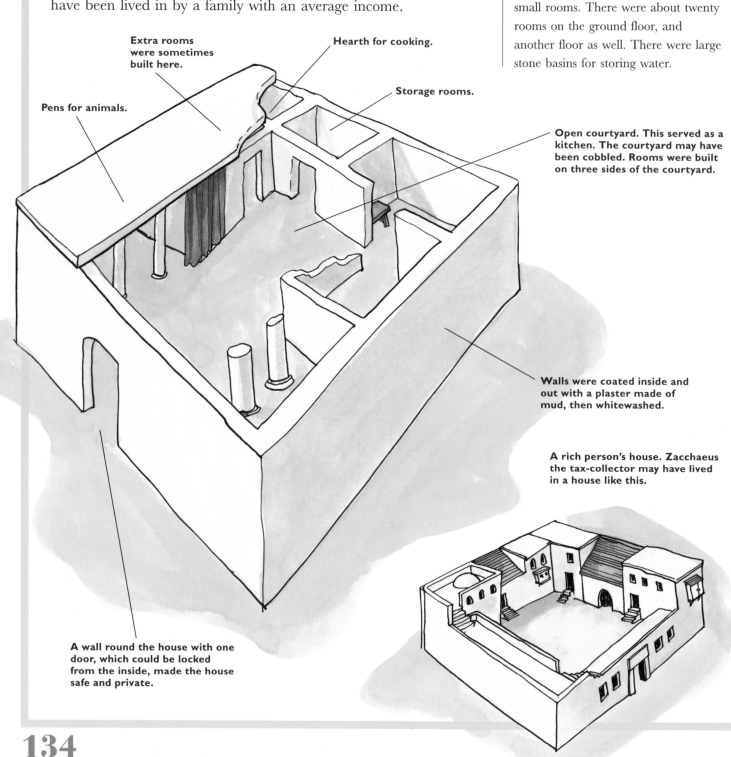

Extra rooms were sometimes built here.

Hearth for cooking.

Storage rooms.

Pens for animals.

Open courtyard. This served as a kitchen. The courtyard may have been cobbled. Rooms were built on three sides of the courtyard.

Walls were coated inside and out with a plaster made of mud, then whitewashed.

A rich person's house. Zacchaeus the tax-collector may have lived in a house like this.

A wall round the house with one door, which could be locked from the inside, made the house safe and private.

HOPE AND ENDURANCE

T he world today is short on hope. Often, people look at the wars, pollution and destruction, and think that there is no hope for the future. When we do speak of hope, the word is often used in a weak sense, for example, "I hope everything will be all right." But this is the exact opposite of what the Bible teaches about hope.

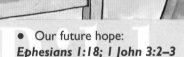

People today often think there is no hope

HOPE IS...

Christian hope is something definite. It means knowing for certain that in the end, everything is going to be all right. This is because Christian hope is based on the love and goodness of God.

Everything will be all right

HOPE FOR WHAT?

In the New Testament, "hope" refers to our future in heaven: our own happiness when we see Jesus, and the love and goodness God will give us. It also refers to the time when Jesus will come again.

SO WHAT?

When you are young it is difficult to think of the future

When we are young, the future in heaven often seems far away and unimportant. But God has given those who trust Jesus a sort of deposit, which guarantees future happiness. This deposit is the Spirit of Jesus in us.

Paul called it "Christ in you, the hope of glory". Good things will happen, and bad things are nothing to be afraid of.

Bible Search

- Our future hope:
Ephesians 1:18; 1 John 3:2–3

- Courage from hope:
2 Corinthians 3:12

- Faith and love from hope:
Colossians 1:5

- Endurance from hope:
*1 Thessalonians 1:3;
Hebrews 10:23–25*

A RACE

In a long-distance race, what keeps the runners going lap after lap? It's the thought of the glory of winning! The writer of the Letter to the Hebrews said that Christian life was like a long-distance race. In this race, everyone who finished would be a winner!

One of the most important teachings in the Bible is that we must persevere, that is to say we must keep going to the end. Hope keeps us going: Paul said, "We remember your endurance inspired by hope."

Christian life is like a race

HOSEA THE BOOK OF

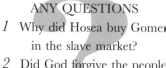

Hosea's children had to cope with a broken home. His wife, Gomer, had gone off with other men, leaving Hosea with three children to look after. One day, he saw Gomer again. She was up for sale in a slave market. Hosea bought Gomer and freed her from slavery.

Hosea buys Gomer

Hosea and his three children

UNDERSTANDING HOSEA

Hosea said that the people in Israel were just like his wife. They had left God, and were worshiping idols. But God still loved them. Baal was one of the gods that the people were worshiping. He was a god of war, storm and rain.

An idol of Baal

READING HOSEA

- *Chapter 1*: Hosea's marriage and family.
- *Chapter 2–3*: Israel is like Gomer.
- *Chapter 4–10*: Israel's crimes and God's punishment.
- *Chapter 11–14*: Hosea says, 'Come back to God'.

Four other prophets were preaching at about the same time as Hosea. To find out more, turn to the pages on Isaiah, Micah and Amos.

GOD'S PUNISHMENT

Hosea predicted the downfall of the Israelite people. God said, "I will come upon them like a lion, like a leopard I will lurk by the path." Hosea saw his warnings come true. In 722 B.C., the Assyrian army destroyed Samaria.

Hosea's book has a happy ending. He said God would forgive his people and love them freely.

ANY QUESTIONS
1 Why did Hosea buy Gomer in the slave market?
2 Did God forgive the people for worshipping idols?

Bible Search

- Hosea buys Gomer back:
  Hosea 3: 2
- A happy future:
  Hosea 14: 4-8
- Idol worship:
  Hosea 4: 2
- Animals:
  Hosea 13: 7-8

The Assyrian army destroyed Samaria

Fetching water

HOUSEWORK A DAY IN A VILLAGE HOME

T he mother was in charge of the home. The Book of Proverbs shows how important she was and how much she had to do: weaving wool and flax, providing food, buying land, and making clothes for her family.

GETTING UP

The family was woken by the crowing of a cockerel at dawn. Cockerels were the first alarm clocks! The smallest houses only had one room, with a raised area where people slept and ate. When everyone got up, the flat mattresses which were their beds were rolled up.

People didn't sit down to breakfast. Instead, bread and dried fruit or cheese was eaten on the move.

Then the father and the older boys set off for work. Younger children stayed at home. Some learned about God, and how to read and write, from priests or other religious leaders.

Making the bed

CHORES

The younger children looked after the animals. Many people kept sheep and goats. At night, the animals were kept in the lower part of the room, next to the raised area. Older girls were often sent to fetch water from the well. Most villages were on a hill, and most wells were at the bottom of the hill!

There was little or no furniture to dust. The earth floor was swept with a broom made from corn stalks tied to a stick.

SHOPPING

Food did not keep well in the hot climate. Vegetables and fruit had to be bought fresh from the market. Grain was ground into flour to make bread, or bread could be bought from the baker. Grain was ground between two stones. Poor families used barley, and rich families used wheat.

IN THE AFTERNOON

During the middle of the day, which was the hottest part, everyone slept. Then, in the afternoon, clothes were made and mended, or washed in the river and spread out to dry on the flat roof. Other jobs to do were weaving and spinning, and preparing the evening meal. The women and girls worked outside in the shade.

THE EVENING MEAL

The family often sat outside to eat. There might be a big pot of soup, and everyone would dip pieces of bread in it. This meant no dishwashing! When it got dark, the family went to bed.

IDOLS
WORSHIPING FALSE GODS

An idol was an object, like a statue, which represented a god. People worshiped the image as a god. It may seem strange that anyone should want to bow down and worship a lump of metal or wood. But in the times before their exile to Babylonia, the Israelites were often tempted to copy their neighbors and worship idols instead of God.

THE GOLDEN CALF

The Israelites were waiting for Moses to come down from Mount Sinai, where he had gone to talk to God. Moses was gone for a long time, and nobody knew what had happened to him. So the people asked Aaron to make them a new god. They gave him all their gold jewelry, and Aaron made it into a gleaming idol in the shape of a calf. The people began to pray and offer sacrifices to it.

In Egypt (which the Israelites had recently left), a bull stood for fertility and power.

Worshiping the golden calf

FORBIDDEN

Moses said to the Israelites, "You saw no form of any kind the day the Lord spoke to you at Horeb (Sinai). Therefore…do not make for yourselves an idol, an image of any shape…"

Other nations believed in gods which looked like people or animals. They made idols of their gods, and sometimes worshiped these idols.

GODS

Baal was the god of storms and war. He was the most important of the gods of the people of Canaan.

Astarte, or Ashtaroth, was a mother goddess, a goddess of fertility, love and war.

Astarte was a mother goddess

Baal was the god of storms and war

Teraphim were sometimes called "household gods". They were small images of human figures used in worship and magic, and for getting in touch with evil powers.

A teraph

EVIL

In New Testament times, Greeks and Romans sometimes worshiped idols. Paul said that while idols were not real, people who worshiped them could be trapped by evil spirits.
See also the page on Worship.

Bible Search
- Moses: *Deuteronomy 4:15–16*
- Isaiah makes fun of idols: *Isaiah 44:9–20*
- Teraphim: *2 Kings 23:24*
- Paul: *1 Corinthians 10:19–20*

ILLNESS
AND MEDICINE

I llnesses such as dysentery, cholera, typhoid and beriberi were common. Skin diseases, especially leprosy, affected many people. (See the page on Beggars and Lepers.) People often suffered from worms. Many children had an eye infection called ophthalmia, which was passed on by flies.

Many children had ophthalmia

- Wine for the stomach:
  I Timothy 5:23
- Oil and wine for a wound:
  Luke 10:34
- Wine and myrrh for Jesus:
  Mark 15:23
- A sick woman:
  Mark 5:25–29; Luke 8:43

- Honey was used as an ointment for open wounds.
- Wine was drunk for stomach disorders.
- Wine mixed with a drug called myrrh made a simple painkilling drink. Jesus was offered this drink when he was dying on the cross.

Wine and myrrh was used as a pain-killer

DOCTORS

In Old Testament times, there were not many doctors. The Egyptians tried to cure illnesses by magic spells. The Israelites thought of health as a gift from God, and asked for God's help when they became ill.

By the time of the New Testament, there were many more doctors. Jewish religious teachers said no one should live in a town without a doctor.

A woman came to Jesus to be cured. Mark and Luke both wrote about it in their Gospels. Mark said, "She had suffered a great deal under the care of many doctors, and spent all she had…" But Luke, who was himself a doctor, was kinder to doctors! He wrote: "No one could heal her."

MEDICINES

People used all sorts of things, such as herbs, as medicines:
- Olive oil mixed with herbs could be used to bathe the head of a sick person.
- A solution of olive oil and wine was put on wounds.

Olive oil was used on wounds

- Figs were used to cure boils. When King Hezekiah had a bad boil, Isaiah made a hot paste from figs to put on it.

DENTISTS

There were no dentists. Garlic was used for toothache, and yeast was rubbed on painful gums.

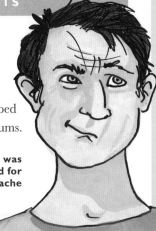

Garlic was used for toothache

INSECTS AND REPTILES

Insects are the largest group of animals in the world, with over a million species. Ants, bees, flies, gnats, grasshoppers and moths all have walk-on parts in the Bible story.

Reptiles are animals with scales instead of fur, skin or hide. Only lizards and snakes appear in the Bible.

LOCUSTS

Locusts are a kind of grasshopper. They can destroy crops.

People ate locusts because they were a good source of fat and protein. You could have boiled locust, roasted locust or even locust cake. John the Baptist ate locusts with honey, which helped to take away their bitter flavor.

BEES

Sugar was not known, so honey was used to sweeten food. People did not have beehives, but they did put up hanging baskets or pots, hoping that bees would nest there.

Locusts eating crops

Ants

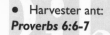

Bible Search

- Harvester ant:
  Proverbs 6:6-7
- Wicked people and snakes:
  Psalm 58:4-5
- Paul on Malta:
  Acts 28:1-6
- Jonathan finds honey:
  1 Samuel 14:24-28

SNAKES

In the Garden of Eden, the Devil made himself look like a snake, so snakes were thought of as evil. The Old Testament has eight different words which all mean 'poisonous snake'. Different translations describe snakes as adders, asps, cobras, serpents and vipers. The New Testament Greek word for all snakes is viper. Snake charmers appear once in the Bible. A psalmist says that evil people who refuse to listen to God are rather like snakes that refuse to listen to the snake charmer's pipe.

Snake charmer

PAUL AND THE VIPER

Paul was shipwrecked on Malta. While collecting sticks for a fire, Paul was bitten by a viper. The islanders expected the poison would kill him, but nothing happened. They were amazed and decided Paul must be a god.

Viper

ISAAC A BABY FOR SARAH AND ABRAHAM

One day, three strangers arrived at Abraham and Sarah's tent. They brought exciting news for Abraham. Sarah, who was listening, laughed aloud when she heard the strangers say that she would have a baby. "Whoever heard of such a thing," she said. "I'm ninety years old!" When the baby was born, he was called Isaac, which means "Laughing."

Sarah, Isaac and Abraham

FARMER ISAAC

When famine came, people moved to live where they could find food. But God told Isaac, "Don't leave this land. I will look after you." Isaac became a rich farmer. This was a different life from his father Abraham, who had been a traveling nomad.

Isaac became a farmer

A MAN OF PEACE

A well

Abimelech, the local chief, was jealous of Isaac. Again and again his men blocked up Isaac's wells. Isaac dug new wells in new areas. Each time, God blessed him. Wells were very important because there wasn't much rain to provide water.

One day, Abimelech rode up with his army general. But he came to make peace, not war. Abimelech had realized that God was on Isaac's side. Isaac and Abimelech celebrated their peace treaty with a feast.

- Isaac's birth: *Genesis 21:1-6*
- A peace treaty: *Genesis 26:26-31*
- Isaac meets Rebekah: *Genesis 24:62-67*

A feast

REBEKAH: AN ARRANGED MARRIAGE

It was important to find the right wife for Isaac, because Isaac's family were to be part of God's plan for the world. Rebekah was God's choice. (To find out how Rebekah was found, turn to the page on Esau.) Rebekah put on a long veil when she first saw Isaac. This was a sign that she was not married.

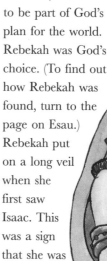

ESAU AND JACOB

Sadness came to Isaac from inside his own family. Isaac and Rebekah had twin sons, Esau and Jacob. But the sons were rivals, not friends. To find out what happened, look up the page on Esau.

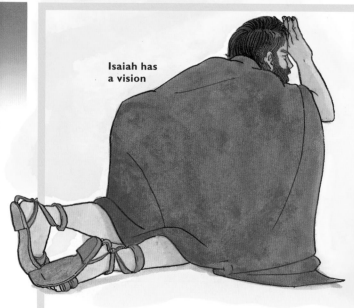

Isaiah has a vision

ISAIAH

THE BOOK OF

The prophet Isaiah lived in Jerusalem. He was a friend of kings. His book is one of the most beautiful and best loved in the Bible. Isaiah was preaching in about 740–700 B.C. At about the same time, the prophet Hosea was preaching in Samaria.

UNDERSTANDING ISAIAH

Isaiah had an awesome vision of God in heaven. He saw flying seraphim (angels) calling, "Holy, holy, holy is the Lord Almighty." When Isaiah saw the greatness of God, he felt very sinful and small. Then one of the angels touched Isaiah's mouth with a burning coal, and told him that his sins were forgiven. He heard God say, "Who can I send?" "Send me," said Isaiah. God told him to go and tell people about his teachings, but warned that they wouldn't listen or understand.

'Send me,' said Isaiah

READING ISAIAH

- *Chapter 1–39*: The northern kingdom of Israel had fallen to the Assyrians. Isaiah warned the people of Judah to watch out, or it would be their turn. But he said the people would be saved by a great king.
- *Chapter 40–55*: Isaiah looked ahead and saw his people would be prisoners. But God would set them free again one day. A "suffering servant' would come to heal them.
- *Chapter 56–66*: Isaiah looked even further ahead. He saw the people struggling to make a living. But he said they must keep going and God's glory would shine again.

ANY QUESTIONS
1 Isaiah wrote about a suffering servant. Who was he?
2 What happened to the kingdom of Judah?

HE PROPHECIES CAME TRUE

- Jerusalem fell to the enemy about 150 years later.
  - The people were taken away and then returned home again.
  - Jesus came as the great king and suffering servant. To find out more, turn to the pages on Amos, Hosea and Micah.

FAMOUS POEMS FROM ISAIAH

- Unto us a child is born: Isaiah 9:1–7.
- Future joy: Isaiah 35.
- Comfort my people: Isaiah 40.
- He was despised…a man of sorrows: Isaiah 52:13–53:12.

Bible Search

- Jesus reads from Isaiah: *Luke 4:19–20*
- Suffering servant: *I Peter 2:23–25*

JACOB
AND THE NATION OF ISRAEL

Jacob at Haran

T he story of Jacob takes up a quarter of the book of Genesis. That shows how important he was. God had promised Jacob's grandfather, Abraham, that he would make his descendants into a great nation. And God passed that promise on to Jacob. God named Jacob "Israel" and the nation was called after him. His sons were the founders of the twelve tribes of Israel.

RIVER JABBOQ

On the journey to **Aram** Canaan, Jacob was a worried man. He thought Esau would be waiting to kill him. Jacob stopped for the night at the River Jabboq. Suddenly, a stranger appeared and began to fight Jacob. They fought all night, until dawn. Then the stranger left, telling Jacob he would now be called Israel instead of Jacob. Jacob realized the stranger was God.

BETHEL

Jacob had to leave home after he tricked Esau out of his birthright. (See the page on Esau.) He set off to stay with his uncle at Haran. One night on his journey, Jacob dreamt of a stairway leading to heaven, with angels on it. God appeared at the top of the stairs and told Joseph he would give him the land he slept on. When Jacob woke up, he named the place where he had slept "Bethel," meaning "House of God."

Shechem

Bethel

River Jabboq

MAHANAIM

Esau came to meet Jacob with 400 men. Esau forgave his brother.

Jacob realized it was God

SHECHEM

Jacob bought land outside this strong-walled city. But he had to leave when his sons made war on the local people.

HARAN

Jacob stayed with his uncle Laban, and fell in love with Laban's daughter, Rachel. Laban tricked him into marrying his other daughter, Leah, before he allowed him to marry Rachel too.

Beersheba, birthplace of Jacob and Esau

ARAM OF THE TWO RIVERS (NOW SYRIA)

Jacob was a clever shepherd, and soon he increased the numbers of his flocks of sheep and goats.

Laban and his sons were jealous of Jacob. So Joseph, after living with Laban for twenty years, decided to go back to Canaan. He took his family and all his flocks with him.

BETHEL

Jacob and his family made a new start. God promised the country of Canaan to his family for ever.

HEBRON VALLEY

Jacob settled here, but his adventures were not over.

143

JAMES THE LETTER OF

The Letter of James is probably the earliest, or second earliest, New Testament book (the other is Paul's letter to the Galatians). One of Jesus' half-brothers, James, is the most likely author of this letter. Christians in Jerusalem were being thrown into prison, and many had run away to other countries. This letter was probably written to help these new followers of Jesus.

Bible Search

- James: *I Corinthians 15:7; Galatians 2:9; Acts 15:13*
- The importance of prayer: *James 5:13–20*

JAMES

At first, James did not believe Jesus was the son of God. But when Jesus was brought back to life after the crucifixion, he went to see James. After that, James became one of the leaders of the Church in Jerusalem. Paul called him 'a pillar of the Church'.

UNDERSTANDING JAMES

Jesus said that real Christians obeyed God. People who said that they had faith in God, but didn't show their faith by their actions, weren't real Christians. James gave many examples of true faith:

Gossip

- James said that real Christians could control their tongues. Phoney Christians gossiped, told tales and cursed. He warned that just as a great forest fire could be started by a small spark, so a great deal of harm could be done by one person's words.

- Real Christians helped people in need. James wrote: "Suppose a brother or sister is without food and clothes. If one of you says to him, "Go, I wish you well; keep warm and well fed," but does nothing about his physical needs, what good is it?"

- Real Christians treated everyone equally. James said, "Suppose a well-dressed rich man and a shabbily dressed poor man come to a meeting. You must not give the rich man the best seat and tell the poor man to sit on the floor"

Feeding and clothing a poor man

READING JAMES

- *Chapter 1*: A guide to true religion.
- *Chapter 2*: Faith and action.
- *Chapter 3*: Controlling the tongue.
- *Chapter 4:1–12*: Yes to God; no to the Devil.
- *Chapter 4:13–5:19*: Warnings, patience and prayer.

A poor man sitting on the best seat

JEREMIAH THE BOOK OF

The Book of Jeremiah gives the prophet Jeremiah's view of the last years of the kingdom of Judah. It contains his messages, poems and prayers, and describes his suffering. Jeremiah has been called "the weeping prophet." He warned the people they were heading for disaster, and was bitterly sad when the people would not listen to him.

Jeremiah was treated like an enemy

JEREMIAH

Jeremiah came from a family of priests. He was a young man when God called him to be a prophet. The king of Judah, Josiah, was his friend. They worked together to make the people trust God. When Josiah died, Jeremiah was treated like an enemy. He spent a lot of time in prison. His enemies, and even his own family, tried to kill him. But he continued to speak God's words.

Josiah and Jeremiah

UNDERSTANDING JEREMIAH

A potter

Jeremiah watched a potter at work at his potter's wheel. When the pot went wrong, the potter started again. "God is like that potter," Jeremiah said. "You people of Judah are like the clay. You are going wrong. God has to put you right."

BARUCH

Baruch was one of Jeremiah's few friends. He was also his secretary. When Jeremiah was told not to preach, Baruch wrote down his sermons. One day, some of the sermons were read to the king, Jehoiakim. The king slashed the scroll with his penknife, and threw the pieces on to a fire. So Baruch and Jeremiah wrote the sermons out again, with more added.

THE END OF JERUSALEM

Everything looked black. Nebuchadnezzar's army was all around Jerusalem. Jeremiah told the people, "You will be taken away as prisoners, but God will bring you back." His words came true.

READING JEREMIAH

- *Chapter 1*: Jeremiah's call.
- *Chapter 18:1–12*: The potter.
- *Chapter 19:14–20:18*: Stocks.
- *Chapter 30–33*: New hope.
- *Chapter 36:20–32*: Burning the scroll.

JERUSALEM
IN THE TIME OF JESUS

I t is about 3,000 years since King David captured the small hilltop town of Jerusalem and made it his capital city. David's son, King Solomon, built the Temple in Jerusalem, making it a holy city. Nearly a thousand years later, King Herod rebuilt the Temple. Then, as now, tourists from all over the world came to Jerusalem.

ANY QUESTIONS
1 Who founded the city
of Jerusalem?
2 Where did the Devil
tempt Jesus?

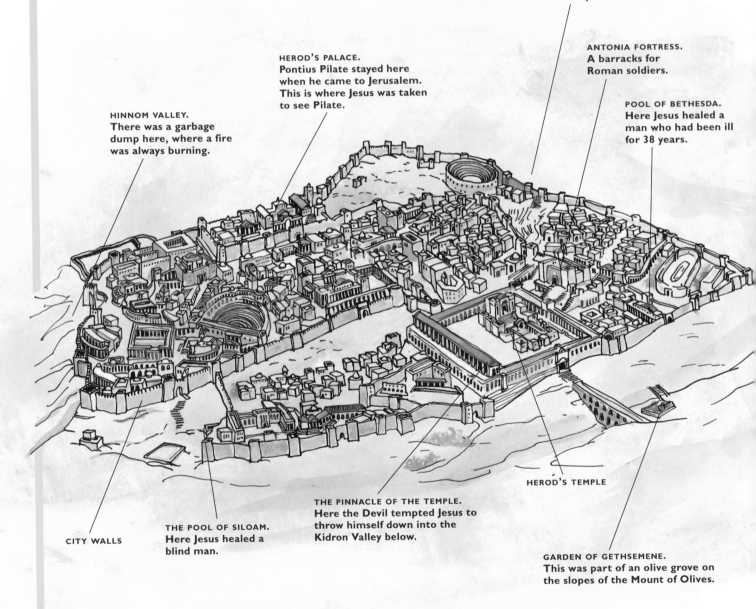

CRUCIFIXION SITE.
Jesus was taken outside
Jerusalem to be crucified.
This is a possible site.

ANTONIA FORTRESS.
A barracks for
Roman soldiers.

POOL OF BETHESDA.
Here Jesus healed a
man who had been ill
for 38 years.

HEROD'S PALACE.
Pontius Pilate stayed here
when he came to Jerusalem.
This is where Jesus was taken
to see Pilate.

HINNOM VALLEY.
There was a garbage
dump here, where a fire
was always burning.

CITY WALLS

THE POOL OF SILOAM.
Here Jesus healed a
blind man.

THE PINNACLE OF THE TEMPLE.
Here the Devil tempted Jesus to
throw himself down into the
Kidron Valley below.

HEROD'S TEMPLE

GARDEN OF GETHSEMENE.
This was part of an olive grove on
the slopes of the Mount of Olives.

JESUS
WHY HE CAME

Jesus

Jesus did many things in his life. He showed us what God is really like; he told us how God wants us to live; he gave us an example of a perfect human life. But these weren't the reasons why he came. Jesus told us that he had come in order to die.

JESUS' WORDS

Jesus' name for himself was "the son of man." This meant "human being." Jesus took the name from the Old Testament Book of Daniel.

When Zacchaeus, the hated tax-collector, became a friend of Jesus, Jesus said, "The son of man came to seek and to save the lost."

Jesus also said, "The son of man did not come to be served, but to serve and to give his life as a ransom for many." Jesus gave his life as a ransom to set us free.

Being set free

SIN

What did Jesus set us free from? Sin means going our own way instead of God's way. People who do this fall into evil ways. Jesus' death is the ransom that sets us free from the power of evil, and from its punishment, which is being cut off from God for ever.

A SUFFERING SERVANT

Jesus called himself a servant, who had "come to serve". He was quoting from the Old Testament Book of Isaiah. Isaiah wrote: "See my servant… He was wounded for the wrong things we did… Each of us has gone his own way. But the Lord has put on him the punishment for all the evil we have done."

ANY QUESTIONS
1 Why did Jesus come to die for us?
2 Why did Jesus call himself 'the son of man'?

VICTORY

Jesus said, "The son of man must suffer…and after three days rise again." And, "The son of man will sit on his throne in heavenly glory." Then, said Jesus, all those who trusted him would be with him for ever.

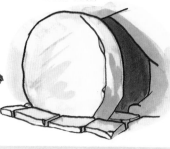

Bible Search

- The lost: *Luke 19:10*
- A ransom: *Matthew 20:28*
- Suffering servant: *Isaiah 53; 1 Peter 2:22–25*
- Son of man: *Daniel 7:13–14*
- Glory: *Matthew 25:31, 34*

A servant

JESUS THE MAN

esus was born about the year 6 B.C. He grew up in Nazareth, a town in the northern part of Palestine called Galilee. Until he was about thirty, he was a carpenter. Then he became a traveling teacher and healer. Three years later, the Romans crucified him. Three days later he came back to life. Since then, billions of people have called themselves Christians.

A REAL HUMAN BEING

Jesus was not an angel, an alien or a superman. Jesus was tempted in every way we are tempted. But he was not weak. He never did anything wrong. When Jesus went into the wilderness for forty days, to fast and pray, the Devil tried to tempt him to stop trusting God. But Jesus refused.

The Devil tempts Jesus

Jesus heals a leper

A MAN FOR OTHERS

Jesus had the power to heal, and he spent his time helping people who were suffering and in need. He showed them how to be happy, forgiving and loving because their father God loved them all.

Bible Search

- Jesus has a rest by a well: *John 4*

- Jesus shows his love for people others despised: *Mark 2:15-17*

- Jesus heals people: *Matthew 8, 9*

A MAN AGAINST EVIL

Throughout his life, Jesus fought a battle against evil. His weapons were truth, love and prayer.

Many of the religious leaders at the time kept the rules and ceremonies of their faith carefully, but did not have a close personal knowledge of God or a real care for needy people. Jesus made them face up to their failure to love God and other people.

JESUS IS GOD

After Jesus died and came back to life again, his friends thought about everything he had said and done. And they became certain that Jesus was God in human form. A writer in the New Testament summed it up when he said, "The Son reflects the glory of God. He is an exact copy of God's nature."

Jesus rose from the dead

A REAL HUMAN

Jesus had a human mother, Mary, but hr did not have a human father. He was formed in Mary's womb by the power of God's Spirit.

JESUS' ACTIONS SHOW HE IS GOD

Jesus told a storm at sea to calm down, and it did! Jesus' friends knew that only God could control the weather. Jesus said to a man who could not walk, "Your sins are forgiven…Take your mat and walk." The man was healed! Everyone knew that only God could forgive sins.

JESUS' WORDS SHOW HE IS GOD

When Jesus said he had seen Abraham, the Jews asked how that could be, since he wasn't old enough. Jesus said, "I tell you the truth. Before Abraham was born, I am!" In the Old Testament the words "I am" were God's name for himself.

Jesus said, "Anyone who has seen me has seen the Father."

Jesus said, "The Father and I are one." When Jesus said this, the Jews tried to stone him. They said, "You are only a man, but you say you are the same as God." Stoning was the Jewish way of carrying out the death penalty. It was the punishment for claiming to be God.

JESUS' FRIENDS REALIZE HE IS GOD

At times, Jesus' friends did not understand Jesus fully. But Peter once realized Jesus was 'the Christ, the son of the living God'. Thomas, the doubter, saw Jesus after he had come back to life and said, "My Lord and my God." Later, Paul was to describe Jesus as being the same as God.

Jesus' friends see Jesus is alive again

JESUS' RESURRECTION SHOWS HE IS GOD

Because Jesus was God, he could not die forever. God the Father brought him back to life, and many people saw him alive.

- Jesus' words:
John 8:58; 14:9; 10:29-31

- Man who could not walk:
Mark 2:1-12

- Storm at sea:
Mark 4:35-41

- Jesus' friends opinion:
Matthew 16:16; John 20:28

Bible Search

A storm at sea

JESUS IS BORN

In about the year 5 B.C., two people were planning to get married. Their names were Mary and Joseph, and they lived in Nazareth, a town in the hills of Galilee.

One day, something very exciting happened to Mary. The angel Gabriel appeared and said, "You will give birth to a son. He will be the son of God."

Joseph

JOSEPH

When Joseph found out that Mary was expecting a baby, he decided to break off their engagement, because he knew he was not the father.

But in a dream, an angel told him not to be afraid. "The baby will be born by the power of God," said the angel. "You must call him Jesus (God Saves) because he will save his people from their sins."

ELIZABETH

Mary went to visit her cousin Elizabeth who lived near Jerusalem. Elizabeth was also expecting a baby. Elizabeth's baby grew up to be John the Baptist.

Mary and Elizabeth

BETHLEHEM

The Roman emperor Augustus Caesar gave orders for a register to be taken of all the people living in the Roman empire. Mary and Joseph had to go to Bethlehem to be registered, which was a three-day journey by donkey.

When they arrived in Bethlehem, the city was full and there was nowhere to stay. That night, Mary gave birth. We know from Luke's Gospel that when Jesus was born, Mary wrapped him in strips of cloth and laid him in a manger. A manger was where animals fed. For this reason, it has always been said that Jesus was born in a stable, probably a cave in the hillside by the inn.

Bible Search

- Gabriel: *Luke 1:26–38*
- Mary and Elizabeth: *Luke 1:39–56*
- Joseph: *Matthew 1:18–25*
- Bethlehem: *Luke 2:1–7*
- Shepherds: *Luke 2:8–20*

SHEPHERDS

On the night Jesus was born, shepherds were guarding their sheep in the hills outside Bethlehem. Suddenly, there was a great light, and an angel appeared. "Don't be afraid," the angel said, "I'm bringing you good news of great joy." The angel told the shepherds about Jesus.

At once, the shepherds decided to go and visit Jesus, Mary and Joseph.

Joseph and Mary try to find somewhere to stay in Bethlehem

JESUS AS A BABY

Mary and Joseph take Jesus to the temple

After Jesus was born, Mary and Joseph moved to a house in Bethlehem. After eight days, Jesus was named and circumcised according to Jewish custom. Forty days later, Mary and Joseph took Jesus to the Temple in Jerusalem, to offer a sacrifice and pray for him to serve God all his life.

WISE MEN

When Jesus was born, a group of wise men saw a new star rising in the east. Their books told them that a new star meant a new king. So they set off for Jerusalem.

The Gospel of Matthew doesn't say the men were kings: it called them "magi" which meant "wise men." They were probably astrologers (men who studied the stars) from Persia or Arabia. We think there were three of them, because they gave three gifts to Jesus.

King Herod, who ruled Judea, was very worried when he heard that a new king had been born. He thought he had a rival for his throne. He sent for the wise men and said, "Come back and see me when you've found the king." He wanted to find out where Jesus was.

Bible Search

- In the Temple:
  Luke 2:21–38

- Wise men:
  Matthew 2:1–12

- Escape:
  Matthew 2:13–18

- Return:
  Matthew 2:19–23

THE GIFTS

The star led the wise men to the house where Mary and Joseph were living. They gave Jesus gifts of gold, frankincense (a perfumed incense) and myrrh (an expensive scented ointment).

The wise men were warned in a dream not to go back to Jerusalem and see Herod, so they went home a different way.

MURDER

Mary, Jesus and Joseph escape

Herod was furious when the wise men didn't return. So to make sure that the new king didn't survive, he gave orders for all baby boys in Bethlehem under two years old to be killed.

Joseph, Mary and Jesus escaped to live in Egypt. When King Herod died in 4 B.C., the family went back to Palestine, and settled in Nazareth.

The three wise men

JESUS GROWS UP

Nazareth

Jesus grew up in Nazareth, a quiet market town in the hills of Galilee. The northern region of Galilee was beautiful, with wooded hills, and many wild flowers. Jews from the south did not like the people of Galilee very much. Galileans spoke with a different accent and many had parents from other countries.

HEAD OF THE FAMILY

We think Joseph died when Jesus was a teenager. Mary is always by herself in the Gospel stories. Jesus, as the eldest son, took over his father's business. He was not able to go on to higher education. This is why he was later called 'uneducated'.

FAMILY

Jesus' father, Joseph, was a carpenter and builder. He would have been an important man in his village, as carpentry was skilled work.

Jesus had at least four younger brothers: James, Joseph, Simon and Judas, and several sisters.

Between the ages of five and thirteen, Jesus went to school in the synagogue in Nazareth. He learned to read and write and he studied the Bible (our Old Testament).

JESUS IS MISSING

When Jesus was twelve, he went with his family, relatives and friends to the Passover festival in Jerusalem. While they were there, Jesus disappeared. His parents were frantic with worry, but at last they found him, sitting with a class of students in the Temple. Jesus was surprised that they were so upset. He said, 'Didn't you know I would be in my father's house?'

COMING OF AGE

On their thirteenth birthday, Jewish boys were considered to be adults. There was a special service in the synagogue, called the Bar Mitzvah, to celebrate. Most boys left school at about this age, and went to work with their fathers. A few went on to study in Jerusalem.

Jesus works as a carpenter

- Nazareth: *John 1:46*
- Jesus' family: *Mark 6:1–3*
- No education: *John 7:15*
- Jerusalem: *Luke 2:41–50*
- Growing up: *Luke 2:51–52*

Joseph and his children

JESUS
IS BAPTIZED AND TESTED

Jesus was about thirty years old when news reached Nazareth of a new prophet called John the Baptist. He was telling people to turn back to God, and get ready to welcome God's Messiah. He was preaching at Bethany, on the eastern banks of the River Jordan, and baptizing people.

Bethany

JESUS' BAPTISM

John was shocked when he saw his cousin Jesus coming to be baptized. "You should baptize me!" John said. Jesus came to be baptized to show he was ready to do what God wanted, and that he was willing to take people's wrongdoing on himself.

People were baptized by dipping their whole body into the water of the lake or river. When Jesus came up out of the water, the Holy Spirit came to him in the form of a dove. And God's voice said, "You are my son, whom I love; with you I am well pleased."

Bible Search

- Baptism: *Matthew 3:13–17;*
- Testing: *Matthew 4:1–11; Mark 1:12–13*
- Moses quoted: *Deuteronomy 8:3; 6:16; 13*
- Temptation: *Hebrews 4:15*

John baptizes Jesus

TESTING

After the baptism, the Holy Spirit led Jesus away to the desert wilderness of Judea. There he spent forty days without food, with only the wild animals for company. Then the Devil came to tempt, or test, Jesus.

The Devil asked Jesus to turn stones into bread, to prove he was the son of God, as he claimed. Jesus replied that man could not live on bread alone, but had to find strength from God's words.

Then the Devil transported Jesus to the top of the Temple, and told him to throw himself off. "If you really are the son of God," he said, "you won't come to any harm." But Jesus said that God was not to be tested in that way.

Finally, the Devil offered Jesus all the kingdoms of the Earth, if he would worship the Devil. Jesus refused, shouting, "Away from me Satan." The Devil gave up, defeated, and disappeared.

With these tests, the Devil was trying to tempt Jesus to use his power in wrong ways.

JESUS' DISCIPLES

Matthew, also called Levi (left). Matthew was a tax-collector who worked for the Romans.

The word *disciple* means "learner". When Jesus started to preach, people flocked to hear him, and many became his friends and followers. Jesus chose twelve men to be with him all the time, to share his life and his work, and to learn from him. Jesus prayed for a whole night before he finally chose the disciples.

DISCIPLES AND APOSTLES

After Jesus' death, the disciples became known as apostles. The word *apostle* meant someone who was sent out as a messenger. The apostles became messengers of the teachings of Jesus.

Andrew (below left).
Andrew was a fisherman, and the brother of Simon.

Simon Peter (above right).
Simon Peter and Andrew were fishing when Jesus called them to follow him. They were to catch men, instead of fish!

Bible Search

- Andrew, John and Simon:
  John 1:35–42

- Fishing:
  Mark 1:14–20

- Praying:
  Luke 6:12–16

James and John (below).
These brothers were also fishermen. Jesus nicknamed them the 'sons of thunder', because they had bad tempers.

Philip (below left).
Philip came from the lakeside town of Bethsaida. As soon as Jesus called him, he went off to find his friend Bartholomew.

Bartholomew, also called Nathanael (above right).
Jesus told Bartholomew, 'You are a true man of Israel. There is nothing false in you.'

Simon (right).
Simon was a zealot. Zealots believed in fighting to get rid of the Romans.

Thomas (right).
Thomas is sometimes known as "Doubting Thomas." because at first he would not believe Jesus had risen from the dead.

James (below).
James was the son of Alphaeus.

Thaddeus (above).
He was also called Judas, son of James.

Judas Iscariot (below).
"Iscariot" means "from Kerioth," which was a town in Judea. So if Judas came from Kerioth he was the only southerner in the group of Galileans. He looked after the disciples' money. It was Judas who betrayed Jesus. In the end, he killed himself.

JESUS HEALS

Jesus made his base in the lakeside town of Capernaum. He traveled all over Galilee, teaching in synagogues and in the open air, and working miracles. Great crowds of people came to see him. Those were exciting, golden days for the disciples.

HEALING

Most of Jesus' miracles were healing miracles. He healed every type of illness, including blindness, fever, leprosy and epilepsy. The Bible tells of three people he brought back from the dead.

Jesus' heart went out to the suffering people he saw. He healed out of love, for he had come to set people free from bad things of every kind. The miracles showed that Jesus was the Messiah the people were waiting for.

HOW JESUS HEALED

Jesus healed in different ways. Sometimes he just commanded, "Be healed," and sometimes he put his hands on the suffering person. Once, in a great crowd of people, a woman touched the hem of his cloak, and she was healed.

Jesus heals a blind man

Another time, Jesus spat on some dirt to make mud, which he put on the eyes of a blind man making him able to see.

A woman touches the hem of Jesus' cloak

TRUST

Jesus healed people without any fuss; he did not use long prayers, special words, or ceremonies. He simply asked people to trust him. Then he often told them not to talk about it, because he didn't want to be known as a wonder-worker. He wanted people to see the miracles as signs which pointed to truths about God.

FAITH

When Jesus returned to his home town of Nazareth, he could do very few miracles. The people didn't believe that someone who was once the village carpenter could be God's special agent, and Jesus refused to do miracles if people did not trust him.

Some people did not believe Jesus could heal

Bible Search

- Healing: *Mark 1:32–34; 3:7–12*
- A woman in the crowd: *Mark 5:26–29*
- In Nazareth: *Mark 6:1–6*
- Pity: *Matthew 14:14*
- A mudpack: *John 9:6*

JESUS TEACHES

Jesus opened people's eyes

In the synagogue in Nazareth one day, Jesus was reading aloud: "The Spirit of the Lord is upon me...to preach good news...to make the blind see...to set prisoners free..." Jesus closed the book. "Today," he said, "these words have come true." Wherever Jesus went, he opened people's eyes to the truth about God. He did it in many different ways.

THE MESSAGE

Jesus' message to the people was:
- God is a loving father and a great king.
- God's kingdom of love is quite different from the kingdoms of this world.
- Friendship with Jesus is the way into God's kingdom.

TEACHING WITH PARABLES

Jesus taught people by telling stories. We call Jesus' short stories "parables." A parable tells a story, but the story also has a special Christian message. For example, this is one of Jesus' parables:

A woman lost a silver coin. She cleaned and swept until she found it. Then she called all her friends, and said, "Great news. I've found my lost coin."

The special message in this parable was that people who rebelled against God were like the lost coin, and God was like the woman searching for it.

TEACHING BY ACTIONS

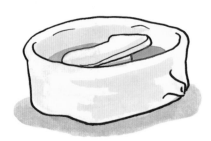

One day, Jesus got a bowl of water and washed his friends' dirty feet. This was a job a slave normally did. "You must be servants to one another," Jesus said.

The parable of the woman and the coin

TEACHING BY DISCUSSION

Jesus talked to anyone who came to him. He asked questions, and listened carefully to the replies. He talked to everyone; from Pharisees who thought they knew everything, to the poorest beggar.

TEACHING BY HIS LIFE

Jesus lived without seeking power. He was not greedy. He made friends with all sorts of people. He depended on God. To him, prayer was as natural as breathing. He fought against evil and died for his friends.

Bible Search

- In Nazareth: *Luke 4:16–21*
- Washing feet: *John 13:1–5*
- The lost coin: *Luke 15:8–10*
- Jesus prays: *Mark 1:35*

156

JESUS' FRIENDS

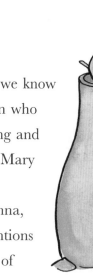

Jesus had many friends about whom we know very little. Luke names three women who probably helped with the shopping, cooking and washing for Jesus and the disciples. One was Mary Magdalene. The others were Joanna, whose husband worked in Herod's court, and Susanna, who we know nothing else about. Mark mentions Salome, too, who was probably the mother of James and John.

Joanna

Susanna

NICODEMUS

Nicodemus was a Pharisee, and a member of the Sanhedrin (a council of religious leaders in Jerusalem). He came to Jesus and said, "Nobody could do what you do without God's power." Later, he spoke up for Jesus in the Sanhedrin, and was laughed at.

Nicodemus helped Joseph of Arimathea to bury Jesus' body.

Nicodemus was a member of the Sanhedrin

MARY AND MARTHA

Martha became upset

When Jesus was passing through the village of Bethany, Martha invited him to stay at her house. This meant a lot of work. Martha became upset because while she did all the work, her sister Mary sat listening to Jesus and not helping her.

Very gently, Jesus said to Martha, "You're worried about many things. Only one thing is necessary. Mary has chosen what is better." He meant that it was more important to listen to his teaching than to do the housework.

Bible Search

- Nicodemus: *John 3:1–21; 7:50–52*
- Martha and Mary: *Luke 10:38–41*
- Supporters: *Mark 15:40–41; Luke 8:2–32*

MARY MAGDALENE

Mary Magdalene had done many wrong things, and was very distressed when Jesus met her. She had "seven evil spirits." Jesus healed her, and she became one of his closest friends. She was the first person to see Jesus alive, after he was raised from the dead.

Also see the page headed Zacchaeus.

Mary Magdalene

157

Jesus calms the storm

JESUS RULES

Jesus was asleep in a boat on the Sea of Galilee. Suddenly, a violent storm blew up. The disciples woke him. "We're going to drown!" they shouted. Jesus stood up. "Silence!" he commanded the storm, and everything went quiet. The disciples were awestruck. They realized that Jesus had power over the Earth.

JESUS FOR KING

One day, Jesus and his disciples went to a quiet area near Bethsaida, to spend time away from the crowds of people who wanted to see him. But the crowds followed him. So Jesus spent the day talking to people, and healing the sick.

Later on, Jesus told the disciples to find food for everybody. There were over 5,000 people! One boy brought Jesus five loaves and two fish. Jesus thanked God for the food, and told the disciples to give it out. Somehow everybody present had enough to eat.

A boy brings loaves and fish

It was another miracle. Excitement rose. Everybody wanted to make Jesus king to lead a rebellion against the Romans, but Jesus sent them all away. After this, many people stopped supporting him.

Everyone had enough to eat

- King of the waves: *Mark 4:35–41*
- King of the loaves: *Mark 6:30–44*
- King of the universe: *Mark 9:2–7*

TURNING POINT

Jesus left Galilee. He visited foreign countries to the east, north and west. He kept clear of crowds and spent his time teaching his friends.

"Who do you think I am?" Jesus asked. "You're God's special agent," Peter replied. "God has shown you this," Jesus said.

"Don't tell anyone. I must go on to Jerusalem. There I'll be killed and rise again."

Jesus visited foreign countries

ON MOUNT HERMON

Six days later, Jesus went further north, to Mount Hermon. He took Peter, James and John up the mountain with him. Suddenly, Jesus' clothes became dazzling white. The three friends saw Moses and Elijah (great leaders of long ago) talking to Jesus. Then God spoke: "This is my beloved son. Listen to him." God was telling them that Jesus had the same kingly power as God himself.

Jesus talks to Moses and Elijah

JESUS' ENEMIES

Lazarus

Jesus went around doing good. He healed people who were ill, and taught about God. He never tried to stir up rebellion against the Romans who occupied the country. Yet almost all the Jewish leaders wanted to get rid of him. Those who hated the Romans, and those who didn't mind them, all joined forces to kill him. Here are some of the reasons why.

TOO MUCH POWER

In Bethany, just outside Jerusalem, Jesus' friend Lazarus died. Jesus brought him back to life. It was the talk of Jerusalem. This led the Pharisees to join forces with the Sadducees.

The Sadducees were the leading group on the Sanhedrin (a council of religious leaders in Jerusalem). They loved power, and were friendly with the Romans. Usually Pharisees and Sadducees were enemies, but the problem of Jesus was a crisis they needed to work on together to solve.

CLAIMING TO BE GOD

Jesus forgives a man's sins

"Your sins are forgiven," Jesus said to a man lying flat on a stretcher. The Pharisees muttered, 'That's blasphemy. Only God can forgive sins.'

Jewish law said that the punishment for making yourself equal to God was stoning.

BREAKING RULES

One Sabbath, Jesus healed a man with a crippled arm. The Pharisees were furious, because Jesus had broken the rule about working on the Sabbath. (That was the day they first started plotting to kill Jesus.)

The Pharisees thought that the way to get into heaven was to keep the thousands of rules set out by Bible teachers (see the page on Pharisees).

Jesus showed that they were wrong, and that what God wanted from people was love and forgiveness.

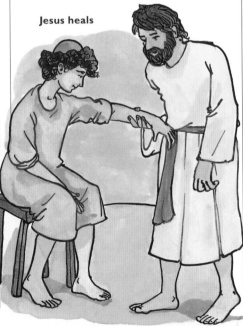

Jesus heals

THE SANHEDRIN

The Sanhedrin held an emergency meeting. They said: "If we let Jesus go on like this, everyone will believe in him, and the Romans will come and take away both our place and our nation."

Caiaphas, the High Priest, said, "It is better that one man die for the people than that the whole nation die."

Bible Search

- Jesus' claim to be God: *Mark 2:1–12; John 8:58–59*
- Breaking rules: *Mark 3:1–6*
- Crisis: *John 11:45–50*
- Troublemaker: *Mark 11:12–18*

JESUS
COMES TO JERUSALEM

After Jesus was baptized, three years went by. By now he was famous. His friends knew he was the Messiah, the great king. They couldn't understand why he said he must die. "A prophet has to die in Jerusalem," Jesus said, and set off. Jesus had been to Jerusalem before, but this time was to be different. Christians always remember this day as "Palm Sunday".

An angry Pharisee

The Pharisees were furious, and tried to make the people keep quiet. But Jesus said, "If they keep quiet, the stones will cry out." He was throwing down a challenge to his enemies.

A PROPHECY

When Jesus rode over the top of the Mount of Olives and saw Jerusalem ahead, he wept. "One day," he said, "you will be in ruins." Forty years later, Jesus' words came true.

THE PASSOVER

It was spring, and nearly time for the Passover festival. Every adult Jew was supposed to go to Jerusalem for the Passover. The population of the city grew to six times its normal size. All the nearby villages were crowded, and many visitors slept in tents outside the city walls.

ON THE LOOK-OUT

A donkey for Jesus

In Jerusalem, everyone was looking out for Jesus, and wondering whether he would come. The Pharisees sent out their spies.

Jesus sent two of his friends ahead of him to Bethany. "As you enter the town you'll see a young donkey," he said. "Untie it and bring it to me." Jesus planned to ride the last part of the journey into Jerusalem.

THE KING COMES

Five hundred years earlier, an Old Testament preacher had written: "Shout, daughter of Jerusalem! See your king comes to you… gentle and riding on a donkey." Everyone knew these words.

The road into Jerusalem was crowded. Many people knew Jesus. When they saw him on the donkey, they tore down branches from the palm trees, and put their cloaks on the road. They yelled, "Blessed is the king who comes in the name of the Lord."

Bible Search

- Death in Jerusalem: *Luke 13:33*
- Is he here?: *John 11:55–56*
- Palm Sunday: *Mark 11:1–10*

Palm Sunday

JESUS' LAST WEEK

Jerusalem was a dangerous place

During the week-long Passover holiday, Jerusalem was a dangerous place to be in. Many Jews were boiling with hatred against the Romans. Armed freedom fighters moved among the crowds. There had recently been one uprising against Rome, and its leaders were still in prison. The city was ready for another rebellion. We can piece together something about every day of Jesus' last week.

SUNDAY

Jesus rode into Jerusalem amid cheering crowds. He looked around the Temple, and then left with his friends to spend the night in Bethany.

MONDAY

The Temple building stood in a vast courtyard. This was the only place where non-Jews could pray. Here money-changers had set up their scales, and traders sold lambs and birds for Temple sacrifices. They often charged too much and made an unfair profit.

Jesus knew what he had to do. He strode into the Temple and threw them all out. "You've turned the house of prayer into a robbers' den!" he shouted.

This was the very thing the Old Testament preachers had said the Messiah would do. The religious leaders trembled. "We must kill him," they said.

Jesus spent the night back in Bethany.

Jesus throws the traders out of the Temple

Bible Search

- A true forecast:
  Malachi 3:1–3; Zechariah 14:21
- A robber's den:
  Mark 11:15–19
- Traitor:
  Mark 14:10–11

TUESDAY

Jesus went back to the Temple courtyard and talked to the crowds of people. The Pharisees and Sadducees tried to trap him with trick questions, but he was too clever for them.

WEDNESDAY

Jesus' enemies were desperate. Jesus was a hero. If they arrested him now, there would be a riot. They couldn't believe their luck when one of Jesus' disciples turned traitor.

The traitor was Judas. He told the enemies: "I'll take you to him, when there are no crowds." They agreed to give Judas thirty silver pieces as a reward.

Turn to the next page to find out what happened during the next few days.

161

JESUS' LAST SUPPER

A man directs the disciples to an upstairs room

Jesus' enemies wanted him out of the way before the Passover festival started. Jesus arranged to have the Passover meal with his friends. He made careful plans. "Go into the city," he said to two disciples. "You will see a man with a water pot. He will lead you to an upstairs room. There you can get our meal ready."

A SLAVE'S WORK

Before the meal started, Jesus washed his friends' feet. This was the work a slave normally did. Jesus said, "Never forget, you must be servants to one another."

A WARNING

Jesus knew there was an informer among his friends. He said, "One of you will betray me." All the disciples began talking at once. John whispered, "Who is it?" Jesus said quietly, "It's the man I give this bread to," and he gave a piece of bread to Judas. Then Judas went out into the night.

Peter announced, "I'll die for you." Jesus said, "Peter, before the cock crows, you'll have said three times that you don't know me."

REMEMBER

Then Jesus broke some bread and gave it to his friends. He said, "This is my body, given for you." He passed round a cup of wine, and said, "This is my blood poured out for you, for the forgiveness of sins." (See also the page on the Lord's Supper.)

Jesus breaks bread and gives it to his friends

LAST ORDERS

John gives up five chapters of his Gospel to Jesus' teaching during that last meal.

"You must love one another," Jesus said. "When I am gone, the Holy Spirit, the Helper, will come to be with you."

The next day, when the Passover lambs were killed, Jesus was killed. By his death and by rising again, he would set his people free from the power of evil.

- A secret sign:
  Mark 14:13–15
- Foot-washing:
  John 13:1–17
- Judas and Peter:
  John 13:18–38
- The Lord's Supper:
  Luke 22:14–23

162

JESUS UNDER ARREST

L ate in the evening after the Passover meal, Jesus and his friends left Jerusalem. In the darkness they crossed the deep Kidron Valley, and climbed the Mount of Olives. At the Garden of Gethsemene, Jesus told his friends to stay awake while he went to pray.

Jesus prays

JESUS PRAYS

Horror and a terrible sadness filled Jesus. He knelt down. "Everything is possible for you," he prayed to God, "Let this pass away. But may your will be done, not mine." Jesus went back to his friends, but they had fallen asleep. Three times he woke them, but they couldn't stay awake while he prayed.

Bible Search

- Praying: *Mark 14:32–42*
- Arrest: *Mark 14:43–52*
- Annas: *John 18:12–14*
- Sanhedrin: *Mark 14:53–65*
- Peter: *Mark 14:66–72*

ARREST

Judas kisses Jesus

Suddenly, lights and noise filled the garden. Judas arrived, followed by Temple guards armed with swords and clubs. Judas kissed Jesus. This was a sign for the guards to arrest Jesus. Peter struck out with a sword and cut off the ear of one of the guards. But Jesus rebuked Peter and healed the man's ear.

Terrified by what was happening, the disciples ran away.

ON TRIAL

Jesus was taken away and immediately put on trial. This lasted many hours. The Gospel writers summarized what happened during that long night in slightly different ways, but here are some of the main events.

First, Jesus was questioned by Annas, the father-in-law of the High Priest. He was then brought before the Sanhedrin (a council of religious leaders). Witnesses were produced to give evidence against Jesus, but their accounts contradicted each other. During the trial, Jesus watched and said nothing.

Witnesses gave contradictory evidence

ALL NIGHT LONG

The trial by the Sanhedrin lasted a long time. At last the High Priest asked, "Are you the Messiah, the son of God?" "I am," replied Jesus. There was uproar! This was all the evidence that they needed.

Blasphemy such as this was a crime punishable by death.

Outside in the courtyard, Peter denied knowing Jesus.

163

JESUS PRISONER OF ROME

Roman law did not allow the Jews to put anyone to death. The Jewish leaders had to take Jesus to the Roman governor, Pontius Pilate. They hurried through the streets to King Herod's old palace, which was where Pilate was staying.

Pilate hated Jews.

PILATE

"Jesus is a dangerous man," the Jews said to Pilate. "He says he's the king of the Jews. He's stirred up trouble in Galilee." Jesus wouldn't defend himself.

When Pilate learned Jesus was a Galilean, he sent him to Herod Antipas, ruler of Galilee, who was also staying in the palace.

HEROD ANTIPAS

Herod Antipas questioned Jesus, but Jesus remained silent. So Jesus was sent back to Pilate.

Before Jesus returned to Pilate, the Jewish leaders gathered together a mob that they paid to speak against Jesus.

Jesus remains silent

JESUS SPEAKS TO PILATE

Pilate questions Jesus

"Are you king of the Jews?" asked Pilate. "The word is yours," said Jesus. "My kingdom is not of this world. Everyone on the side of truth listens to me." Pilate was sure that Jesus was innocent.

Every Passover festival, a prisoner was set free. Pilate decided that this would be Jesus, and he told the crowd he would let Jesus off with a flogging. But the crowd demanded, "Set Barabbas free!" (Barabbas was another prisoner, a murderer.) "Crucify Jesus," they shouted. In the crowd was the mob paid by the Jewish leaders to speak against Jesus.

The crowd demands Jesus' crucifixion

DEATH SENTENCE

Pilate washes his hands of Jesus

Pilate did all he could to set Jesus free. The Jews said, "If you let him go, you're no friend of Caesar." This was a threat, meaning that if he did this, Pilate would be shown to be disloyal to the Roman emperor, Caesar.

In the end, Pilate gave in. He took a bowl of water and washed his hands. "I'm innocent of this man's death," he stated. He handed Jesus over to be crucified

Bible Search

- Pilate and Herod: *Luke 23:1–12*

- Jesus and Pilate: *John 18:28–19:16*

- Pilate washes his hands: *Matthew 27:24*

JESUS DIES

Death by crucifixion was a hideous torture. Cicero, a Roman writer, called it "the most cruel and revolting punishment." Yet Jesus had an extra pain to bear as well. As he hung on the cross, he carried the sin which separated people from God. (See the page on Jesus, Why He Came.)

Jesus carries the cross through the streets of Jerusalem

IN JERUSALEM

Jesus was made to carry the heavy wooden cross on which he would be crucified, through the streets of Jerusalem and out of the city gates. He fell down, and Simon from Cyrene was forced to help carry the cross.

GOLGOTHA

Jesus was taken to Golgotha, which means 'the place of the skull'. Some women offered him a painkilling drink, but he refused it. The soldiers nailed his hands to the cross. A block of wood halfway up the cross took the weight of his body (or the nails would have torn through his flesh). His feet were tied or nailed to the cross. Over his head, a notice in three languages said: 'The king of the Jews'.

THIEVES

Two thieves were crucified with Jesus. One made fun of him. The other said, "We deserve our fate, but this man is innocent." And he said to Jesus, "Remember me when you come to your kingdom.' Jesus replied, "Today you will be with me in paradise."

Bible Search

- In Jerusalem: *Luke 23:26–31*
- Forgive them: *Luke 23:34*
- Mary: *John 19:25–27*
- Jesus' death: *Luke 23:44–49; Matthew 27:45–56*

DARKNESS

Jesus prayed, "Father forgive them. They don't know what they are doing."At midday, the sky turned black. For three hours, there was darkness. At three o'clock Jesus cried out, "My God, my God, why have you left me?" (This was a quotation from Psalm 22.)

Then Jesus shouted, "It is finished. Into your hands I give my spirit." And in this way, with a clear mind, and with a prayer, Jesus gave himself to God and died.

When one of the Roman guards saw how Jesus had died, he said, "Surely this was the son of God."

Jesus is crucified

JESUS IS ALIVE

The Gospel writers do not tell identical stories about Jesus' resurrection. But the main part of their stories is the same: the earth-shattering fact that Jesus died on Friday, and was brought back to life again on Sunday. He was then seen by many people.

Mary and Jesus

BURIAL

Joseph of Arimathea, a rich landowner, and Nicodemus, a member of the Sanhedrin, found the courage to ask Pilate for Jesus' body. They rubbed it with sweet-smelling spices, and wrapped it in cloth. Jesus was then taken to a tomb for burial. The tomb was a cave with a garden in front.

Jesus' body is prepared for burial

The Pharisees were afraid Jesus' friends might steal the body. So Pilate gave them permission to seal the tomb, and put Roman guards on duty. A large stone was rolled in front of the cave.

AN EARTHQUAKE

Very early on Sunday morning, there was an earthquake. An angel, in dazzling white clothes, rolled back the stone and sat on it. The guards were petrified! (Later, the chief priests bribed them to say they had fallen asleep.)

JESUS' FRIENDS

Mary Magdalene, James' mother, and Salome went the tomb to put more spices on Jesus' body. To their amazement, they found that the stone had been rolled away and Jesus' body was gone. The angel said to them, "Jesus is alive. Tell his friends, and Peter."

An angel opens the tomb

MARY MAGDALENE

The women raced back and told the disciples, who wouldn't believe them! Peter and John ran to the tomb. They went inside and saw Jesus' burial clothes, but not his body.

As Mary stood crying outside the tomb, a man spoke to her. "Why are you crying?" he asked. Mary thought it was the gardener. "Sir, if you've taken the body, tell me where you've put it," she begged. "Mary!" said the man. And then she saw he was Jesus.

- Guards: *Matthew 27:62; 28:4, 11–15*
- Burial: *John 19:38–42*
- Peter and John: *John 20:3–9*
- Mary Magdalene: *John 20:10–18*

JESUS
THE EMPTY TOMB

"If Jesus Christ has not been raised, our preaching is useless, and so is your faith." These were Paul's words.

We cannot go back into the past and see for ourselves what happened to Jesus, but we can examine the evidence. If Jesus did not rise from the dead, what did happen? Here are some theories.

DISCIPLES

Did the disciples steal the body?
The evidence:
• They were too scared. They all ran away.

• Some were put in prison and killed for preaching that Jesus was alive. Would they have died for a lie?
• If only one or two of them stole the body, how was it that so many saw Jesus alive?

Prison keys

• Roman soldiers guarded the tomb. They would have been punished by death if they had fallen asleep on duty.

Did the guards fall asleep?

THIEVES

Did thieves steal the body?
The evidence:
• What was the point?
• Roman soldiers guarded the tomb.

What's the point?

JESUS

Maybe Jesus was not dead?
The evidence:
• But how did he get out of the tomb? He was exhausted even before he was crucified, and couldn't have moved the stone in front of the tomb. What did he wear? The grave clothes were left behind.
• Would Jesus have preached a lie (that he had risen from the dead)?
• Roman soldiers were sure he was dead.

WOMEN

Perhaps the women went to the wrong tomb?
The evidence:
• In that case, why didn't the Jews produce the body from the right tomb?

A LIE

Perhaps someone made it all up years later?
The evidence:
• The disciples changed from terrified followers to brave preachers. Something made them change.
• The Gospel accounts seem to contradict each other in some details. If they had been invented, the writers would have made sure the stories all agreed.
• The first witnesses were women. No Jew would have made that up. It had to be true!

OTHER EVIDENCE

The Jewish leaders said the body was stolen. If the body was there all the time, why did they put out this story?

CONCLUSION

Conclusion: everyone has to decide for himself or herself.

Bible Search

• Paul: *I Corinthians 15:14, 17*
• Guards bribed: *Matthew 28:11–15*
• Grave clothes: *John 20:3–8*
• Women: *Mark 16:1–8*
• Alive: *I Corinthians 15:3–8*

JESUS' SPIRIT IS HERE

Just before he went back to heaven, Jesus said to his friends, "I am going to send you what my Father has promised. But stay in the city until you have been clothed with power from on high." What did that mean? The friends had to wait!

DISCIPLES

Jesus' disciples were staying in a large upstairs room, and also spending a lot of time at the Temple. In the Temple there were many small rooms, and they may have rented one of these. Every day, 120 Christians met together to pray and praise God. Jesus' mother was there, and so were his brothers.

Jesus' family

PENTECOST

Ten days went by. Jerusalem was crowded: visitors had come from all over the world for the festival of Pentecost.

It was early in the morning. The disciples were all together in the room where they were staying. Suddenly, a tremendous wind roared through the house, and fire flashed around them. A flame rested over each disciple, and they were filled with the Holy Spirit.

Visitors came from all over the world for Pentecost

Bible Search

- An upstairs room: *Acts 1:12, 12:12*

- Wait in Jerusalem: *Luke 24:49; Acts 1:4–5*

- The Holy Spirit: *Acts 2:1–13*

- Peter's sermon: *Acts 2:14–41*

VOICE POWER

The disciples suddenly found they were able to speak different languages. They went out into the streets, where they were able to speak to people from other countries in their own languages. People were amazed, and asked, "What's going on? These men are from Galilee, but they're speaking our language!"

A SERMON

Peter stood up and spoke to the crowd. "This is the Holy Spirit. He's come to us, just as the prophet Joel promised." And Peter told them all about Jesus, how he had died, and risen again.

That day, 3,000 people became Christians.

WHITSUN

The day the Christian Church began is often called Whitsun, which is short for White Sunday. In the past, new believers were baptized on that day, and always wore white clothes.

A flame appears above each disciple

JESUS IS KING

The resurrection showed that Jesus is God's perfect son: if he had been just an imperfect human, he would have stayed dead. Paul said, "He was declared with power to be the son of God, by his resurrection from the dead." When his friends saw Jesus on Easter Sunday evening, they touched him. Jesus ate some fish. This proved he was certainly not a ghost.

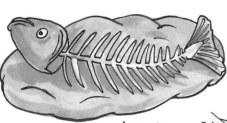

Jesus ate some fish

ALIVE!

The Gospels tell us about eleven meetings people had with Jesus when he was brought back to life.

Meeting: At the empty tomb
Date: Early Sunday
People: Women friends
Place in Bible: Matthew 28:1–10

Meeting: Outside the tomb
Date: Early Sunday
People: Mary Magdelane
Place in Bible: Mark 16:9–11; John 20:11–18

Mary Magdelene

Meeting: On the road to Emmaus
Date: Sunday, midday
People: Cleopas
Place in Bible: Luke 24:13–32

Meeting: In Jerusalem
Date: Sunday
People: Peter
Place in Bible: Luke 24:34; 1 Corinthians 15:5

Meeting: The upper room, Jerusalem
Date: Sunday evening
People: 10 disciples, Cleopas
Place in Bible: Luke 24:36–43; John 20:19–25

Meeting: The upper room, Jerusalem
Date: One week later
People: 11 disciples
Place in Bible: John 20: 26–31

Meeting: Sea of Galilee
Date: One day at dawn
People: Disciples
Place in Bible: John 21:1–23

Meeting: Mountain in Galilee
Date: Unknown
People: 11 disciples
Place in Bible: Matthew 28:16–20; Mark 16:16–18

Meeting: Possibly in Jerusalem
Date: Unknown
People: More than 500 people
Place in Bible: 1 Corinthians 15:6

Meeting: Possibly in Jerusalem
Date: Unknown
People: James, Jesus' brother
Place in Bible: 1 Corinthians 15:7

Meeting: Mount of Olives
Date: After 40 days
People: 11 disciples
Place in Bible: Luke 24:50–53

THE ASCENSION

Forty days after Easter Sunday, Jesus and the disciples were on the Mount of Olives. As Jesus was praying for them, he was lifted up into the sky, hidden by a cloud. The cloud represented the presence and glory of God. In this way, Jesus showed his friends that he had gone to heaven.

JEWELS AND METALS

The Israelites knew six metals: gold, silver, iron, lead, tin and copper. Of these, only iron and copper were found in their country. Gold, silver, tin and lead had to be imported. Precious stones were bought from other countries such as Arabia, Egypt, India, and Africa.

Bible Search

- A smith at work:
  Isaiah 44:12
- Any old iron?:
  1 Samuel 13:19–22
- A chest full of jewels:
  Exodus 28:15–29

JEWELS

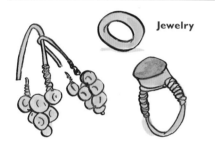

Jewelry

Precious stones were made into smooth shapes and polished. Then they were set in silver, gold or copper to make nose-rings, earrings, rings, bracelets, necklaces, brooches and diadems.

The High Priest wore a breastplate set with nine beautiful jewels. These were ruby, topaz, beryl, turquoise, sapphire, emerald, jacinth, agate and amethyst.

The High Priest

SEALS

Seals

Seals were stamped into a plug of soft wax which was put on letters, or sometimes boxes, to keep them private. A broken seal showed that the letter had been opened.

A seal might be made out of a small jewel, cut to an oval shape, polished and then engraved.

Archaeologists have found thousands of seals. Some have pictures of gods or animals. Seals found in Israel are engraved with patterns, plants and names. Often, a hole was drilled through the seal so it could be worn as a necklace or ring.

METALWORKERS

The men who worked iron, copper, silver, gold and lead were very respected craftsmen.

Gold and silversmiths had small furnaces where the metals were melted. Molten gold was poured into moulds. Gold was also hammered into thin sheets and then cut into strips. These were used for embroidery.

COPPER

Three thousand years before the birth of Jesus, people dug copper ore out of the earth. It was heated (in a process called smelting) to extract the copper. A thousand years later, people learned to make bronze by adding tin to copper. Bronze is stronger than copper, but not as strong as iron.

SMITHS

The Israelites only learned to make iron in the time of David (see the page on Philistines). Iron was beaten out on an anvil to make weapons and tools. It was hard work!

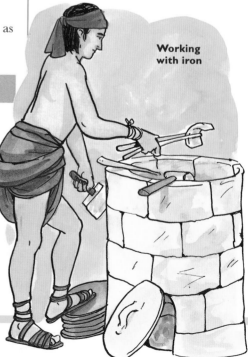

Working with iron

JEWS, GENTILES, AND SAMARITANS

The Samaritans wanted to help rebuild the Temple

A Jew is someone who is descended from Jacob, the grandson of Abraham, or someone whose religion is Judaism. Jews are often called "the chosen people," because God chose to work with the Jews to save the people of the world. Jesus and the first Christians were Jews.

CHANGE OF NAME

Jews were first known as Hebrews, or Israelites, and their country was Israel. (Jacob was given the second name "Israel" by God.) Later the country split into two: Israel in the north, and Judah in the south. Over three hundred years later, the people of Judah were taken prisoner to Babylonia. After this time they were called Jews, from the word Judah.

GENTILES

Jews call non-Jews "Gentiles." In New Testament times, many non-Jews were attracted to the Jewish faith.

JUDAISM

Jews stress the importance of keeping the Old Testament laws. They are waiting for the coming of a great king.

Bible Search

- Samaritan religion: *2 Kings 17:25–34*
- A Samaritan woman: *John 4*
- The Good Samaritan: *Luke 10:25–37*

SAMARITANS

Samaritans take their name from Samaria. When King Solomon died and the country split into two, Samaria became the capital city of the northern kingdom, Israel. Two hundred years later, Israel was invaded by the Assyrians, and large numbers of the people were taken prisoner. The invaders married among the remaining Israelites, and added the worship of God to their own religions.

Old Testament scrolls

When the Jews came back from exile in Babylonia, the Samaritans wanted to help them to rebuild the Temple. But the Jews would not let them.

Samaria was a small area right in the middle of the country. Samaritans and Jews did not like each other. Jews who wanted to travel from Galilee to Jerusalem would usually not go through Samaria. They went a long way round, across the Jordan River .

Taking the long way around

SAMARITAN RELIGION

About 330 years before the birth of Jesus, the Samaritans set up their own temple on Mount Gerizim, with priests and sacrifices. Their Bible was the first five books of the Old Testament.

JOB THE BOOK OF

The writer of the Book of Job knew the teachings of the prophets and wise men. He was a traveler who had visited other countries. He probably wrote about 500 years before Jesus was born.

Job was tested by Satan, but didn't lose his faith in God.

Job

UNDERSTANDING JOB

If God is good and fair, why does he let good people suffer? This is one of the big questions Christians must face. The Book of Job shows that there is no easy answer.

The story shows us that we must trust God even when we don't understand why something happens. We see how Job's faith holds strong in the face of suffering.

THE CHARACTERS IN THE BOOK OF JOB

● Job: He was the greatest and richest man in the eastern world. He loved God and did nothing wrong. Job had 7,000 sheep, 3,000 camels, 500 oxen, and 500 donkeys.
● Satan: He wanted to prove that Job was only good because it paid him to be good, and that was really selfishness.
● Elihu: a young man.
● Eliphaz, Bildad and Zophar: Job's three friends.

Bible Search

● My redeemer lives:
Job 19:25
● Job's riches:
Job 1:3
● A silly bird:
Job 39:13–18

READING JOB

● *Chapter 1:1–2:10*: God allowed Satan to test Job. Satan made Job lose everything he owned and his children died. Then his body was covered with hideous sores. His wife cried, "Curse God and die" But Job would not say anything against God.
● *Chapter 2:11–31:40*: Enter Job's three friends. They were full of good advice, but it had nothing to do with Job's situation. They thought Job was suffering because he had sinned against God. Job cried out to God: "Why should I suffer when I am innocent?"
● *Chapter 32–37*: Elihu joined in. His verdict was that Job was suffering because God was teaching him a lesson.

Elihu

● *Chapter 38:1–42:6*: God showed Job something of his power.
● *Chapter 42:1–6*: Job said, "Now my eyes have seen you and I repent."
● *Chapter 42:7–17*: God told off the four friends, or "comforters." They had not understood Job or helped him. Job prayed for God to forgive his friends, and God made him even happier and richer than before.

172

JOEL, OBADIAH AND NAHUM – THE BOOKS OF

J oel, Obadiah and Nahum were three preachers. Their books are three of the shortest in the Old Testament: Nahum has only one chapter. Nahum preached between 664 and 612 B.C., and Obadiah after 586 B.C. Joel may have been preaching at the same time as Obadiah.

The people of Edom laugh at Jerusalem

UNDERSTANDING JOEL

A locust

"A terrible army has invaded the land," wrote Joel, "an army with the teeth of a lion." This army had millions of soldiers, who scaled walls, climbed houses, and marched straight ahead in long lines.

The army was a gigantic swarm of locusts. They left the land bare. They even ate the bark on the trees!

Those locusts were a sign from God. God's terrible day of judgment and punishment was close.

READING JOEL

- *Chapter 1*: Locusts.
- *Chapter 2:1–11*: Judgment for the people.
- *Chapter 2:12–33*: Hope for those who change their ways.
- *Chapter 3:1–17*: Punishment for God's enemies.
- *Chapter 3:18-21*: New life.

UNDERSTANDING OBADIAH

Obadiah's poem was addressed to the country of Edom. The people of Edom had been delighted when Jerusalem was destroyed, and had joined in the killing.

"You wanted us to suffer," Obadiah said. "Watch out. One day it will be your turn, along with all God's enemies."

UNDERSTANDING NAHUM

The city of Nineveh was soon to be destroyed. Nahum was delighted. This was God's punishment for the cruel people of Nineveh.

Nineveh, the strongest city on earth, was the capital of Assyria. It had been built as a city to last. It was surrounded by very thick, high walls, and a deep moat. The walls had 200 fortified towers and were very wide.

- *Chapter 1*: The destruction of Nineveh.
- *Chapter 2*: Nineveh is destroyed.
- *Chapter 3*: The reason why.

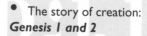

- The story of creation: *Genesis 1 and 2*
- God, the great creator: *Psalm 33:6–9* *Isaiah 40:26* *Nehemiah 9:6* *Hebrews 11:3*
- What Jesus said: *Matthew 26:28–32*

The city walls of Nineveh

JOHN THE DISCIPLE

Jesus nicknamed John and his brother James the "sons of thunder". It was probably because they both had a bad temper! When a village wouldn't welcome Jesus, the brothers would say, "Call down fire from heaven and destroy it!" In the New Testament, we see a change taking place in John, and he becomes less angry.

John

FISHERMEN

John and his brother James lived in Capernaum, by the Sea of Galilee. They were fishermen. One day, they were mending their nets with their father Zebedee, when they saw Jesus walking towards them. "Come with me," Jesus said. At once, they decided to follow him.

Together with Peter, John and James became Jesus' closest friends.

POWER-SEEKING

One day, James and John, encouraged by their mother, asked Jesus: "May we have the seats of power on your right and left-hand side when you come as king?" The other disciples were furious when they found out!

But John let go of his longing for power. In his Gospel, he didn't even put his name, but just described himself as "the disciple Jesus loved."

James and John are encouraged to seek power

JESUS' MOTHER

When Jesus was dying, John stood close to the foot of the cross, next to Mary. Jesus said to John, "Here is your mother." And he said to Mary, "Here is your son." From then on, John looked after Mary.

COURAGE

When Jesus was raised from the dead, John and Peter went to tell the people of Jerusalem. For this, they were thrown in prison. John and Peter refused to be silenced. "We cannot help speaking about what we have seen and heard," they said. It was a dangerous time for the disciples: King Herod arrested James, and had him killed.

John is arrested

THE WRITER

John wrote the Gospel of John and the Book of Revelation. He also wrote three letters, known as 1, 2, and 3 John, when he was an old man living in Ephesus. Above all else, these letters stressed the importance of love.

Bible Search

- Follow Jesus: *Mark 1:19–20*
- Sons of thunder: *Luke 9:51–55*
- Power-seeking: *Mark 10:35–45*
- Love: *1 John 4:7–21*

174

JOHN THE GOSPEL OF

T he Gospel of John is the story of Jesus, told by the apostle John. John never mentions his own name: he always calls himself simply "the disciple whom Jesus loved." There are no parables in his Gospel, but there are some very important conversations which tell us a great deal about Jesus.

UNDERSTANDING JOHN'S GOSPEL

At the end of his Gospel, John tells us why he wrote it: "These (miraculous signs) are written that you may believe that Jesus is the Christ, the son of God, and that believing you may have life in his name."

SEVEN 'SIGNS'

To a Jew, the number seven was a very important number. It stood for perfection. John wrote about seven miracles Jesus performed, which he called signs. They showed that Jesus was the perfect son of God.

● Sign 1: Jesus changed water into wine at a wedding. (John 2:1–11)

● Sign 2: Jesus healed a very sick boy. (John 4:46–54)

● Sign 3: Jesus healed a man who had not been able to walk for 38 years. (John 5:1–14)

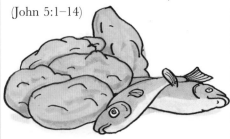

● Sign 4: Jesus made a meal for 5,000 people, from five barley loaves and two fish. (John 6:1–15)

● Sign 5: Jesus walked on the Sea of Galilee. (John 6:16–21)

● Sign 6: Jesus made a blind man see. (John 9)

● Sign 7: Jesus brought Lazarus back to life. (John 11:1–44)

I AM

In the Old Testament, God's name for himself was "I Am". Jesus said, "I am" seven times:

● 1. "I am the bread of life." (John 6:35)
● 2. "I am the light of the world." (John 9:5)
● 3. "I am the gate for the sheep." (John 10:7)
● 4. "I am the good shepherd." (John 10:11)
● 5. "I am the resurrection and the life." (John 11:25)
● 6. "I am the way, the truth and the life." (John 14:6)
● 7. "I am the true vine." (John 15:1)

FAMOUS VERSE

The most famous verse in the Bible comes in John's Gospel: "For God so loved the world that he gave his one and only son, that whoever believes in him shall not perish but have eternal life." (John 3:16)

READING JOHN'S GOSPEL

● *Chapter 1*: Jesus starts his work.
● *Chapter 2–12*: The Book of Signs.
● *Chapter 13–19*: Jesus' last week.
● *Chapter 20–21*: Jesus is alive again.

Bible Search

● The author of the Gospel: *John 21:20–24*

● Why John wrote his Gospel: *John 20:30–31*

● Best friends: *John 13:25; 19:26*

JOHN THE FIRST, SECOND AND THIRD LETTERS OF

T he apostle John wrote these three letters when he was an old man, living in Ephesus. Letters were written with pen and ink on long pieces of parchment or papyrus. They were rolled up and tied with a cord, then sealed.

John wrote because he wanted Christians to "know that you have eternal life."

UNDERSTANDING JOHN'S LETTERS

A group of men were teaching weird and sinister ideas. The men's teaching was an early type of Gnosticism. "Gnosticism" comes from the Greek word for "knowledge". The Gnostics believed:

● Human bodies were evil. Jesus could not have had an 'evil' human body. Therefore his body was not a human body. Or else he took over a human body, and left it before he was killed.

Gnostics believed the human body was evil

Gnostics believed that you could do wrong and still be a Christian

● Christians could do as many wrong things as they wanted; because as they held Christian beliefs their spirit would remain good.
● To get to heaven, you needed more than faith in Jesus: you needed a secret knowledge of God, which only some people discovered.

This was a lie! John set out to prove this teaching was wrong.

Secret knowledge

KNOCKING THE GNOSTICS

John wrote to prove that the Gnostics were wrong. He said that:
● Jesus was flesh and blood. (John knew that was true because he had seen and touched Jesus.) Jesus really died on the cross.
● Anyone who thought it was all right to keep doing wrong things, was not a Christian. A true Christian was loving in his words and actions.
● Everyone who trusted Jesus and obeyed him was forgiven and would go to heaven.

BE MY GUEST

At the time John wrote these letters, Christians met in each other's homes, and Christian teachers led the meetings. John warned the Christians not to let the Gnostics into their homes.

READING JOHN'S LETTERS

1 John
● *Chapter 1-3*: Walking with God.
  ● *Chapter 4–6*: Truth, love and faith.
  2 John
    ● Guard against Gnostics.
    3 John
      ● Good Gaius, and dangerous Diotrephes.

Bible Search

● God forgives us: *I John 1:8–10*
● Jesus, a real person: *I John 1:1*
● Jesus really died: *I John 4:1–3*
● A true Christian: *I John 3:6–7*
● Love and hate: *I John 2:9–11*

A voice calling in the desert

JOHN THE BAPTIST

J ohn the Baptist was Jesus' cousin. He was six months older than Jesus. Jesus said that John the Baptist was the greatest prophet there had been, who would get people ready for the coming of God. John said of himself, "I am a voice of one calling in the desert, 'Prepare the way for the Lord.'"

- Clothes: *Matthew 3:4*
- His message: *Luke 3:7–14*
- Prison: *Matthew 11:2–19*

Bible Search

ZECHARIAH

Zechariah was an elderly priest. One day, the angel Gabriel came to Zechariah in the Temple and said, "You will have a son, called John. He will prepare the people for the coming of God." Zechariah didn't believe the angel, so Gabriel made him unable to speak until John was born. That taught him not to doubt an angel!

Zechariah's wife was called Elizabeth. John was her only child, and she was old when he was born.

Gabriel comes to Zechariah

THE DESERT

When he grew up, John went to live in the desert. He wandered from place to place, preaching to the people. Everybody came to hear him. He said, "Turn from your evil ways. The Deliverer is coming. I am not fit even to untie his sandals."

THE BAPTIST

John baptized people when they became Christians. Baptism was a sign that they were sorry for the wrong things they had done. When Jesus came to be baptized, John was surprised. "You ought to baptize me!" John said.

Many of John's followers left him to follow Jesus, and John was delighted. He said, "Jesus must become greater and I must become less."

JOHN AND KING HEROD

King Herod had married his brother's wife, while his brother was still alive. John told Herod that what he had done was against the law. Herod threw him in prison.

John began to have doubts while he was in prison. He sent a message to Jesus, asking: 'Are you really the one we are expecting?' Jesus assured him he was, by telling him what was happening.

Herod's wife, Herodias, detested John. Turn to the page on Queens to read how she had him beheaded.

John in prison

177

JONAH THE BOOK OF

Jonah was a prophet preaching in Israel at the same time as Amos. The Book of Jonah tells the story of a lesson he learned. "Go to preach in Nineveh," God said. "What? Not likely!" thought Jonah. He didn't like the people there, who were very wicked and the enemies of Israel. So he set off by ship in the opposite direction.

A FISHY TALE

A violent storm began. The waves were so fierce that the ship was in danger of breaking up. The sailors began to throw cargo overboard, to lighten the ship.

The frightened sailors thought that somebody on the ship must be the cause of the terrible storm. They drew lots to try and discover who it was, and Jonah's name was drawn.

Jonah was brought on deck. He realized that God had sent the storm to punish his disobedience. "Throw me over the side," he told the sailors, "and the storm will die down."

The sailors didn't want to be responsible for Jonah's death. But the storm still raged furiously, and so they threw Jonah into the swirling waters.

Jonah is thrown into the sea

THE GREAT FISH

As Jonah struggled in the sea, he was swallowed by a great fish. For the next three days, he lived in its stomach, until the fish vomited him on to dry land. The 'great fish' described in the Bible may have been a whale.

UNDERSTANDING JONAH

The story of Jonah shows God's love for everyone, even his enemies.

When Jonah was saved by the fish, God again told him to go to Nineveh. This time Jonah did what he was told. He warned the people that their city would be destroyed. The people decided to change their ways, and asked God to spare them.

Jonah in the stomach of the fish

READING JONAH

- *Chapter 1*: Jonah runs away.
- *Chapter 2*: Jonah in the fish.
- *Chapter 3*: Jonah preaches in Nineveh.
- *Chapter 4*: Jonah sulks.

- Jonah:
  2 Kings 14:25

- Jesus talks about Jonah:
  Matthew 12:39–41

Joseph

JOSEPH
THE COAT OF MANY COLOURS

Joseph was the son of Jacob and Rachel. He had eleven brothers: Reuben, Simeon, Levi, Judah, Issachar, Zebulun, Gad, Asher, Dan, Naphtali, and Benjamin. The family lived in tents in Canaan. Joseph was Jacob's favorite son, so Jacob gave him a beautiful coat made in many different colors. His brothers were very jealous.

JOSEPH'S STORY AT A GLANCE

• Joseph dreamed that he and his brothers were sheaves of corn, and his brothers were all bowing down to him. He told his brothers about the dream. The brothers decided to get rid of him.

• They sold Joseph to traders going to Egypt.

• The traders sold Joseph to be a slave in Egypt. His master's wife fell in love with him. When Joseph refused to fall in love with her, she had him thrown into prison.

• The pharaoh who ruled Egypt had a strange dream. He wanted to know what it meant, but no one could tell him. A man who had been in prison with Joseph remembered that Joseph was good at interpreting dreams. The pharaoh sent for Joseph, who told him that it meant there would be a famine in seven years' time.

• The pharaoh was so impressed that he made Joseph chief minister, with the job of storing up corn before the famine.

• When famine came, Joseph's brothers traveled to Egypt to find food. They went to the chief minister, Joseph, to beg for corn, but didn't recognize him until he made himself known to them. They were amazed!

• Joseph brought his father and all his family to live safely in Egypt.

Joseph's dream

JOSEPH'S COAT

Did Joseph wear a technicolor coat? The Hebrew word for the coat could mean it was brightly colored, or that it had long flowing sleeves, or that it was beautifully decorated.

Joseph is sold to traders

THE TRIBES OF ISRAEL

Joseph's brothers became the founders of the twelve tribes of Israel, which were named after them. Joseph's name does not appear because his two sons, Ephraim and Manasseh, each founded a tribe.

Joseph refuses to fall in love with his master's wife

• The story of Joseph: *Genesis 37–50*

• Joseph's dreams and coat: *Genesis 37:1–11*

• Joseph in charge: *Genesis 41:41–43*

Bible Search

JOSHUA AND THE LAND OF CANAAN

Joshua's name meant "The Lord Saves," and that sums up his exciting life. He was a slave in Egypt, until Moses led him and the Israelites to freedom. He became the commander of the Israelites' desert army, and Moses' assistant. God chose Joshua to lead the invasion into Canaan. He was a brilliant army commander, and a man who trusted God.

Bible Search

- Desert warrior: *Exodus 17:8–14*
- The spies: *Numbers 13*
- God's promise to Joshua: *Joshua 1:1–9*
- Shechem: *Joshua 24*

SPIES!

From their desert camp, twelve Israelites went to see what the new land of Canaan was like. Ten of the spies said, "It's a great land! But you should see the people. They're giants. And they live in strong cities."
The other two spies were Joshua and Caleb. They said, "Don't be afraid. We'll cut them down to size: we have God with us."

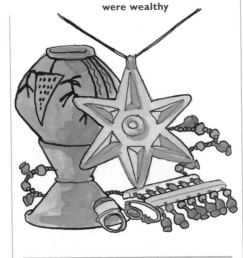

The Canaanites were wealthy

CANAAN

Canaan was the Promised Land, the land God had given to Abraham for the Israelites to live in, hundreds of years before.

There were many strong, walled cities in Canaan, ruled over by different kings. The kings often fought each other. It didn't occur to them that it would be a better idea to gang up together to fight the invading Israelite army.

The Canaanite people had become wealthy by trading with other countries. They had comfortable homes, fine furniture, and gold jewelry.

The Canaanites gave the world one big gift: they invented a simple alphabet (see the page on Writing).

THE RELIGION OF CANAAN

The chief Canaanite god was Hadad, known as Baal (meaning Lord). He was the god of storms and weather. There was also a female god called Asherah.

When the Israelites finally came to live in Canaan, the Canaanite religion proved to be one of the biggest problems they faced. Many Israelites were persuaded that they should worship Baal instead of God.

JOSHUA'S FAITH

Joshua called everyone to a great meeting at Shechem, his capital city. He asked them to choose between Baal and God. All the Israelites made an agreement (called a covenant) to serve God. (Turn to the next page to find out more about the story of Joshua.)

"They're giants," say the spies

JOSHUA
THE BOOK OF

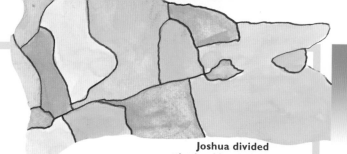

Joshua divided
the land into areas

After Moses sent twelve spies to find out what Canaan was like, the Israelites gave up the idea of invading Canaan. They stayed in the desert for nearly forty years, before Joshua finally led them into their Promised Land. The Book of Joshua is a book of battles. It tells the story of the invasion of Canaan. The Israelites had no chariots and no iron weapons, yet they terrified their enemies.

The Israelites'
enemies are terrified

UNDERSTANDING JOSHUA

The Book of Joshua starts when Joshua had become the new leader of the Israelites, after the death of Moses. The key to the book lies in God's words to Joshua in chapter one: "Be careful to obey all the laws my servant Moses gave you...Do not be terrified; do not be discouraged, for the Lord your God will be with you wherever you go."

RAHAB

The city of Jericho was the first city in Canaan that the Israelites came to. Joshua sent spies into the city to find out how well it was defended. They were spotted, but a woman called Rahab hid them on her roof. "Remember me when you attack Jericho," she said. "Do not harm my family." The spies escaped and reported back to Joshua.

THE BATTLE OF JERICHO

The gates of Jericho were bolted fast against the Israelites. "I have given you this city," God said. He told Joshua that the Israelites should walk round outside the city walls for the next six days. On the seventh day, the priests were to blow their trumpets and the people were to shout as loud as they could.

The Israelites followed God's plan, and on the seventh day, they made a huge din with trumpets and shouting. The walls of the city crumbled to the ground! Everyone living there was killed, except Rahab and her family.

The Israelites
make a huge din

DIVIDING THE LAND

The land of Canaan had to be divided between the Israelite tribes (family clans), and Joshua had to be fair. So he split the land into areas, and each tribe drew lots to see who would get what. Joshua's town was called Timnath-Serah, which means 'what is left'.

READING JOSHUA

- *Chapter 1:1–2:24*: Getting ready.
- *Chapter 3:1–5:12*: The first moves.
- *Chapter 5:13–12:24*: The fight for the land.
- *Chapter 13:1–21:45*: Dividing the land.
- *Chapter 22:1–24:33*: Agreeing to serve God.

False teachers are like clouds with no rain

JUDE THE LETTER OF

The Letter of Jude is a short letter from Jude to a group of Christians. Jude was the half-brother of Jesus. Jude had planned to write about Jesus, but bad news had reached him: impostors had secretly crept among the Christians. Jude wrote to tell the Christians how to spot these false teachers.

SPOT THE ALIEN

Jude's letter gave guidelines on how to spot which teachers were false. Here are some of the things he said:

- They do not obey Jesus.
- They are money mad.
- They flatter you for their own ends.
- They boast.
- They grumble and find fault.
- They are greedy and wicked.
- They are like fruit trees in autumn without fruit.
- In a dry land, where people are longing for water, they are like clouds that sail by without giving any rain.

Money

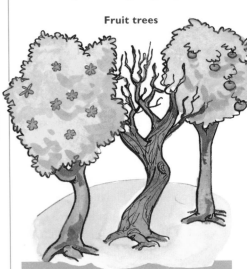

Fruit trees

UNDERSTANDING JUDE

In the first years after Jesus died, small groups of Christians formed in many cities. But the New Testament had not yet been written. How could these new Christians get to know Jesus' teaching?

Christian teachers began to travel from church to church. In return for teaching, they got free meals and somewhere to sleep. This is where the impostors came in. False teachers, who were out for what they could get, had begun to work their way among the Christians.

A HORRIBLE WARNING

Jude was very worried by this. To drive his point home, he gave examples of horrific things that had happened in Old Testament times:

- The evil cities of Sodom and Gomorrah were destroyed by fire and brimstone. (Probably this was a volcanic eruption.)
- Wicked angels were thrown out of heaven.

Sodom is destroyed

HOW TO BEAT THE CHEAT

Jude advised the Christians to steer clear of the false teachers. Instead, they should fix their minds on God and his love, on Jesus and his life, and pray. They should also be kind and helpful to people who were full of doubts.

READING JUDE

- *Verses 1–16*: The false teachers.
- *Verses 17–23*: Keep strong in the faith.
- *Verses 24–25*: A prayer of praise.

JUDGES THE BOOK OF

T he Book of Judges carries on from the end of the Book of Joshua. Joshua took over as leader of the Israelites after Moses. His orders were to make sure the Israelites obeyed God, had nothing to do with the worship of idols, and took over the whole land of Canaan. The book covers two hundred years, and shows how the Israelites mostly failed to follow these orders.

- Summary:
  Judges 2:11–23
- Deborah:
  Judges 4:1–5:31
- Gideon:
  Judges 6:1–8:35

Bible Search

JUDGES

"Judge" was the title given to a leader of a tribe or group of tribes. He, or she, kept law and order and led the people in battle against the enemy. Deborah, Gideon and Samson are the three most famous judges.

HELP

Some of the Israelites thought that God was a desert God, who didn't know about growing crops or getting rain to fall. Often they turned to worshiping the Canaanite gods, to ask for help with farming.

Worshiping the gods of Canaan

PROBLEMS

Under Joshua's leadership, the Israelites had settled in Canaan. Now they had to build cities, plow fields and plant vineyards. But this wasn't easy. Because the Israelites had lived in the desert for so long, they didn't have many of the necessary skills.

Archaeologists have found the ruins of some of the cities the Israelites captured. There are layers of ash showing old buildings destroyed by fire, then come new houses, which are much rougher and less well built than Canaanite houses.

UNDERSTANDING JUDGES

The Philistines attack the Israelites

The Israelite tribes were under attack. Philistines on the coast and desert tribes from across the Jordan River were invading the land. God used the invaders as part of his plan to teach the Israelites to follow him.

The Book of Judges goes round in circles. The amazing thing about the Book of Judges is that God never gave up on the people.

READING JUDGES

- *Chapter 1:1–3:6*: Summary of the invasion.
- *Chapter 3:7–16:31*: Stories of the judges.
- *Chapter 17:1–21:25*: Two nasty stories.

Desert warriors

JUDGES
THE LEADERS OF THE PEOPLE

The Book of Judges is a story of heroes, cowards and traitors. The cowards and traitors were the Israelite people. They were traitors to God, who had loved them and looked after them. The heroes were the judges.

JUDGES

A judge was a cross between a sheriff from the wild west, a tribal warrior chief and a preacher. The Book of Judges gives the names of twelve judges. They ruled over tribal districts, not over the whole country, but sometimes God called them to deliver the nation from its enemies.

EHUD

Ehud was left-handed. He hid his sword on the inside of his right leg, and pulled it out with his left hand. This tactic caught his enemy by surprise.

Ehud

DEBORAH

Deborah would sit under a palm tree, and people came to her for advice.

The Israelites' enemy, King Jabin, had 900 iron chariots. "Go and fight Jabin," Deborah said to Barak. "I dare not," he said. "I'll only go if you go with me." "God has given the enemy to you," Deborah said.

So Barak and his troops waited on a mountain. Sisera, King Jabin's army commander, and his chariots were in the valley below. God sent a heavy rainstorm. The Kishon River flooded, making the chariots useless, and the army was routed.

Deborah tells Barak to fight Jabin

SAMSON THE STRONG

Samson was a fierce fighter. He killed a hungry lion with his bare hands. His story shows that even heroes were sometimes bad.
(Look at the page on Samson to find out his story.)

Samson fights a lion

Bible Search

- Deborah's victory song: *Judges 5*
- Lawless days: *Judges 21:25*
- Samson the strong: *Judges 13–16*

KINGDOM OF GOD

The kingdom of God is not a place

Jesus' first words when he started preaching were: "The kingdom of God is near." The kingdom is not a place, but it exists wherever people obey God. Anyone who lives according to God's rules is part of God's kingdom. This is summed up in the Lord's Prayer: "Your kingdom come, your will be done on Earth as it is in heaven."

MIRACLES

Matthew wrote: "Jesus went through all the towns…preaching the good news of the kingdom and healing every disease." Jesus' miracles of healing were a sign that he was the Messiah, or deliverer, that the people had been waiting for.

A SEED

Jesus said, "The mustard seed is the smallest seed, but it slowly grows until it's the biggest plant in the garden, and birds nest in it." The kingdom of God seemed small to the friends of Jesus, but one day it would be known all over the world.

The growth of a mustard seed

TREASURE

A man and his treasure

Jesus said that the kingdom of God was like a man who finds a treasure hidden in a field and sells everything he has to buy that field. He meant that belonging to the kingdom of God is worth everything you've got.

BELONGING

As members of the kingdom of God, Christians can live worry-free lives. God has promised to give them all they need and to turn even bad things into good.

Jesus said, "Not everyone who says to me, 'Lord, Lord', will enter the kingdom of heaven; but only he who does the will of my Father in heaven." God's will is that everyone should let him control every part of their lives.

Living a worry-free life

Bible Search

- Entry: *Matthew 7:21*

- God's care: *Matthew 6:25–34*

- Bad into good : *Romans 8:28*

KINGDOM OF ISRAEL

When King Solomon died, his kingdom split into two: Judah in the south, and Israel in the north. Israel was the larger and richer of the two countries. That made it appealing for other countries to grab. Israel only lasted 200 years, before it was destroyed by the Assyrians.

THE SPLIT

When Solomon died, the twelve tribes of Israel had to decide who would be the new king. Solomon had two sons, Rehoboam and Jeroboam. Rehoboam was made king. Because taxes had been very high under Solomon, and the people had been forced into slave labor, Jeroboam and others asked Rehoboam to make life easier. He promised to make it even harder!

So the kingdom split into two. Ten of the tribes made Jeroboam the king of Israel, and Rehoboam became king of the other two tribes in Judah.

Rehoboam promises to make life even harder

JEROBOAM I

Jeroboam made a fatal mistake. He wanted to stop people from rushing to Jerusalem to worship God. So he built temples at Dan and Bethel, and put a gold statue of a bull in each. Jeroboam may have installed the bulls in God's honor. But the people began to worship the bulls as well as God. That started the bad times in the country of Israel.

KINGS

One bad king followed another. Some, especially Omri and Jeroboam II, were strong kings and almost made Israel a world power again. But none gave wholehearted service to God. They worshipped stars, and served the god Baal. Some even sacrificed their own children to these gods. In 200 years, there were nineteen kings.

TEN LOST TRIBES

When the Assyrians conquered Israel, they had a devastating way of stopping future rebellion. They took away part of the population as prisoners of war.

The calamity hadn't come without warning. Over and over again, the prophets had been telling the people that they must turn to God and obey him.

Find out more on the pages headed Elijah, Elisha, Amos and Hosea.

Prisoners of war

- Summing up Israel's kings: *2 Kings 17:7–23*

- The split of the kingdom: *1 Kings 12*

- Red alert: *Amos 6:4–7; 8:3–4*

A bad king sacrifices his child

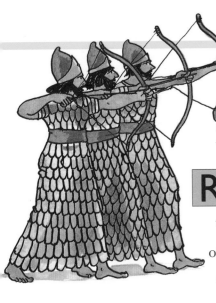

KINGDOM
OF JUDAH

Read the page on the Kingdom of Israel, first.

When King Solomon died, the tribes of Judah and Benjamin formed the small mountain country of Judah, ruled by Solomon's son Rehoboam. The people of Judah believed that God wanted David's descendants to be their kings. So each king was followed by his son.

ENEMIES FROM THE OUTSIDE

The country was often at war. Judah's main enemies were:

● Israel and the city state of Damascus, until they were swallowed up by Assyria.

● Assyria. Then Assyria was beaten by Babylonia.

● Babylonia. In 586 B.C., Babylonia destroyed Judah.

ENEMIES FROM THE INSIDE

Worship of the Canaanite god Baal was common. On hilltops and in little groves of trees, sacrifices were offered to idols. Some kings were true to God: Asa, Jehoshaphat, Joash, Hezekiah, and Josiah.

HEZEKIAH

When the Assyrian army attacked Jerusalem, King Sennacherib of Assyria wrote, "I shut King Hezekiah up like a bird in a cage." But Hezekiah prayed to God for help. The prophet Isaiah said, "You have trusted God, so God will save you." A plague swept through the Assyrian army, killing many men. The soldiers who survived packed up and left.

JOSIAH

Josiah was eight when he became king. When he was sixteen, he made up his mind to work for God. He told the priests to mend the broken-down Temple in Jerusalem.

One day, the workmen found an old scroll. It was a lost copy of God's teachings. Josiah called a meeting of all the people and read the book aloud. The people promised God that from now on they would keep his laws. And they did, for as long as Josiah was alive.

To find out about the fall of Jerusalem, see the page on Exile. Turn also to the pages on 1 and 2 Kings and 1 and 2 Chronicles.

Bible Search

● Hezekiah:
Isaiah 37 and 38

● Asa:
2 Chronicles 14; 15

● Josiah:
2 Kings 22 and 23

KINGS THE FIRST AND SECOND BOOKS OF

The First and Second Books of Kings cover nearly 400 years (975–586 B.C.) of the history of the Jews. The First Book of Kings starts with the death of King David, and describes the glory of his son Solomon's kingdom. It goes on to describe the civil war and the breakdown of the people's trust in God. The Second Book of Kings ends with the saddest moment in the people's history: the fall of Jerusalem.

AUTHOR

The books were probably written by a prophet living in Babylon. He wrote when the people of Judah had been taken away to Babylonia by King Nebuchadnezzar's soldiers. He collected stories and records of kings and prophets. The books 1 and 2 Chronicles also describe this period in history.

A Babylonian soldier

UNDERSTANDING 1 AND 2 KINGS

Years before, at the foot of Mount Sinai, the people had made a covenant with God, and promised that they would obey his laws. The Books of 1 and 2 Kings show how the kings of Israel and Judah often did not keep their side of the agreement.

1 and 2 Kings were probably written by a prophet

THE TEMPLE

Many chapters in 1 Kings describe the building of the Temple. God said to Solomon, "As for this temple you are building…if you keep all my commands…I will not abandon my people Israel."

PROPHETS

The disasters which overtook the kingdoms of Israel and Judah didn't come without warning. Over the years, many prophets had warned the kings of the dangers of refusing to obey God. Chief among them were:
- In Israel: Elijah, Elisha, Amos, Hosea.
- In Judah: Joel, Nahum, Isaiah, Micah, Zephaniah, Habakkuk, Jeremiah.

READING 1 AND 2 KINGS

1 Kings
- *Chapter 1–2*: Solomon becomes king.
- *Chapter 3–11*: Solomon builds the Temple.
- *Chapter 12–22*: The two kingdoms.
- *Chapter 17–21*: Elijah.

2 Kings
- *Chapter 1–16*: The two kingdoms.
- *Chapter 17*: The fall of Samaria and Israel.
- *Chapter 18–23*: The kingdom of Judah.
- *Chapter 24–25*: The fall of Judah.

FAMOUS READINGS IN 1 AND 2 KINGS

- *1 Kings 3*: Solomon prays for wisdom.
- *1 Kings 8*: The Temple is dedicated.
- *2 Kings 17*: Samaria is captured.
- *2 Kings 25*: Jerusalem and the Temple are captured.

The Temple

KNOWING YOURSELF

S ome people think that a human being is made up of a body with a spirit, or soul, living in it. When a person dies, the spirit flies away, like a bird out of a cage. But in the Bible, the word *soul* and the word *body* both mean the same thing: the whole person.

Some people think that the spirit flies away

ME

We can think, choose and act for ourselves; we can feel things and know right from wrong; we can make friends and relate to God. All this makes us unique people. But even if we are hurt or handicapped in some way, so that we can't do all these things, God still knows us and cares for us, and we are special to him.

Everybody is special to God

GOD'S IMAGES

When God made people, he said, "Let us make man in our image, in our likeness." This doesn't mean God has a physical body. It means God is a person. We can create, think, and love because that's the way God is.

A PURPOSE

Human beings need to know that their lives have a meaning and purpose. God made us to worship and love him, to love and help other people, and to look after the world.

Paul wrote: "God gives us all things richly to enjoy." Everything is a gift from God.

A STORY

Jesus told a story about a rich man who was going on a journey. He gave his money to his three servants to keep until he returned. The first two servants doubled their money. The third servant hid the money in the ground!

When the man came back, he was furious with the third servant and took his money back.

This story showed that we must not waste the abilities God gives us.

The three servants

Bible Search

- God's image: *Genesis 1:26*
- Use our gifts: *Matthew 25:14–30*
- Love: *Mark 12:30–31*

LAMENTATIONS
THE BOOK OF

The Book of Lamentations is a funeral song for the city of Jerusalem, after it was destroyed by King Nebuchadnezzar and the Babylonian army in 586 B.C.

Each of the five chapters in the Book of Lamentations is a poem. The first four chapters are acrostic poems, meaning each verse starts with a letter of the Hebrew alphabet. Verse 1 begins with the first letter and verse 22 starts with the last letter of the alphabet. This is repeated twice in chapter three.

Jeremiah comforts the people

JEREMIAH

It is thought that the prophet Jeremiah wrote these poems. At the time of writing, he was living in the captured city of Jerusalem. His poems were inspired by his sadness at seeing hungry people, and children searching for their parents.

UNDERSTANDING LAMENTATIONS

When they lost their city and their Temple, many of the people of Jerusalem felt they had lost God.

A BETTER FUTURE

Jeremiah had warned the people that disaster would come. But instead of saying, "I told you so!", he tried to comfort the poor and elderly people who had been left behind in Jerusalem. (The Babylonian army had taken many of the other people back to their own land as prisoners.)

The Wailing Wall

THE WAILING WALL

Today, in the center of Jerusalem, one part of the wall of Herod's Temple is still standing. It is known as the Wailing Wall. Each Friday evening, for the last 600 years, Jews have met by the wall to read aloud from the Book of Lamentations.

HOPE

Although he was very sad, Jeremiah still trusted God. He wrote:

"Because of the Lord's great love we are not consumed, for his compassions never fail. They are new every morning; great is your faithfulness."

READING LAMENTATIONS

- *Chapter 1*: Judah's great sadness.
- *Chapter 2*: God is not defeated.
- *Chapter 3–4*: Judah's trust in God for the future.
- *Chapter 5*: A prayer.

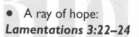

Bible Search

- A ray of hope: *Lamentations 3:22–24*
- Jeremiah writes sad songs: *2 Chronicles 35:25*

LANGUAGES
AND WRITING

The earliest writing we know about takes the form of drawings on cave walls. The earliest cave pictures are about 30,000 years old. Pictures, instead of words, were used to describe objects.

Later civilizations also used picture symbols. The ancient Egyptians drew beautiful pictures, which we call hieroglyphics. They had 800 picture symbols.

Hieroglyphics

THE ROSETTA STONE

For a long time, no one could read the hieroglyphics on Egyptian tombs. But in 1798, near the city of Rosetta in Egypt, one of Napoleon's soldiers dug up a large stone with writing all over it. It was a royal command dating from about 200 B.C. The command was written in Greek, in everyday Egyptian and in old hieroglyphic Egyptian. At last translators were able break the code and unlock the secrets of ancient Egypt. The stone became known as the Rosetta Stone.

The Rosetta Stone is discovered

CUNEIFORM

The Babylonians used a very simple form of picture writing. They pressed shapes into soft clay with wedge-shaped sticks or bones. The clay was baked in the sun.

These "books" can still be read today (see the page on Schools).

ALPHABET

In Canaan, in about 1500 B.C., a genius invented the alphabet. He or she divided language into twenty simple sounds and wrote down a symbol for each sound. Over the years, each symbol became a letter.

HEBREW

Nearly all our Old Testament was written in Hebrew. Hebrew has twenty-two consonants, but no vowels. It is read from right to left, perhaps because the first Hebrew writing was chiseled on stone. It was easier for most people to chisel from right to left! Hebrew books start from the back.

Chiselling from right to left

GREEK

All our New Testament books are written in Greek. This was the language spoken by the Romans, who ruled most of the world in New Testament times.

ARAMAIC

Small parts of the Old Testament are written in Aramaic. This was the language of the Persian empire, which was the world superpower before the Romans.

Jesus and his disciples spoke Aramaic, and there are a few Aramaic words in the New Testament. *Abba* is Aramaic for "father", or "daddy."

191

LEADERS
AND GOVERNMENTS

Any group of people living or working together needs rules. Leaders decide rules and make sure they are kept. Leaders of a country work together in a government.

When Noah and his family came out of the ark, God said, "Whoever sheds the blood of man, by man shall his blood be shed." With those words, God put people in charge of keeping law and order: that was the beginning of government.

Teams need leaders

GOOD GOVERNMENT

In the time of the Judges, there was no government. Everybody "did what was right in his own eyes," and the result was chaos. Every country needs a good government. That's why the New Testament writers told people to pray for the leaders of governments, and to obey them.

Chaos

BAD GOVERNMENT

In Old Testament times, the leaders of Israel and Judah were often very bad people.

The prophets didn't sit back and say nothing: they got involved, and told the leaders where they were going wrong.

Amos stood up in the marketplace at Bethel and said God would punish the leaders. He complained, 'You trample on the poor and force them to give you grain.'

JESUS

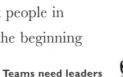

Taxes

Jesus lived in an occupied country, but he didn't try to rebel against Roman government. He paid his taxes, saying, "Give to Caesar what is Caesar's." But Jesus did not respect King Herod, who ruled for the Romans, and hung on to power and wealth by any means. He thought Herod was cunning, like a fox, and refused to answer his questions. The religious leaders had added many extra laws to God's laws. These laws made life hard and did not help people to love God or each other. Jesus refused to keep them.

King Herod

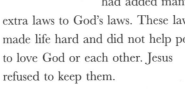

A cunning fox

PETER AND JOHN

Peter and John were brought before the Sanhedrin (a council of religious leaders in Jerusalem) and told to stop preaching. 'We must obey God rather than men,' they said.

The Sanhedrin

- Obey leaders and pay taxes: *Romans 13:1–7; I Peter 2:13–17*

- Pray for leaders: *I Timothy 2:2*

- Speaking out: *Jeremiah 21:11–22:19*

- Obey God: *Acts 5:27–29*

LETTERS
AND NEWS

Many people today are "news-aholics." We have TV, radio, newspapers, phones, fax machines and computers to tell each other what is going on in our lives and in the rest of the world. How did people spread news in Bible times?

Television, faxes and telephones

Computers and radios

CUNEIFORM

Cuneiform writing

The Babylonians wrote letters by pressing a wedge-shaped stick into soft, thin, clay bricks (called tablets). These were left to harden in the sun. This type of writing is called cuneiform. Thousands of cuneiform tablets have been found by archaeologists.

PAPYRUS

The Egyptians made a rough paper from papyrus reeds. Reeds were also used as pens, cut at one end to a sloping point. Black ink was made from soot, olive oil, resin and water.

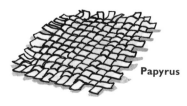

Papyrus

PARCHMENT

The Hebrew word for *book* comes from the word "scrape". Skins of sheep and goats were dried, scraped and softened to make a smooth surface. This was called parchment, and was used for writing on.

ROMANS

The Romans sometimes used two pieces of wood covered with wax for letters. Leather bands held two edges together so that the letter opened like a book. The letter would be written with a bone, bronze or silver stylus. This was pointed at one end, and flat at the other for smoothing the wax.

SENDING LETTERS

A letter might be written on a scroll, which was a long roll of parchment or papyrus. The letter was signed, rolled up, and tied with a cord. Then the knot was covered with wax, and the wax was stamped with a seal. Every man of any importance had his own seal. (See the page on Jewels.)

Bible Search

- Paul signs off: *Galatians 6:11*
- Scrolls and parchments: *2 Timothy 4:13*
- A Roman notice: *John 19:19–22*

POSTAL SERVICE

The first postal service was started by the Persian king, Darius, in about 500 B.C. The Romans copied his idea. Letters were taken by messengers on horseback. The messengers rode in relays. Every 15–20 miles, there were rest houses and fresh horses.

Messengers were only used by the Romans and their employees. Other people could hire letter-carriers. These men carried messages in wooden tubes round their neck or waist. Or people sent slaves, or relied on friends, to take messages.

93

LEVITICUS
THE BOOK OF

L eviticus is the third book in the Bible. Here you find many of the laws which God gave to Moses on Mount Sinai.

Jews called Leviticus "the Priests' Book". The priests were in charge of the worship at the Tabernacle, and the Levites helped them. The name 'Leviticus' comes from "Levite". Levites were named after Levi, one of Jacob's sons.

Levites were one of the twelve tribes of Israel.

A Levite

UNDERSTANDING LEVITICUS

"You are my holy people," God said. "You belong to me." How should God's holy people live? Leviticus tells us in great detail.

- God is good and wants us to be good and loving.
- Every day is God's holy day.
- Wrongdoing must be punished. Some of the laws in Leviticus only apply to the times they were written in, such as the laws about hygiene and what food to eat. Other laws always apply, such as those about caring for people.

A sacrifice

SACRIFICES

There are instructions on making sacrifices. Specially chosen animals were killed on an altar as a way of saying "thank you" or "I'm sorry" to God. The people also brought "thank offerings" of food to God.

FOOD

Moses gave laws for healthy living and eating. Only certain animals could be eaten. It was all right to eat cows, sheep, fish with fins and doves.

Dove   Sheep

Cow

Pigs, birds of prey and shellfish were forbidden.

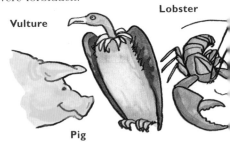

Vulture   Lobster

Pig

SOME OTHER RULES IN LEVITICUS

- Love your neighbor as yourself.
- Don't eat all the fruit on your trees. Leave some for poor people.
- Stand up when old people enter.
- You shall not steal, cheat or deceive.

READING LEVITICUS

- *Chapters 1–7*: Five types of offering.
- *Chapters 8–10*: The priests.
- *Chapter 11–15*: Clean and unclean.
- *Chapter 16*: Atonement or how to be 'at-one-with-God'.
- *Chapters 17–27*: Rules for right living.
- *Chapter 23*: Holy days and holidays.

LIGHTING AND HEATING

I n the time of Jesus, lamps were kept burning all night. Most houses had only one or two small windows, and so houses were dark. A lamp was often kept lit all day as well. Lamps were very important, and in Bible stories sometimes represented life itself.

LAMPS

The earliest lamps were clay dishes, with one end pressed to make a lip. A wick of rush, flax or rag was put in the lip. It soaked up oil contained in the dish. These lamps would burn for two or three hours before they needed to be refilled with oil.

By New Testament times, potters had learned how to make lamps with tops. They were safer because the oil couldn't spill out.

Some lamps had room for several wicks to give more light.

Most lamps burned olive oil, but sometimes animal fat was used. Olive oil was expensive.

Oil jar

TORCHES, CANDLES AND LANTERNS

Outside, in processions, torches were often used. To make a torch, you drenched rags in oil, fastened them to a stick and then lit them. About every fifteen minutes, the charred ends of the rags had to be cut, and more oil added.

Candles were only used in funeral processions, and by the poorest people who could not afford oil for lamps.

To make a lantern, a lamp could be put inside a pottery or metal container. The container had an opening at the side.

FIRES

Houses didn't have fireplaces or chimneys. A brazier (a container for burning things) might be taken indoors, or a fire would be lit in a hollow in the floor lined with stones. The fuel was animal dung, charcoal or wood.

Bible Search

- Five silly girls and their lamps: *Matthew 25:1–13*

- What Jesus said about a lamp: *Matthew 5:15–16*

- Lamp means life: *Pslam 18:28*

In one of Jesus' stories, five bridesmaids at a wedding ran out of oil for their lamps

LORD'S SUPPER
AND HOLY COMMUNION

T he Lord's Supper is also called the Holy Communion, Breaking Bread, the Eucharist (which means thanksgiving) and, in Roman Catholic churches, the Mass. It was started by Jesus during his last meal with his friends.

Receiving
Communion

THE PASSOVER

Each year, every Jewish family sits down for a special meal of roast lamb, bitter herbs and unleavened bread. This Passover meal celebrates the time when the Israelites in Egypt were spared by God, while in Egyptian families, every firstborn son was killed.

- The first Lord's Supper:
  Matthew 26:17–30; John 13–17

- As described by Paul:
  1 Corinthians 11:17–26

JESUS' LAST SUPPER

Jesus' last meal with his friends was the Passover meal. During the supper, Jesus broke pieces of bread and gave them to his friends. He said, 'This is my body which is given for you.'

He passed around a cup of wine. He said, "This is my blood, the blood of the new covenant, which is shed for the forgiveness of sins." A covenant is an agreement. In the Old Testament, agreements between God and his people were sealed with a blood sacrifice.

Jesus told his friends to keep on meeting together after his death, and to drink wine and eat bread in the same way, in memory of him.

Today, Christians eat a small piece of bread (or a wafer) and drink a sip of wine as part of the communion service. There have been many arguments about what Jesus' words at the Last Supper mean, but in Protestant churches most people take Communion

- In memory of Jesus' Last Supper and his death for us.
- As a way of saying that they are sorry for the wrong things they have done.
- As a way of saying that they belong to Jesus and to one another; that they are part of the family (or body) of Jesus.
- As a symbol of their need to receive Jesus' power to live for him.

The Last
Supper

LOT, SODOM AND GOMORRAH

Lot grew up in the beautiful city of Ur. God told his uncle Abraham to leave Ur and travel to Canaan. Lot went with him, and so did other members of the family and all their servants. They lived a nomadic life, moving from place to place, and living in tents.

Lot

SODOM

Lot drifted to the plains south of the Dead Sea. He settled in a town called Sodom, near to a town called Gomorrah. The people of Sodom were very wicked, and God decided to destroy the city. He sent two angels to rescue Lot and his family. They led them out of the city and told them to hurry away without looking back. But Lot's wife turned to look at the city. She instantly became a pillar of salt.

WHAT HAPPENED?

Sodom was probably destroyed in a great volcanic eruption. Boiling tar and minerals rained down on the city. The quaking, shaking land may have dropped slightly, and the waters of the Dead Sea overflowed into nearby cities.

Lot's wife looks back

ABRAHAM AND LOT SEPARATE

Both Lot and Abraham had flocks of sheep and goats, and many servants. At the place in Canaan where they decided to settle, there wasn't enough good land and water for everyone. "We must not fight," Abraham said. "Choose where you want to live." Lot decided to go eastwards.

FACT OR FICTION?

Today, there is no trace of Sodom. Did it ever exist? In 1975, archaeologists working hundreds of miles away found 20,000 flat clay bricks covered with writing. And on some of those old bricks, dating from 2400 B.C., are the names of cities ruled over by the kings of Ebla. Among the names are Sodom and Gomorrah.

Bible Search

- Lot's choice: **Genesis 13**
- Abraham prays for Sodom: **Genesis 18:16–33**
- Lot escapes: **Genesis: 19:15–29**

LOVE

'I love my mum'

"I love fish and fries." "I love my mom." Our English word *love* has lots of meanings!

In the New Testament, there are four different words for love. These mean close, loving friendship; the love that you have for your family; love between a man and a woman; and the love God has for his people.

'I love fish and fries'

TWO COMMANDS

The New Testament word *agape* means the love God has for his people. It is also the love we are told to show to other people. It means wanting the very best for others, and trying to bring that about.

Someone asked Jesus, "What is the greatest command?" Jesus replied, "Love (*agape*) the Lord your God with all your heart, and with all your soul, and with all your mind, and with all your strength. The second is this: Love your neighbor as yourself."

Love your neighbour

A STORY

The Samaritan takes the Jew to an inn

"Who is my neighbor?" asked someone else. So Jesus told a story. A Samaritan found a Jew lying on a mountain road, where he had been attacked. He bathed his wounds, took him to an inn and paid the innkeeper to look after him. (This was surprising because Jews didn't like Samaritans.)

So the answer to the question was that anyone who needs your help is your neighbor.

Bible Search

- Love from God: *I John 4:7–12*
- Jesus' last command: *John 15:9–17*
- The greatest command: *Mark 12:28–31*
- Who is my neighbor?: *Luke 10:25–37*
- A gift: *Galatians 5:22*

LOVE IS...

What is love like? Jesus gave us a guide. He said, "Love each other in the way that I have loved you."

Paul described *agape* love in 1 Corinthians 13. Paul said something startling in this chapter. He said that anything we do for Jesus without love, anything at all, is useless.

Paul said something startling

198

LUKE
THE GOSPEL OF

Luke wanted his friend Theophilus to have a clear and true account of the start of the Christian faith. He checked all his facts, and made sure that dates were correct. He wrote his Gospel in Greek. Unlike the other Gospel writers, Luke was a Greek, not a Jew.

Luke

UNDERSTANDING LUKE

Luke showed that the Christian message was for the whole world, and not just for Jews. We can tell what was important to Luke by looking at the things he included in his Gospel, which do not appear in the other Gospels. Most Jewish men considered certain people, such as the sick, shepherds, Samaritans, and tax-collectors, to be unimportant. Luke showed that Jesus cared about these people as much as anybody else.

A sick person

WOMEN AND POOR PEOPLE

In the time of Jesus, religious Jews looked down on women and the poor. But Luke showed how important they were, by writing about them in his Gospel. Only Luke tells of the healing of Peter's mother-in-law, and writes down Mary's song of praise to God, thanking him for making her the mother of Jesus. Only Luke tells the story of the beggar Lazarus being accepted by God, and the story of how a runaway son who wasted his money was forgiven.

A shepherd

A tax-collector

THE GOOD SAMARITAN

The Jews did not like the Samaritans. But in Luke's Gospel, we read Jesus' story about the Samaritan who helped a wounded Jew. Luke also tells us about the healed Samaritan leper who came back to say thank you to Jesus.

The Good Samaritan

READING LUKE

- *Chapter 1:1–4:13*: Jesus' early days.
- *Chapter 4:14–9:50*: Jesus in Galilee.
- *Chapter 9:51–19:44*: Jesus goes to Jerusalem.
- *Chapter 19:45-25:53*: Jesus' last week, his death and resurrection.

- Mary's song: *Luke 1:46–55*
- Good Samaritan: *Luke 10:25–38*
- The returning son: *Luke 15:11–24*
- The rich man and Lazarus: *Luke 16:19–31*
- Ten lepers: *Luke 17:11–19*

MAKE-UP, HAIRSTYLES, PERFUME, JEWELLERY

A comb

Make-up was popular in all the lands of the Bible. Archaeologists have found hundreds of little cosmetic pots made from ivory, bone and metal. Exquisite jewelry, combs, jewels, ornaments and mirrors have also been discovered.

A cosmetic pot

Bible Search

- Jewels:
Isaiah: 3:18–23

- A warning:
1 Peter 3:3–4

- Jezebel:
2 Kings 9:30

PERFUME

Perfume was made by crushing flower petals, such as jasmine or rose, and mixing them with oil. Herbs and spices were used in the same way.

At parties, women might be given cones of perfume. They put them on their heads, where the scented oil dripped a fragrant perfume on their clothes.

Scented oils and creams were rubbed on the body to protect against sunburn and insect bites.

MAKE-UP

Eyes were outlined in black; eyebrows were darkened; eyelids were shaded; eyelashes were thickened with blue coloring. Cheeks were powdered, and rouge was added to lips and cheeks. Women also painted their fingernails and the palms of their hands with a yellowy-orange paste made from henna plant leaves, mixed with oil.

Make-up and jewelry

JEWELLERY

Egyptian jewellery

Egyptians were especially gifted at making jewelry. They would wear wide collar-like necklaces, studded with jewels. Some jewelry was worn as magic charms. A precious stone in the shape of a scarab beetle was said to be a powerful charm.

The Jews liked to wear jewelry: bracelets, rings, necklaces, earrings, nose-rings, and tiaras. Sometimes it was all worn at the same time! Jewelry was made from gold, silver, bronze, ivory, precious jewels and glass.

HAIRSTYLES

In Old Testament times, men and women wore their hair long. By the time of Jesus, many Jewish men had short hair and beards. But they didn't cut their sideburns, so these grew into long tassel-like lengths of hair.

Women did not usually wear their hair loose in public. They used curlers, hairpins, hairnets, and gold, ivory and wooden combs. They twisted their hair into tight curls. They also braided their hair and put flowers, ribbons and jewels in it.

MALACHI THE BOOK OF

T he Book of Malachi contains the teachings of the prophet Malachi, whose name means "my messenger". Malachi was the last Old Testament prophet. Four hundred years were to pass before God sent another prophet to his people.

Bible Search

- John the Baptist: *Malachi 3:1; Matthew 11:10*
- Priests: *Malachi 1:6–2:9*
- People: *Malachi 2:10–16*
- Happiness: *Malachi 3:10–11; 4:2*

PRIESTS

At the rebuilt Temple in Jerusalem, the priests were not worshiping God properly. They were bringing sick, and even stolen, animals to sacrifice to God. Malachi said, "When you sacrifice crippled or diseased animals is that not wrong? Try offering them to your governor! Would he be pleased with you?"

God said, "You insult me when you sacrifice worthless animals."

A worthless sacrifice

PEOPLE

Malachi turned his piercing gaze on the people. He saw lots of bad things:
- Men had married women who worshiped idols.

Some wives worshiped idols

A man divorces his wife

- Men were divorcing their wives. Malachi said, "Make sure none of you breaks his promise to his wife."
- Employers were greedy.
- People were cheating God, and not giving a tenth of their crops, as the law said they should. (The money was used to pay for the Temple.)

People were cheating God

A FUTURE MESSENGER

The book ends hopefully. Malachi promised that a messenger would come from God to get the people ready for the arrival of God himself.

John the Baptist was to be this messenger, 400 years later. Jesus said, "For John is the one of whom the Scriptures say, 'God said, I will send my messenger ahead of you to open the way for you.' "

Malachi promised that one day, when they had turned back to God, the people would know God's happiness.

John the Baptist was born 400 years later

READING MALACHI

- *Chapter 1:1–2:16*: A scolding.
- *Chapter 2:17–4:6*: God's judgment, and kindness.

201

MARK THE GOSPEL OF

The Gospel of Mark is the story of the last three years of Jesus' life. Papias, who lived about 150 A.D., said it was based on the preaching of Jesus' friend, Peter. It is the shortest Gospel, and probably the first to be written. Mark's real name was John Mark, but he was known as Mark.

Mark's Gospel is full of swift-moving action. The words *at once* are used forty times. It is written very simply, with many little details which paint a picture of the events Peter saw.

For example, only Mark tells us that Jesus picked up the children in his arms to bless them.

UNDERSTANDING MARK'S GOSPEL

Murder!

The apostles Peter and Paul were both murdered in Rome, on the orders of the Roman emperor, Nero. Mark probably wrote his Gospel to help the Christians in Rome to be brave. This may be one reason why over one third of the book is about Jesus' last week on Earth, his death and coming to life again.

Christians in Rome

MARK

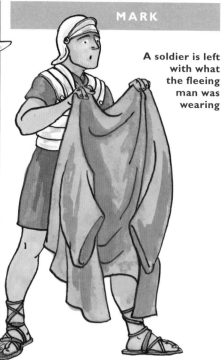

A soldier is left with what the fleeing man was wearing

After Jesus died, the Christians used to meet at Mark's mother's house. Jesus' last supper may also have been held there.

On the night Jesus was captured, the soldiers grabbed a young man. The cloth he was wearing came off and he ran away naked. This story only appears in Mark's Gospel, in two short verses. Why bother to include it? In the dark, who even knew what had happened? Probably only the young man! Perhaps the young man was Mark himself.

READING MARK

- *Chapter 1:1–13*: Beginnings.
- *Chapter 1:14–9:50*: Jesus' work in Galilee.
- *Chapter 10:1–52*: From Galilee to Jerusalem.
- *Chapter 11:1–15:47*: Jesus' last week
- *Chapter 16*: Jesus is alive.

Bible Search

- Peter and Mark: **1 Peter 5:13**
- Mark's house: **Acts 12:12**
- A walk-on part: **Mark 14:51–52**

GOOD NEWS

Gospel comes from a Greek word meaning "good news". The good news was about Jesus: Mark wrote about many of Jesus' miracles. The miracles showed that Jesus really was the son of God.

Jesus blesses some children

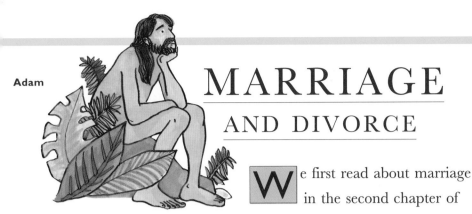

Adam

MARRIAGE
AND DIVORCE

We first read about marriage in the second chapter of Genesis. Adam was lonely, so God gave him a friend: Eve. Then the writer adds, "For this reason a man will leave his father and mother and be united to his wife, and they will become one flesh."

ADULTERY

Commandment number seven in the Ten Commandments is: "You shall not commit adultery." This means that husbands and wives must be faithful to each other. They must not have a sexual relationship with another person.

Married people must not be unfaithful

KING DAVID

King David broke the seventh commandment when he fell in love with beautiful Bathsheba, the wife of the soldier Uriah. David made sure Uriah was sent to the front line of the fighting, where he was killed. David then married Bathsheba. God sent Nathan the prophet to tell David how wrong he had been. David was very sorry, and God forgave him.

DIVORCE

In the time of Jesus, a husband was allowed to divorce his wife, but a wife could not divorce her husband. Some Jewish teachers said that a husband could only divorce his wife if she had done something very wrong.

Other teachers said that a husband could divorce his wife for almost any reason: if he didn't like her looks, for example, or if she kept burning the dinner.

A burnt dinner – reason for divorce?

JESUS AND DIVORCE

Jesus was once asked if it was lawful for a man to divorce his wife for any and every reason.

He said that God had never planned that people should divorce at all. The only possible reason for divorce was unfaithfulness.

Paul compared marriage to two oxen

DOUBLE TROUBLE

The Old Testament teachers often said that Jews should not marry people who worshiped other gods. They had different goals in life.

Paul said it was like two oxen, yoked (tied) together to a plow, trying to pull in opposite directions. He advised: "Do not be yoked with unbelievers… What does a believer have in common with an unbeliever?"

- God's gift: *Genesis 2:24*
- Adultery is wrong: *Exodus 20:14*
- Jesus and divorce: *Matthew 19:1–12*
- Double trouble: *2 Corinthians 6:14–18*

Bible Search

Matthew was in his office when Jesus found him

- Happy people:
  Matthew 5:3–12
- The two houses:
  Matthew 7:24–27
- Don't keep on worrying:
  Matthew 6:25–34

Bible Search

READING MATTHEW

- *Chapter 1–4*: Jesus' early life.
- *Chapter 5–7*: The Sermon on the Mount.
- *Chapter 8–19*: Jesus heals and teaches.
- *Chapter 20–25*: Jesus' last days in Jerusalem.
- *Chapter 26–28*: The first Easter.

MATTHEW
THE GOSPEL OF

Matthew's Gospel is the first book in the New Testament. It tells the story of the birth, life and death of Jesus.

The writer was Matthew, one of Jesus' twelve disciples. Matthew, also called Levi, was a tax-collector. He was in his office when Jesus saw him and said, "Follow me."

THE ADVENTURE GOES ON

When Jesus was brought back to life after being crucified, he gave his friends an exciting command. Only Matthew writes about this at the end of his Gospel. The words sum it up. Jesus said, "All power in heaven and Earth is given to me. So go and make all people in the world my followers…Teach them how to live according to what I have shown you…I will be with you always."

UNDERSTANDING MATTHEW

The Old Testament taught that one day a great king, the Messiah, would rescue his people. Matthew quotes the Old Testament sixty-five times, showing how Jesus matched up to the Old Testament picture of the Messiah.

WRITING THE GOSPEL

Matthew took Mark's Gospel as his framework and added to it.

Out of the four Gospels, only Matthew speaks of the church. In his writing, Matthew emphasizes the teaching of Jesus. He wrote to teach the members of the rapidly growing Christian church that Jesus fulfilled all the Old Testament hopes.

Matthew writes the Gospel

MICAH THE BOOK OF

Micah

The prophet Micah lived at a time when his country was split into two. Israel (capital city Samaria) was in the north. Judah (capital city Jerusalem) was in the south.

Samaria was destroyed by the Assyrians, and Micah warned that Jerusalem would be destroyed too.

UNDERSTANDING MICAH

Micah was disgusted at the wickedness of the people. "Get rich quick" was their motto. Micah wrote: "They lie on their beds and make evil plans."

Micah told the people: "Cut off your hair to show you are sad…Make yourself bald like a vulture because your children will be forced to live in a foreign land." Micah was not a very popular preacher.

'They lie on their beds and make evil plans'

THE ASSYRIANS

For 300 years, from 911 to 609 B.C., Assyria was the greatest power in the world. Its kings built magnificent buildings. They paid for their temples and palaces, sculptures and engravings, with the riches they grabbed from other countries. The fierce Assyrian army destroyed Samaria, just as Micah said it would. Micah warned that the same thing would happen to Jerusalem.

THE FUTURE

Micah said that one day a great ruler would be born in Bethlehem and that there would then be universal peace and trust in God. He said, "Nations will no longer fight other nations. They will make their swords into plows."

Micah prophesied universal peace

READING MICAH

- *Chapter 1–3*: God's judgment is coming.
- *Chapter 4–5*: God will make things good again.
- *Chapter 6–7*: Turn back to God.

To find out more, turn to the pages on Hosea, Amos and Isaiah.

- Micah's warning: *Micah 1:16*
- Universal peace: *Micah 4:3*
- Plotting and doing evil: *Micah 2:1–4*
- What God wants: *Micah 6:8*

Bible Search

Jesus made lame people able to walk

MIRACLES
IMPOSSIBLE
THINGS HAPPEN

Jesus cures Jairus' daughter

A miracle is when God makes something happen that could not happen in any natural way. Jesus made many miracles happen. John's Gospel calls Jesus' miracles "signs". They pointed to truths about God.

ASKING FOR A MIRACLE

Sometimes we may pray for a miracle to happen, but it doesn't. God knows better than we do. Sometimes God lets us live with a problem, as a better way of showing his love.

The apostle Paul had a problem: a "thorn in the flesh". He prayed for God to work a miracle, but God did not. Instead God said, "My power is made perfect in weakness."

Should you ask God to make it stop raining on sports day?

Jesus walks on water

JESUS WALKS ON WATER

Jesus sent his disciples to go ahead of him by boat across the Sea of Galilee. A strong wind blew up, and the disciples found it hard to row. Jesus walked out across the water. When the disciples saw him, they thought Jesus was a ghost and were frightened. Jesus told them not to be afraid, and got into the boat. The wind dropped, and they continued their journey.

JESUS HEALS A LITTLE GIRL

Jairus, who was head of the synagogue, begged Jesus to heal his daughter, who was dying. But by the time they got to Jairus' house, they were told that the girl had died. Jesus said, "The child is not dead: she is asleep." He went inside and took hold of the girl's hand, telling her to get up. Immediately, the girl got up and walked about. She was completely better. Everyone was amazed. It was a miracle.

Bible Search

- Jesus on the water:
Mark 6:45–50

- A storm at sea:
Matthew 8:23–27

- Paul's thorn in the flesh:
2 Corinthians 12:7–10

- Jairus' daughter:
Luke 8:40–56

MONEY A ROOT OF EVIL?

n the Old Testament, people thought that having lots of money was a sign of God's blessing. If you were good, then God loved you and made you rich. That's why Jesus' friends were shocked when he said it was hard for a rich man to get into heaven.

Jesus tells a rich man how to be his follower

A RICH MAN

"I want to belong to your kingdom," said a rich young man to Jesus. "What must I do?" "Keep the Ten Commandments," said Jesus. "But I do already," said the man. "Give away all your money, and follow me," said Jesus. The man could not do it.

Jesus told his friends, "It's hard for a rich person to follow me. It's harder than for a camel to squeeze through the eye of a needle."

WHAT'S WRONG WITH MONEY?

There's nothing wrong with money: we can use it to do a lot of good. But it's always wrong to rely on money to make us happy.

A TEST

If we spend a lot of time thinking about how to get money, then the love of money has got us in its grip.

Paul said, "People who want to get rich fall into a trap…Be content with what you have…The love of money is a root of all kinds of evil."

DON'T WORRY ABOUT MONEY

Jesus said that God fed the birds and he gave the flowers beautiful petals to wear, so he would look after his followers too. By loving God and helping people, followers would get a better sort of wealth: they would gain a happiness that lasted forever.

Bible Search

- A rich young man:
Matthew 19:16–24

- Do not worry:
Luke 12: 22–34

- Danger of money:
1 Timothy 6:3–10

- Treasure in heaven:
Matthew 6:19–24

Bartering
for goods

Bible Search

- A very rich man:
Job 1:2–3

- Buying a slave:
Hosea 3:2

- Lambs for money:
2 Kings 3:4

- Abraham buys a field:
Genesis 23:16

COUNTING SHEEP

A conquered nation paid taxes with farm produce as well as with silver and gold. King Mesha of Moab gave the king of Israel 100,000 lambs and the wool of 100,000 rams.

MONEY
IN OLD TESTAMENT TIMES

F or much of the Old Testament period, there was no money as we know it. At first, people got the things they wanted by bartering, that is, by swapping or trading. But this had snags. It was hard to work out what was fair. How much corn did you trade for five sheep?

THE FIRST COINS

In about 600 B.C., Croesus, the King of Lydia (present-day western Turkey) hit on the idea of making gold coins and stamping them with their weight. The idea quickly caught on.

Coins were used to pass on news. When a new king came to power, he minted coins with the image of his head on them, to tell the world who he was. Poor countries made coins of copper or bronze.

THE FIRST MONEY

As well as bartering, people began to pay with silver jewelry or pieces of gold and silver. Hosea bought his wife back from slavery with silver and barley.

SHEKELS OF SILVER

Gold was not as common as silver, so it was more precious. Gold was used for payment between kings.

The Old Testament word for money is "silver". Silver and gold were weighed on scales and measured in shekels and talents. *Shekel* comes from a word meaning 'weigh'. *Talent* meant a large amount.

Gold and silver

MONEY
IN NEW TESTAMENT TIMES

B y the time the New Testament was written, there were Roman, Greek and Jewish coins circulating in Palestine. All had different values, so shopping could be rather confusing. There was plenty of work for the money-changers.

ROMAN MONEY

Roman taxes had to be paid with Roman money:

• Quadran. The smallest Roman coin, made of bronze.

• As. One as was worth four quadrans. It was made of bronze. In Matthew we read that two sparrows cost one as.

• Denarius. This was a large silver coin, worth sixteen times more than one as. Matthew tells us that a workman was paid one denarius for a day's work.

Denarius

• Sparrows:
Matthew 10:29

• Workman's wage:
Matthew 20:1–16

• The king's servants:
Luke 19:12–27

• A poor widow:
Luke 21:1–4

GREEK COINS

• Drachma. One drachma was worth one Roman denarius. It was made of silver.

• Didrachma. A silver coin worth two drachmas. Taxes due to the Temple were paid in didrachmas because they contained more silver than Roman coins.

• Tetradrachma or stater. One tetradrachma was worth four drachmas.

Tetradrachma

This coin was made of silver. The thirty pieces of silver paid to Judas were probably tetradrachmas.

• Mina. A silver coin worth 100 drachmas. In Luke there is a story about a king giving his servants ten minas (about three months' wages).

JEWISH MONEY

• Lepton. This was the smallest possible coin, worth half a Roman quadran. In Luke we read about a widow who gave all she had to the collection in the Temple: two lepta.

The widow in Luke's story

• A talent. This was not a coin. It meant a large amount of money.

LOOKING AFTER MONEY

There were no safes, and probably no banks. To keep their money safe, people buried it in the ground or put it in the Temple treasury in Jerusalem.

Archaeologists have found hoards of money, often in clay pots, buried in the ground.

Money was buried in the ground

MOSES THE LEADER

Moses was a great leader. He took a large group of scared slaves and shaped them into an army able to conquer a country. He gave them a code to live by and showed them a God to love.

He had a fiery temper, but became known as the most humble man on Earth, a man who prayed and relied on God.

EGYPT

In the time of Moses, Egypt was at the height of its power. The rulers of Egypt, the pharaohs, made many peoples living in their land into slaves. These included the Israelites, descendants of Joseph.

Slaves carried out most of the work on building sites. To make bricks, water was scooped from a pool and made into a stiff paste with earth. The paste was mixed with chopped straw, and pressed into wooden boxes. The shaped bricks could then be tipped out, stamped with the name of the king, and left to dry in the sun.

A pharaoh

MOSES' CHILDHOOD

You can read about baby Moses on the page on Aaron. Moses was born an Israelite, but was adopted by an Egyptian princess.

Moses grew up in a palace on the Nile Delta. He learnt to read and write, and probably studied science, medicine, maths and archery.

MOSES IS OUTLAWED

Moses longed to help his own people. One day, Moses killed an Egyptian who was beating a Hebrew slave. Now he had to leave Egypt because his own life was in danger.

He fled to the bleak desert land of Midian. There he became a shepherd, and learned how to live in the desert. Forty years went by.

THE STORY CONTINUES

In Egypt, the Israelite slaves cried out to God to help them. Now turn to the page headed Plagues, to find out more about Moses.

Bible Search

- Slavery in Egypt: *Exodus 1:1–14*

- A humble man: *Numbers 12:3*

- All the wisdom of Egypt: *Acts 7:22*

An Egyptian slavemaster

MUSIC AND INSTRUMENTS

The Israelites filled their lives with music. They became so good at music-making that their fame spread to other countries. When King Sennacherib of Assyria attacked Jerusalem, he took away with him silver, gold, and male and female singers. We know this because he boasted about it in his court records!

PLENTY OF RHYTHM

Usually, songwriters took well-known tunes and put new words to them. Musicians improvised on the tunes as they played.

Tunes were not very tuneful. Mostly, the songs and hymns were chanted. Often the singers sang alternate lines. But what the songs lacked in tune, they made up for in rhythm. The music was great for dancing to!

INSTRUMENTS

There were all sorts of instruments: timbrels, trumpets, horns, pipes, sistrums, lyres, cymbals, lutes and flutes.

TIMBREL
A timbrel, or tambourine, was made from animal skin stretched over a hoop.

TRUMPET
There were different kinds of trumpet. The shofar was a long horn which turned up at the end. It was used to call people to battle or to worship.

HORN
The horn, or cornet, was one of the instruments that Joshua's priests blew when they attacked Jericho.

PIPE
A pipe probably made a wailing, moaning sound. It was played at funerals.

LYRE
A lyre, or harp, was the instrument David played.

LARGE LYRE
The sound box of this instrument was probably round and flat, and it would have made a low, rich sound.

SISTRUM
This was rather like a baby's rattle.

CYMBALS
"Loud cymbals" were two shallow metal plates which were clashed together. "High sounding cymbals" were hollow metal cups.

LUTE
A lute was shaped like a triangle, with three strings.

FLUTE
The Hebrew word for *flute* means "hiss" or "whistle".

Bible Search

- A victory song:
Exodus 15

- A king's wedding song:
Psalm 45

- A sad song:
2 Samuel 1:17–27

- A marching song:
Numbers 10:35

NAMES
BLASPHEMY, SWEARING

The name Deborah means 'bee'

Names are important to us: we like to know their meaning, and we like to give people nicknames. But in Old Testament times, names were even more important. People were careful about naming their babies. They thought that a baby grew to be like his or her name. So, if a stranger told you his name, you thought you knew what sort of person he was.

THE NAME OF JESUS

Jesus said, "I am the good shepherd… The good shepherd calls his own sheep." Jesus meant that he knows us through and through. Jesus said, "Ask for anything you want in my name and I will do it." A prayer which asks for something in the name of Jesus must be the sort of prayer that Jesus might make.

THE SONS OF SCEVA

In the town of Ephesus, the seven sons of Sceva claimed to be able to rid people of evil spirits. One day they decided to use Jesus' name to do so. They said to a man with an evil spirit, 'Come out in the name of Jesus.' But the brothers were not Christians and the man attacked all seven of them. This shows Jesus' name is not a magic charm.

The sons of Sceva were attacked

BLASPHEMY

Blasphemy means using God's name in wrong ways. It means telling lies about him to cause trouble, or saying his name aloud because you are in a bad mood. Blasphemy is forbidden in the Ten Commandments. It is hateful for Christians to misuse the name of someone they love.

SWEARING

Swearing means using unpleasant or embarrassing words as a way of getting rid of your angry feelings. It's unkind to upset people by swearing. A lot of today's swearwords were once thought to be blasphemous. But they no longer count as blasphemy because no one remembers their first meaning!

Bible Search

- In the name of Jesus: *John 14:14*
- The sons of Sceva: *Acts 19:11–20*
- The third commandment: *Exodus 20:7*
- The Good Shepherd: *John 10:3*

NEHEMIAH THE BOOK OF

Nehemiah

Nehemiah was wine steward to the king of Persia. It was Nehemiah's job to taste the king's wine to make sure it was not poisoned. The Book of Nehemiah is Nehemiah's diary. Nehemiah describes some of the events in the Book of Ezra from his own point of view. He tells the exciting story of the rebuilding of the walls of Jerusalem.

People laughed at Jerusalem

UNDERSTANDING NEHEMIAH

Years earlier, the king of Persia had sent all the captured Jewish people back home. Nehemiah heard that the Jews who had gone back to Jerusalem had not been able to rebuild its walls. A city without walls meant that anyone could attack it. People laughed at Jerusalem.

Nehemiah asked the king if he could go to Jerusalem to help with the rebuilding. The king agreed, and made Nehemiah the governor of Jerusalem.

Rebuilding the walls of Jerusalem

ENEMY ALERT

But not everyone who lived around Jerusalem was Jewish, and these people didn't want a strong Jewish city. They tried every nasty trick they knew to stop Nehemiah.

Nehemiah met every new threat with prayer. 'Remember the Lord, he is great,' he said. He put all the men of Jerusalem to work on the broken walls. Half the men were on guard duty, with bugles to blow in case of attack. The builders kept their swords close at hand.

The wall was finished in fifty-two days. Nehemiah wrote: 'When our enemies heard about this they realized that this work had been done with the help of our God.'

A SIX-HOUR SERMON

The people asked Ezra, the priest, to read God's law to them. They began to cry when they realized all the wrong things they had done. "Don't be sad," said Nehemiah. "The joy of the Lord will make you strong." And they had a great feast to praise and thank God for his goodness to them.

READING NEHEMIAH

- *Chapter 1–2*: Nehemiah goes back to Jerusalem.
- *Chapter 3–7*: The walls are built.
- *Chapter 8:* Ezra reads the law.
- *Chapter 9–10*: The Jews agree to obey God.
- *Chapter 11–13*: Other reforms.

Bible Search

- Nehemiah's sadness: *Nehemiah 1:4; 2:3*
- Armed builders: *Nehemiah 4:16–18*
- Nehemiah's prayers: *Nehemiah 1:4–11; 4:9*

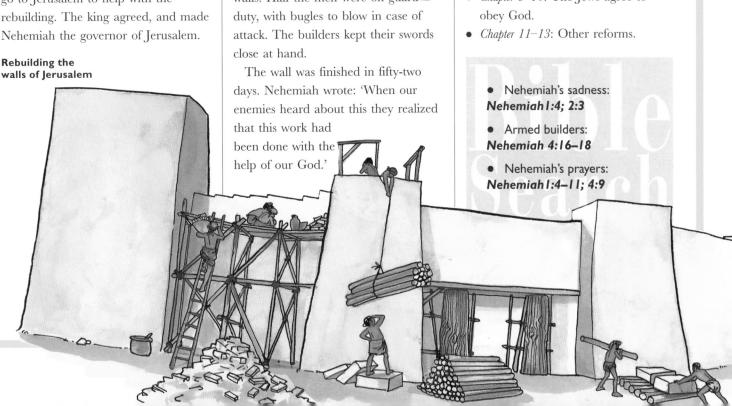

NEW TESTAMENT
WORLD

P alestine in the time of Jesus was quite a small country, about 155 miles from north to south. As far as we know, Jesus did all his traveling on foot. He only rode on a donkey on his last journey into Jerusalem. The map shows some of the places he visited in the Gospel stories.

Mount Hermon.
This may be where Jesus' clothes become dazzling white with the brightness of heaven.

Capernaum.
Jesus' base while he was teaching in Galilee. Capernaum was Matthew's home.

Caesarea Philippi.
Here Peter said to Jesus, 'You are the Son of the living God.'

Cana.
At a wedding, Jesus turned water into wine.

Bethsaida.
Peter, Andrew and Philip's home town. Jesus made a blind man see at Bethsaida.

Nazareth.
Jesus grew up here. He trained to be a carpenter.

Sea of Galilee.
Many of Jesus' miracles took place in the little fishing towns on the shores of this lake.

Caesarea.
King Herod rebuilt the town. It was the headquarters of the Roman army in Palestine. Paul was in prison here.

Sychar.
Here Jesus sat down by a well and asked a Samaritan woman for a drink.

Jordan River

Jabboq River

Emmaus.
On Easter Sunday, Jesus joined two of his friends on the road to Emmaus, after he had risen from the dead.

Jericho.
Here Jesus healed Bartimaeus, a blind man. Zacchaeus the tax-collector worked here.

Jerusalem.
The capital city. Jesus was crucified outside the walls.

Bethany.
The home of Martha, her sister Mary and their brother Lazarus. Jesus brought Lazarus back from the dead.

Bethlehem.
Jesus was born in a stable.

Wilderness of Judea.
Jesus spent forty days here, and was tempted by the Devil.

Dead Sea

NEW TESTAMENT
COMES TOGETHER

Matthew

Mark

Luke

John

After Jesus died, the apostles began preaching about all that Jesus had said and done. Some of Jesus' sayings were written down in the Gospels. The four Gospels were written by, and named after, four of the apostles: Matthew, Mark, Luke and John.

In one or two places, church leaders began to collect together copies of the writings of the apostles.

Between A.D. 200 and A.D. 300, many books were written which claimed to be Christian, but contained wrong teachings. Christian leaders decided to make a list of books that gave the true teaching of the Christian faith.

At two meetings in A.D. 393 and A.D. 397, some Christian leaders agreed on twenty-seven books which form the New Testament *canon* (this word means 'measuring rod').

GOSPELS AND LETTERS

The letters were carefully copied

Matthew and John wrote accounts of the life and death of Jesus. Mark wrote down the sermons of Peter. Luke, who was Paul's friend, also wrote an account of Jesus' life, and then went on to write the Acts of the Apostles.

Some of the apostles wrote letters to help new Christians. All the letters were carefully copied and passed around.

A REMARKABLE DISCOVERY

Papyrus scrolls

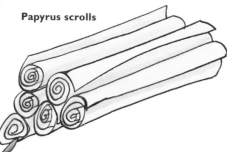

It had been thought that none of the early papyrus scrolls survived. This may still be true. But recently, a man called Dr. Thiede examined an old copy of Matthew's Gospel in a library in Cambridge. He believes that this writing dates from about A.D. 50 or earlier. (Jesus was killed in A.D. 30.)

MAKING THE DECISION

The leaders looked at every book which claimed to be the teaching of the early Church. They asked:
● Did the first Christians say that the book was written by an apostle, or a close friend of an apostle?
● Did the style and teaching of the book match the teaching of the apostles?

Bible Search

● A saying of Jesus: *Acts 20:35*

● Why Luke wrote his Gospel: *Luke 1:1–4*

● Why John wrote his Gospel: *John 20:30–31*

● The Holy Spirit guided the writers: *John 14:26; 16:13*

The letters were passed around

NEW TESTAMENT
THE GREATEST STORY
EVER TOLD

T he New Testament tells the story of the birth, life and death of Jesus Christ, and the beginning of the Christian Church. These events changed the world.

16 10 days later the Holy Spirit comes to the disciples

1 John the Baptist is born

2 Jesus is born

about 6 BC

3 Jesus, Mary and Joseph escape to Egypt

4 The 12-year-old Jesus gets lost in Jerusalem

5 John the Baptist baptizes people in the River Jordan. He also baptizes Jesus

about AD 29

6 Jesus is tempted

7 Jesus calls his disciples

8 John the Baptist is beheaded

9 Jesus spends three years traveling, teaching, healing

10 Jesus enters Jerusalem to waving palm branches

11 Jesus' last week in Jerusalen

12 Jesus' last meal

13 Jesus is crucified

14 Jesus rises from the dead

AD 33

15 40 days later Jesus returns to heaven

17 Peter preaches the first Christian sermon

18 Stephen is killed: the first martyr

19 To escape attack, and prison, Christians spread out all over the world

AD 34 or 35

20 Saul becomes a Christian

21 The Council of Jerusalem decides anyone can become a Christian without becoming a Jew as well

22 Paul goes on missionary journeys throughout the world and writes letters

AD 46 to 53

23 Paul is in prison in Rome

AD 62 to 64

24 The Book of Revelation is written

25 John, the last disciple, dies

about AD 100

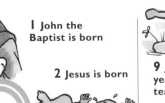

NOAH AND THE FLOOD

The descendants of Adam and Eve lived all over the world. But God saw that the people had become wicked, and he decided to destroy every human being and living creature he had created. Only one man and his family were good: the man was Noah.

THE ARK

God told Noah to build a great ship, or ark. The ship was made of cypress wood. It was covered with pitch inside and out to make it waterproof. There were three decks, which were divided into small rooms. A row of windows ran around the top of the ship.

WHO WENT INTO THE ARK?

God said that Noah, his wife, their three sons, Shem, Ham and Japheth, and their wives were to get into the ark. They also had to take with them a male and female pair of every kind of animal and bird.

THE FLOOD

When they were all safely in the ark, the rains began. It poured down for forty days, causing a flood so deep that it even covered the mountains. Every living creature was drowned. Finally, the rain stopped and the waters began to go down. The ark came to rest on the Ararat range of mountains in eastern Turkey.

THE RAVEN AND THE DOVE

From the small windows, Noah could only see the mountain peaks and the sky. So he sent out a raven and a dove to see if there was any dry land. The birds saw water everywhere, and flew back. A week later, Noah sent the dove for another look. It came back with an olive leaf. Olive trees do not grow on high land, so Noah knew that the floods must have gone right down. They had been shut up in the ark for 371 days.

THE RAINBOW

God told Noah that he would never again destroy everything in the world by a flood. A rainbow would be a sign to remind people of this promise.

ANY QUESTIONS
1 How deep did the water get during the Flood?
2 Which bird told Noah that the waters had gone down and it was safe to get out of the ark?

Bible Search

- Noah and the flood: *Genesis 6–8*
- The rainbow: *Genesis 9:8–17*
- Noah's faith: *Hebrews 11:7*

NUMBERS THE BOOK OF

T he Book of Numbers takes its name from the two occasions when the people were counted in a census, to find out how many men over the age of twenty there were, who could be called upon to fight. The book begins thirteen months after the Israelites had left Egypt, and ends thirty-eight years later, on the borders of the Promised Land. It tells of some of the Israelites' desert adventures, and we see God's love for his people, in spite of their grumbling.

Men eligible to fight

The people stayed in the desert

The people decided not to go into Canaan, so for the next forty years, they stayed in the desert. Most of the people who originally left Egypt died. Now the tribe was made up of their descendants. Moses knew that he would soon die, and he called Joshua to tell him that he must now lead the Israelites into the Promised Land.

Moses and Joshua

UNDERSTANDING NUMBERS

Fifteen hundred years later, Paul wrote to the Christians in Corinth. He mentioned some of the stories in Numbers, saying, "We should not test the Lord, as some of them did, and were killed by snakes… These things happened to them as examples and were written down as

READING NUMBERS

- *Chapter 1:1–8:26*: Putting things in order.
- *Chapter 9:1–10:10*: A Passover feast, the cloud, and trumpets.
- *Chapter 10:11–12:16*: On to Kadesh. Fire, food from heaven, and revolt.
- *Chapter 13:1–20:13*: Mutiny.
- *Chapter 20:14–22:1*: The plains of Moab. Enemies are beaten.
- *Chapter 22:2–32:42*: Life in Moab.
- *Chapter 33–36*: Getting ready to cross the Jordan.

Bible Search

- A talking donkey: **Numbers 22–24**
- A bronze snake: **Numbers 21:4–9; John 3:14**
- Moses fails: **Numbers 20:1–13**

I SPY

Moses sent twelve men to spy out the Promised Land. They came back saying "It's a beautiful, rich land, but its people are like giants. And the walls round its cities reach to the sky! We should not be able to defeat them." Only Joshua and Caleb said, "We should trust God and attack."

Spies investigate the Promised Land

OBEDIENCE
OBEYING GOD

'Love one another'

Jesus said to his friends, "Not everyone who says to me, 'Lord, Lord,' will enter the kingdom of heaven, but only he who does the will of my Father which is in heaven."

Jesus always obeyed God. He said, "I've come down from heaven not to do my own will, but to do the will of him who sent me."

TWO BUILDERS

The two houses

Jesus told a story about two men who each set out to build a house. One man built his house on sand; the other built his house on rock. When winter came, rain poured down, hillside steams turned into torrents, and the winds howled. The house on rock remained firm, but the house on sand fell with a great crash.

Jesus said, "Anyone who hears my words and puts them into practice is like the man who built his house on rock."

The house on rock survives the storm

JAMES

Jesus' brother, James, said, "Don't just listen to God's word: do what it says." James used the example of someone looking into a mirror, seeing a mark on his face, then going away and forgetting to wash it off.

The Bible is like a mirror. It shows us what we need to do, and then we have to do it.

The Bible is like a mirror

Bible Search

- Hard words: *Matthew 7:21*
- Two builders: *Matthew 7:24–27*
- Love: *John 15:17*
- Help: *John 15:5*
- A mirror: *James 1:22–25*

HOW DO WE OBEY GOD?

Jesus was sometimes asked what people need to do to obey God. He gave different answers according to the needs of the person who asked him. One answer was: "Love one another."

HELP TO OBEY

As we go about our everyday lives, we sometimes feel we want to do something loving, or to be truthful, or to stand up for Jesus. That idea comes from the Holy Spirit, and Jesus helps us to carry it out.

Do something loving

OLD TESTAMENT
WORLD

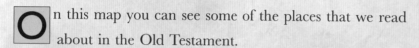

On this map you can see some of the places that we read about in the Old Testament.

CRETE

CANAAN (The Promised Land).
It was later divided into two countries: Israel in the north and Judah in the south.

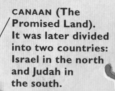

NINEVEH.
Capital city of the warlike Assyrians. Jonah preached in Nineveh.

EUPHRATES RIVER

TIGRIS RIVER

PHILISTIA.
The land of the Philistines, or 'sea peoples'. They came over the sea from Crete.

DAMASCUS.
Capital of Syria, and home town of Naaman, who became a leper.

JERICHO.
Joshua and his army walked around the city, blew their trumpets, and the walls fell down.

GAZA.
Samson died here by pulling a temple down on top of him.

JERUSALEM.
King David captured Jerusalem by sending men up an underground tunnel. He made it his capital city.

UR.
Abraham lived here when God told him to leave Ur for a new land.

GOSHEN.
This is where the Israelites became slaves. They had to make bricks to build cities for the pharaoh.

COUNTRY OF MOAB.
Ruth, and her mother-in-law Naomi, lived here.

SINAI DESERT.
Here the Israelites spent forty years, waiting to go to the Promised Land.

SEA OF REEDS.
Moses led the slaves across the sea out of Egypt. The Bible refers to it as the Red Sea.

MOUNT SINAI.
Moses was given the Ten Commandments here.

RIVER NILE

BABYLON.
Capital city of the Babylonian empire and of King Nebuchadnezzar. Here Daniel's friends were thrown into a fiery furnace.

RED SEA

OLD TESTAMENT
COMES TOGETHER

The earliest stories were passed on by word of mouth

F or a very long time, the only people who could read and write were scribes. Scribes kept records of all the events of the kingdom. The earliest Bible stories were passed on by word of mouth. These stories were so important that people repeated them word for word, without making any changes.

RECORDING THE STORIES

The Israelites copied the Egyptian habit of writing on sheets made from the pith (inside) of the reeds of the papyrus plant. Long sheets of papyrus were rolled up to form scrolls.

Papyrus plant

After one desert battle, God said to Moses, "Write this on a scroll as something to be remembered."

Jews believe that the first five books of the Old Testament were written by Moses.

God said to Isaiah the prophet, "Take a large scroll and write on it." The prophets, or their friends, wrote down their sermons and thoughts.

Pen and ink

A very large scroll

COLLECTIONS

Jews believe that during the Israelites' exile in Egypt, Ezra the priest collected all the writings that had been made up to that time. Each book was written on a separate scroll. Scribes copied the scrolls very carefully. They counted the lines to make sure nothing was missed.

The scribes copied very carefully

After the exile we are told that Nehemiah and, later, Judas Maccabaeus, collected together a library of Old Testament books.

JEWISH MEETING

By the time of Jesus, all the Old Testament books were well-known. In A.D. 90, at a special Jewish meeting called the Synod of Jamnia, it was confirmed that all Old Testament books were the word of God. (See also the pages on Dead Sea Scrolls and Apocrypha.)

Bible Search

• Moses the writer:
Exodus 17:14

• Books of battles and songs:
Numbers 21:14; 2 Samuel 1:18

• Court records:
1 Kings 11:41

• Jesus reads from a scroll:
Luke 4:16–21

OLD TESTAMENT STORY

The Old Testament is God's story. In its pages we see God at work in the lives of ordinary and extraordinary people. God did not only give a list of rules to obey. He showed what happened when people lived as he wanted, and what happened when they ignored him.

Most of all, we see how God prepared his people for the coming of Jesus. This chart shows some of the important events in the history of God's people, and the order in which they came.

16 Jerusalem, the capital of Judah, is destroyed by Babylon

587 BC

17 Exile: the Israelite people are taken away as prisoners and spend 70 years in Babylonia

538 BC

18 The first people return from exile

1 Creation

2 Adam and Eve think they know better than God

3 Noah is saved from a great flood

4 Abraham travels to Canaan
about 2000–1825 B.C.

5 Joseph is taken to Egypt
about 1750–1640 BC

6 Joseph's family follows him

7 The Exodus: Moses rescues the slaves

8 Mount Sinai: God gives Moses the Ten Commandments

9 Joshua leads the people into Canaan
about 1240 BC

10 Gideon and the other tribal judges rule the people

11 Saul, the first king of the Israelites
about 1050–1011 BC

12 David, Israel's greatest king
about 1011 BC

13 Solomon builds the first Temple

14 The kingdom splits into Israel and Judah
931 BC

15 Samaria, the capital of Israel, is destroyed by Assyria
722 BC

19 Zerubbabel rebuilds the Temple

20 Nehemiah returns and rebuilds the walls of Jerusalem

21 Ezra returns and rebuilds religious life

22 The Roman army invades Israel
63 BC

23 King Herod is made king
40 BC

24 Jesus is born
6 BC

Bible Search

- The purpose of the Old Testament: *2 Timothy 3:15–17*

- The Old Testament and Jesus: *Luke 24:25–27*

- An Old Testament picture of Jesus: *Isaiah 52:13–53:12*

OLIVES AND VINES

Olive trees were called "the king of trees." Fresh or pickled olives were eaten with bread, but most olives were made into oil.

Bible teachers often called the Israelites "God's vine." God planted them, looked after them, and wanted them to produce "good grapes."

GROWING OLIVES

Olive trees lived for many hundreds of years, but for the first fifteen years, a tree had no fruit.

To harvest the olives, the branches of the tree were beaten with poles. The olives were gathered into baskets and taken to stone olive presses. A large round stone, turned by a man or donkey, squeezed out the oil. The olive pulp was then put into baskets and pressed with weights. Heavier weights were added to get out as much oil as possible.

USES OF OLIVE OIL

Olive oil was used:

- For cooking.

- To burn in lamps.
- As a hair and skin tonic.

- As a medicine to put on wounds.

- As a scent (it was perfumed first!)

- For anointing. Olive oil was poured over someone's head as a sign that the person was specially chosen to do work for God. Objects could be anointed too.

GROWING VINES

The young vine plants were set out in rows, often in terraces on the hillside. A watchtower was built in the vineyard, so a lookout could be kept for wild animals and thieves.

The vine harvest was a happy time. Families camped out in the vineyards. Ripe bunches of grapes were cut with small hooks and put into baskets.

Grapes were made into wine in wine presses, which were often stone hollows in the vineyards. The workers sang songs as they trampled the grapes with their bare feet. The juice was collected in goatskins or jars, and left to ferment into wine.

As well as being used to make wine, grapes were dried, and pressed together to make raisin cakes.

Bible Search

- The vine and God's people: *Isaiah 5:1–7*

- Jesus the true vine: *John 15:1–8*

- A good person is like an olive tree: *Psalm 52:8*

PAINTING
AND SCULPTURE

In the Ten Commandments, God told the Israelites not to make or worship idols. They understood this to mean that they should not paint, draw, or make a model of any human being, animal, bird or fish. This didn't leave much to paint! Not surprisingly, the Israelites had little interest in painting and sculpture. They were creative in other ways, such as in literature and music, and possibly in embroidery, jewelry and carving.

TOMBS

Egyptian artists painted colorful scenes of everyday life on the walls of their tombs. They thought that these scenes would magically come to life in the spirit world.

But the Jews did not think like this. Hundreds of tombs have been excavated, but only one contains a painting, and that was made much later than the time of the New Testament.

An Egyptian tomb painting

DECORATION

A wall decoration

The Jews decorated the walls and pillars of their synagogues with drawings of plants, flowers, palm trees and fruit, or with objects from the Temple, such as the seven-branched candlestick, and scrolls.

Greek vases were decorated with beautiful pictures. But pots made in Palestine were painted, not very skillfully, with a zigzag lines and simple patterns.

A Greek pot

THE TABERNACLE

When they were slaves in Egypt, the Israelites learnt many artistic skills from the Egyptians. They used these skills to make the Tabernacle, the worship tent. They believed that their artistic abilities were given by God. But they didn't pass on their skills to their children. When Solomon built the Temple in Jerusalem, he employed craftsmen from Phoenicia.

CHERUBIM

The Ark of the Covenant (the box containing the Ten Commandments) had two cherubim on the top.

There were two gold cherubim in the Most Holy Place of the Temple built by Solomon. They were winged creatures, possibly with a human body and a lion's head.

- A nightmare wall painting: *Ezekiel 8:10*
- Making an idol: *Isaiah 40:19–20; 44:12–14*
- A gift from God: *Exodus 35:30–35*
- Cherubim in the Temple: *1 Kings 6:23–28*

A pot from Palestine

PALESTINE
THE HOLY LAND

Palestine is the name of the land Jesus lived in. Bible writers called it "Canaan", "The Land of Israel", or "The Promised Land". It was the Greeks who named it "Palestine". In Jesus' time, Palestine had an amazing variety of scenery: snow-capped mountains, thick forests, and deserts.

In 1948, Palestine was divided and the new country of Israel was formed. This is what we call the country today.

THE COASTAL PLAIN

The coastal plain was about 30 miles wide in the south but only a few meters wide in the north. It was a flat area with sand dunes.

The Shephelah was a line of low wooded hills. When the Philistines were attacking from the coast, the Shephelah was a war zone.

CENTRAL HIGHLANDS

In the central highlands, there were three regions: Galilee, Samaria and Judah. Galilee, with its beautiful inland lake, was where Jesus grew up.

The plain of Esdraelon was a flat stretch of land between the hills of Galilee and the hills of Samaria. It was a corridor to the sea used by armies and traders.

Most of the Old Testament stories took place among the high hills and valleys of Samaria and Judah.

THE JORDAN VALLEY

The Jordan River twisted along the deepest valley in the world. The word *Jordan* means "descender": a good name, because the river dropped a good distance before it reached the Dead Sea. The valley was a thick jungle where lions roamed.

Across the Jordan River was a vast high plateau, like an uneven table-top. This was the Trans-Jordan plateau. It was very fertile land, with forests and vineyards.

DEAD SEA

The Dead Sea was 48 miles long, 10 miles wide and 2,500 feet below sea-level. It was the lowest place in the world.

There was little rain, and the air was still, heavy and hot. There was nothing but cliffs, rocks and swarms of insects. There was no fish or plant life in the Dead Sea. The water was very salty, felt oily, and smelled of decaying minerals.

Galilee

Sea of Galilee

Plain of Esdraelon

Coastal plain

Samaria

River Jordan

Shephelah hills

Jordan valley

Judah

Central highlands

Dead Sea

PAUL MEETS JESUS

More than one third of the New Testament was written by Paul. Yet at first, Paul detested all Christians. The story of how Paul changed, became a Christian, and spread the teachings of Christianity is told three times in the Book of Acts. This shows what a revolutionary story it was.

Saul is blinded

Saul as a student

GROWING UP

Paul is a Roman name. Paul grew up as a Jew in Tarsus, an important Greek city. Paul's Jewish name was Saul.

Saul learned the trade of leather-worker and tentmaker. He also went on to higher education in Jerusalem, where he became a student of the famous teacher Gamaliel. Saul was brilliant, and had a great future as one of the country's leading Pharisees.

Saul learned to make tents and work with leather

- Education: *Acts 22:2–3*

- Paul sees Stephen stoned: *Acts 7:57–8:1*

- Paul sees Jesus, told by Luke: *Acts 9:3–19*

- Told by Paul: *Acts 22:6–16; 26:9–23*

CHRISTIANS

In Saul's view, Christians were stupid, dangerous people who told lies about God. Saul made up his mind to stamp out the Christian faith. He set off for Damascus, with warrants for the arrest of all the Christians.

Just outside Damascus, a very bright light suddenly shone from the sky. A voice called, "Saul, why do you persecute me?" Saul fell to the ground. "Who are you?" he asked. "I am Jesus," said the voice. "Go into the city and you will be told what to do."

Saul falls to the ground

BLINDED

Saul stood up, and found he couldn't see. The men with him led him into Damascus. For the next three days, Saul didn't eat or drink. He was shattered, realizing that the Jesus he had despised, and who had been crucified, was alive.

ANANIAS

Ananias heals Saul

Jesus sent a man called Ananias to Saul. Ananias said, "In the name of Jesus, receive your sight." Saul was baptized. From that moment on, he began to preach about Jesus.

He traveled throughout the Roman empire.

After Saul converted to Christianity, he became known by his Roman name of Paul.

PAUL TIME CHART

Paul was a man under orders. When he met Jesus on the road to Damascus, his life was turned around. His new aim in life was to complete the task Jesus had given him. That task was to preach the good news of Jesus to Jews and non-Jews throughout the Roman world.

Paul meets Jesus.

Paul is baptized in Damascus.

Brief visit to 'Arabia'. **(Galatians 1:17)**

A.D. 35. Paul preaches in Damascus for three years. **(2 Corinthians 11:32; Galatians 1:17)**

Visit to Jerusalem. The Christians think his new faith is a trick! Barnabas makes friends with Paul. **(Galatians 1:18; Acts 9:23–28)**

Return to Tarsus. Paul spends eleven years preaching in the area.

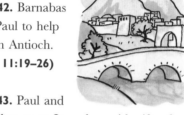

A.D. 42. Barnabas asks Paul to help him in Antioch. **(Acts 11:19–26)**

A.D. 43. Paul and Barnabas go to Jerusalem with gifts of money. At a private meeting, the Jerusalem Christians support Paul's work among non-Jews. **(Acts 11:27–30; Galatians 2:1–10)**

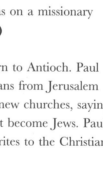

Back at Antioch, the Christians send Paul and Barnabas on a missionary tour. **(Acts 13–14)**

A.D. 46–48. Return to Antioch. Paul hears that Christians from Jerusalem have gone to the new churches, saying all Christians must become Jews. Paul is horrified. He writes to the Christians in Galatia.

A.D. 49. To Jerusalem for a conference to discuss the problems. (See the page on Cornelius.)

A.D. 50–52. Paul and Silas set off from Antioch on a second missionary tour. He writes 1 and 2 Thessalonians.

Return to Antioch. **(Acts 18:22)**

A.D. 53–57. Third missionary trip. Paul spends three years in Ephesus. He writes 1 and 2 Corinthians and Romans.

A.D. 57–59. Paul and his friends go to Jerusalem with more money. Paul is arrested and spends two years as a prisoner. He appeals to Caesar. **(Acts 23–26)**

A.D. 59. Paul is shipwrecked on the way to Rome, and spends the winter on Malta. **(Acts 27–28:10)**

A.D. 60–62. House arrest, probably in Rome. Paul writes letters to Philemon and to Christians in Colosse, Philippi and Ephesus. The Book of Acts ends here.

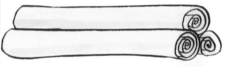

A.D. 62. This is the likely date Paul was set free. He visits his friends in the churches. He writes letters to Timothy and Titus. He may have gone on to Spain.

A.D. 64 or later. Paul is back in Rome, where he is imprisoned again. He is killed on the orders of Emperor Nero.

PAUL ON TOUR

The Christian faith started off from a small group of Jews in Jerusalem. Thirty years later, it had spread throughout the Roman world. This drastic change was managed by Paul. We know about Paul's adventures and travels from the diary Luke kept (given in the Book of Acts).

PAUL'S METHOD

- Paul didn't try to do it alone. He always took at least one helper with him.
- He headed for the important cities, which were centers of communication.
- In each town, he went to the Jews first, then to the non-Jews.
- He revisited the new Christians, and sent letters and teachers to help them understand their new faith.
- He didn't ask for money. When he was short of funds, he worked as a tentmaker.

Bible Search

- Tour 1: *Acts 13:4–14:28*
- Tour 2: *Acts 15:36–18:22*
- Tour 3: *Acts 18:23–21:17*
- Tough times: *2 Corinthians 11:23–29*

TOUR TWO

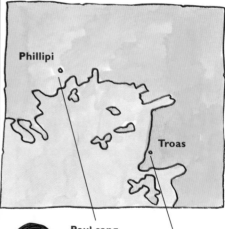

Phillipi

Troas

Paul sang hymns in jail. The jailer believed in Jesus.

In a vision, Paul saw a man begging him to go to Macedonia.

TOUR ONE

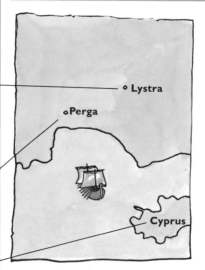

Lystra

Perga

Cyprus

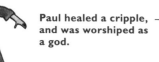

Paul healed a cripple, and was worshiped as a god.

Mark gave up.

Here the Roman governor became a Christian.

Traveling was hard and dangerous. Paul walked, or rode a donkey. He wrote that he had been in danger from bandits, and from rivers. He was shipwrecked three times.

TOUR THREE

There was a riot, started by silversmiths who sold images of the goddess Diana.

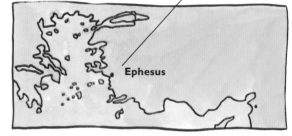

Ephesus

PAUL SPEAKS

The previous pages on Paul may have given you some ideas about what he was like. We know how brave he was; how hard he worked for Jesus; how full of love he was for Jesus and for other people (though he had a quick temper!) Here are a few more glimpses, from some of the things he said about himself.

● Danger:
2 Corinthians 11:23–33

● Enemies:
Philippians 1:15–21

● A secret:
Philippians: 4:10–13

● A race:
Philippians 3:12–14

Bible Search

PAUL'S WORK

"I always want to preach the good news in places where people have never heard of Jesus."

DANGEROUS JOURNEYS

"Five times, the Jews have given me their punishment of thirty-nine lashes with a whip. Three different times I was beaten with rods…many times I have been without food. I have been cold and without clothes…"

Paul was beaten…

…starve

…cold and without clothes

ENEMIES

"I do not care if they make trouble for me… To me the only important thing is to live for Christ."

A SECRET

The secret of being happy

"I have learned the secret of being happy at any time in everything that happens…when I have all that I need, and when I do not have the things I need. I can do all things through Christ because he gives me strength."

'The first time I defended myself no one helped me. Everyone left me…But the Lord stayed with me. He gave me strength…"

LETTERS

Paul may have had bad eyesight. His friends often wrote his letters for him. At the end of one letter he wrote: "I am writing this myself. See what large letters I use."

A RACE

"I intend to be the kind of man Jesus wanted me to be when he called me on the road to Damascus. I know I haven't got there yet; but I've set my heart on one thing: to forget the past and live for the future. I'm like a long-distance runner; I see the tape ahead and I'm going to get there–and win the prize."

Paul compared himself to a long-distance runner

PAUL'S FRIENDS

Paul was not a loner. He had a team of close friends who helped in his work. He also had many other Christian friends. As he finished his letter to the Christians in Rome, he sent greetings to twenty-eight people by name. Here are some of Paul's team.

Barnabas

LUKE

Luke

Paul described Luke as "our dear doctor." He joined Paul on the second journey, and looked after him when he was ill. He wrote the Gospel of Luke and the Book of Acts. He was an excellent writer and an accurate historian.

MARK

Mark set off on Paul's first missionary journey, but gave up after a while and went home.

Barnabas wanted Mark (his cousin) to go with them on their next journey, but Paul refused. So Barnabas went off with Mark, and Paul went with Silas. Later, Mark became Paul's assistant, and also helped Peter. He wrote the Gospel of Mark.

PRISCILLA AND AQUILA

Priscilla and Aquila were a married couple. Paul stayed at their home in Corinth several times, and helped them to make tents. Their house was a meeting place for Christians.

TITUS

Titus was a brave member of the team on Paul's third journey. Paul sent Titus to sort out the trouble in the Church in Corinth. He was successful, so Paul sent him to Crete.

Titus

BARNABAS

When Paul became a Christian and went to Jerusalem, Barnabas helped him to make friends with the other Christians.

Barnabas asked Paul to help him in Antioch. Barnabas and Paul traveled together as missionaries, taking Mark with them.

TIMOTHY

Timothy was one of Paul's closest friends. Paul wrote: "I have no one else like him..." He first joined Paul on the second journey. Paul wrote the First and Second Letter of Timothy to him.

Timothy and Paul

SILAS

Silas

Silas was one of the leaders in Jerusalem, and went with Paul on his second journey. Paul called him "a faithful Christian brother". He also helped Peter.

Bible Search

- Barnabas: *Acts 4:36–37; 9:26–27; 11:25–26*

- Mark: *Acts 15:36–40; Colossians 4:10*

- Timothy: *Acts 16:1–3; 1 and 2 Timothy*

- Luke: *Colossians 4:14; 2 Timothy 4:11*

PEACE

We should not ignore wrong for the sake of an easy life

Adam and Eve disobeyed God

When God made the world it was filled with peace. This peace was lost when Adam and Eve, the first man and woman, took it into their heads to disobey God. Jesus is often called the Prince of Peace. When he was born, the angels sang: "Peace on Earth to men with whom God is pleased."

Christians should be peacemakers. But this doesn't mean going around with the attitude of "anything for an easy life." It means "making *shalom*." It may mean giving in to people, and not getting your own way.

In the world, peacemakers often start off by being troublemakers, and challenging things other people do. That's why Jesus once said, "I did not come to bring peace but a sword."

SHALOM

The Hebrew word for "peace" is *shalom*.

In a person it means wholeness, inner harmony, and knowing you are safe because God is caring for you.

Between people it means trusting and caring; being truthful, forgiving, honest and fair.

In the world, it means taking care of the Earth and the creatures that live there. It means trying to put wrong things, such as pollution, right.

Shalom only comes when people know they are forgiven by God, and when they obey God.

THE PRICE OF PEACE

Sin must be punished. That is just and right. Jesus took the punishment we deserve, so that we can be forgiven and be at peace with God. Paul said that Jesus was "making peace through his blood shed on the cross." During his last supper with his friends, Jesus said, "My peace I give you…"

Bible Search

- Prince of Peace: *Isaiah 9:6*
- Angels' song: *Luke 2:14*
- The price: *Colossians 1:20*
- A gift: *John 14:27*
- Peacemakers: *Matthew 5:9*
- A sword: *Matthew 10:34*

ANY QUESTIONS
1 How did Jesus make us able to be at peace with God?
2 How can Christians be peacemakers?

Shalom

Jesus challenges wrong

231

PEOPLE IN NEED
HELPING OTHERS

Many people today are hungry, poor, lonely, ill, or homeless. Many old people feel that nobody cares about them. The Bible writers showed we must do what we can to stop such suffering. Christians used to argue about whether it is more important to trust God to put things right, or to do good ourselves. Today we know that it is essential to do both.

Many old people feel nobody cares about them

STRONG WORDS

Jesus' teaching on helping other people is summed up in a story he told about the end of the world. Then, Jesus said, he would divide Christians into two groups. One group would go with him into heaven. The other group would be sent away.

This is what Jesus said he would say to the first group. "I was hungry and you gave me food…

I was a foreigner and you took me home with you;

I was in rags and you gave me clothes;

I fell ill and you looked after me…

I was in prison and you came to see me.

When you helped the least of my brothers, you helped me.'

WHAT CAN WE DO?

The poor widow gives money

Sometimes we feel upset because we can't help people very much. But God's idea of help may be different from our own.

Jesus was sitting in the Temple watching people put money in the collection box. Rich people threw in a lot of money. A poor widow gave two tiny coins. Jesus said, "She put in more than all the others. She put in all she had."

GIVING

We can give other things besides money, such as our friendship. Zacchaeus was a tax-collector, and people didn't like him. One day he climbed up a tree to see Jesus. He nearly fell down again when Jesus said, "Zacchaeus, I must stay at your house today."

Turn also to the page on Giving.

ANY QUESTIONS
1 Jesus taught that Christians must help each other. Why is this so important?
2 How could you help an old person living on their own near you?

Bible Search

- Judgment Day: *Matthew 25:31–46*
- Zacchaeus: *Luke 19:1–27*
- A poor widow: *Luke 21:1–4*

PERSECUTION
AND BULLYING

Probably the worst persecution the world has known was by the German Nazis during the Second World War. They murdered over six million Jews in the most horrifying ways.

But persecution takes many other forms. For example, school can be a nightmare place for children who are bullied.

School can be a nightmare for children who are bullied

YOU TOO

Many people attack, hurt, kill, and ridicule other people. Jesus said, "If the world hates you, keep in mind that it hated me first...if they persecuted me, they will persecute you also." Followers of Jesus don't always fit in with the world's ideas of how to live.

WEAPONS AGAINST PERSECUTION

• Love and prayer.
Stephen was stoned to death for preaching about Jesus, but he prayed for his murderers. Jesus said, "Love your enemies and pray for those who persecute you."

• Praise.
The disciples were flogged by the authorities for preaching about Jesus. They came away rejoicing. Peter later wrote: "If you suffer as a Christian...praise God."

• Enlist help.
When Paul was a prisoner, his enemies vowed to kill him. Paul's nephew overheard and told Paul, who alerted his guards. As a result he was given an armed escort of 200 soldiers, 70 horsemen and 200 spear-throwers: all to protect one Christian!

• Courage.
Jesus never let fear keep him from speaking up. It takes courage to tell teachers about bullying. It's easier to keep quiet. But if people do nothing when they see wrong, the situation gets worse.

It takes courage to tell teachers

• Jesus.
Paul was in court, charged with causing trouble. Everyone deserted him. But he later wrote: "The Lord stood by my side and gave me strength...The Lord will rescue me from every evil attack."

LOVE, NOT REVENGE

The Bible tells us not to seek revenge: it only adds to the hatred and suffering. Instead, Christians are called to love and care for their enemies, and to leave God to deal with people who still go on doing bad things.

Bible Search

• Endure: *1 Corinthians 4:12*

• Rejoice and do good: *1 Peter 4:12–19*

• Holy Spirit's help: *Luke 12:11–12*

• Revenge ruled out: *Romans 12:14, 17–20; Matthew 5:11*

PETER THE DISCIPLE

Peter was one of Jesus' twelve disciples. His real name was Simon. Jesus gave him the nickname "Peter", which meant "rock." At first Peter wasn't very strong in his beliefs. He was more like shifting sand than rock! But Jesus said to him, "I have prayed for you." We see how Peter grew strong and became, as Paul later wrote, a "pillar" of the Church.

Peter, the 'rock'

Shifting sand

EARLY DAYS

Peter and his brother Andrew were supporters of John the Baptist. Jesus came to John to be baptized. Andrew met Jesus and knew that he wanted to follow him, so he rushed to tell his brother.

Later, by the Sea of Galilee, Jesus found Peter and Andrew at work fishing. "Follow me and I will make you fishers of men," Jesus said. They went with Jesus right away.

A COWARD

Before he was arrested, Jesus told his disciples that one of them would betray him. When Peter said this was impossible, Jesus turned to him and said, "Before the cock crows at dawn, you will have disowned me three times." That night, Jesus was arrested. Peter, along with John, followed Jesus right into the courtyard of the High Priest's house. Three different people came up and asked Peter if he was one of Jesus' followers. Each time, Peter denied that he was.

Jesus beckons Peter and Andrew to follow him

A LEADER

When Jesus was brought back to life after being crucified, he met Peter and forgave him.

When Jesus returned to heaven, the disciples continued to spread God's word. They became known as the apostles. Peter was beaten, and thrown into prison because he kept on preaching about Jesus. He was one of the first to see that the Christian faith was for everyone, not just for Jews. But he didn't always have the courage to practice what he preached. (See the pages on the First Christians and on Cornelius.)

Peter wrote two letters, which can be found in the Bible as 1 and 2 Peter, to help Christians. His life ended when he was crucified in Rome.

Bible Search

- Who am I?:
  Matthew 16:16

- Jesus' prayer:
  Luke 22:32

- Christianity for all:
  Acts 10:9–48

PETER

THE FIRST AND SECOND LETTERS

A lion

The Roman authorities often persecuted Christians. Emperor Nero took delight in throwing the Christians in Rome to the lions. He even had some daubed with tar and set alight. The apostle Peter wrote these two short letters to Christians who were suffering.

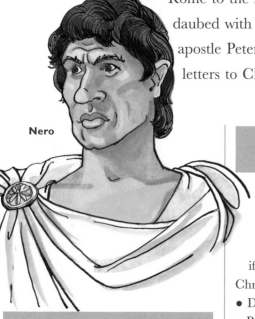

Nero

ROME

Peter seems to be writing his letters from Babylon since he says, "She (the Church) that is in Babylon sends you her greetings." But Babylon was probably a code name for Rome. Like Babylon in the Old Testament, Rome in the time of Nero was a place of great evil and danger. The same code name is used in the Book of Revelation.

PETER

Peter was a fisherman when he first met Jesus. He became one of Jesus' close friends. (See the page on Peter.)

Peter died in Rome in AD 68. He may have been crucified upside-down by Nero's soldiers.

UNDERSTANDING 1 AND 2 PETER

Peter advised the Christians what to do when people attacked them for their beliefs. It is still helpful advice for us to remember today, if anyone teases you about your Christian beliefs.

● Don't let it take you by surprise.
● Remember that Jesus suffered for you.
● Don't let it get you down: it's a privilege to suffer for Jesus.
● Try to be like Jesus. Don't fight back.
● God will make you happy.
● Watch out: make sure you don't bring trouble on yourself by doing wrong things!

Don't let it get you down

Peter also told the Christians what to do when people taught false things about Jesus. He said:
● Spot the false teachers: they are big-headed and out for what they can get.
● The best counter-attack is to put your mind to knowing Jesus.

READING PETER

1 Peter
● *Chapter 1:1–21*: God's rescue plan.
● *Chapter 1:22–4:19*: Grow, Christian, grow.
● *Chapter 5*: Serve others and be humble.
2 Peter
● *Chapter 1*: How to live the Christian life.
● *Chapter 2*: Beware of false teachers.
● *Chapter 3*: Jesus will come again.

(Note: in his second letter, Peter copied out part of Jude's letter.)

Bible Search

● Persecution:
1 Peter 2:21; 3:18; 4:1; 4:12–14

● False teachers:
2 Peter 2:11–22

● The example of Jesus:
1 Peter 2:21–25

235

PHARISEES
A VERY RELIGIOUS PEOPLE

A Pharisee

The Pharisees were a group of very religious people, who kept the Jewish laws very strictly. In New Testament times, there were 6,000 Pharisees. They were powerful people, because everybody looked up to them. Many were members of the Sanhedrin, a council of religious leaders in Jerusalem. The Sanhedrin had the power to judge, punish and imprison people brought before it.

Bible Search

- A good Pharisee: *John 3:1–2*
- A story: *Luke 18:9–14*
- Whitewashed tombs: *Matthew 23:1–27*
- Washing: *Mark 7:1–8*

LAWS

The first five books of the Bible, which the Jews called the Torah, or Law, contain 613 different laws. Bible teachers divided the Law up into many thousands of little rules. They called these rules "the teaching of the elders." Pharisees kept every rule.

WASHING

Pharisees said that before every meal your hands had to be washed. This was a sign that you wanted to be clean from wrong. They laid down strict rules about how to wash your hands. The rules were too strict for most people. Jesus said, "What's the use of having clean hands if your hearts are full of anger and greed?"

The Pharisees' rules were like burdens, and their law was often called a yoke. (A yoke was a frame put on two oxen pulling a plow.) Jesus said, "Come to me all you who are burdened. …My yoke is easy."

Washing

JESUS AND PHARISEES

Some Pharisees were good men. But some thought they were better than everyone else.

Some Pharisees thought they were better than everybody else

Jesus and the Pharisees had many head-on clashes. Jesus once described them as "whitewashed tombs." He meant they looked nice on the outside, but inside they were rotten.

Jesus told a story about a Pharisee and a tax-collector. The Pharisee thanked God for making him good. The tax-collector asked for forgiveness. Jesus said that God accepted the tax-collector, but not the Pharisee.

A whitewashed tomb

SHOW-OFFS

The Pharisees were not very popular. People thought they showed off by having extra-long tassels on their prayer shawls. People grumbled that the Pharisees chose the best seats for themselves in meetings.

PHILEMON
THE LETTER TO

P aul's letter to Philemon is the shortest of all his letters. Usually, one of his friends wrote his letter down for him. But this time Paul says, "I am writing this with my own hand." This is because in this letter he was asking for a personal favor.

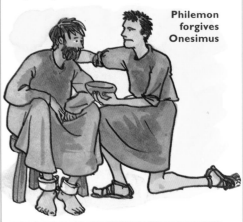

Paul writes the letter himself

DETECTIVE WORK

Philemon was a wealthy Christian. Paul called him his "dear friend and coworker."

Where did Philemon live? In Paul's letter to the Christians at Colosse, there is a message for Archippus. He also mentions a man called Onesimus, and says the Christians met at Archippus' house. Philemon also says: "I am sending Onesimus back to you."

So Philemon lived at Colosse, and Onesimus himself brought this letter.

ONESIMUS

Onesimus was a slave and a thief. He had stolen something from his master, Philemon, and then fled to Rome. In Rome, he met Paul and became a Christian. Paul wrote that Onesimus became like his son during the time that Paul was kept in chains.

F IS FOR FUGITIVE

When a runaway slave was caught, he was punished. The lightest punishment was to branded on the face with 'F' for fugitive (runaway). The most severe punishment was to be killed by the most painful means of torture: crucifixion.

UNDERSTANDING PHILEMON

The Greeks and Romans treated their slaves like tools. Some masters looked after their tools. Some didn't. Slaves were sometimes treated very, very cruelly.

Paul wanted Philemon to forgive Onesimus and take him back "as a dear brother." This was like asking for a miracle. It was revolutionary!

Paul could have written, "Philemon, I am a most important apostle. Do as I say." Instead, he pleaded with Philemon to take Onesimus back out of love. Paul himself offered to pay anything that Onesimus owed.

Colosse

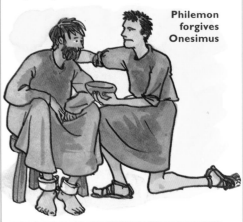

Philemon forgives Onesimus

READING PHILEMON

- *Verse 1–7*: Hello from Paul.
- *Verse 8–22*: The runaway slave.
- *Verse 23–25*: Goodbye from Paul.

PHILIPPIANS
THE LETTER TO

Paul was under house arrest in Rome, guarded day and night by a Roman soldier. He still had to pay for his food and rent. The Christians in Philippi heard about Paul's struggles, and sent him a gift. This letter is Paul's thank you to them.

PHILIPPI

Philippi was the most important city in eastern Greece. Greece was part of the Roman empire.

In 30 B.C., Philippi had been given a great honor: it was made a Roman colony. That meant it had the same privileges as any city in Italy. Its people were counted as Roman citizens. They did not have to pay taxes. Another benefit was that if they broke the law, they could not be flogged.

- The Palace guard: *Philippians 1:13*
- Racing to the goal: *Philippians 3:13–14*
- What to think about: *Philippians 4:8–9*

THE PALACE GUARD

Paul under house arrest

Paul wrote: "It has become clear throughout the whole palace guard and to everyone else that I am in chains for Christ." The soldiers of the palace guard were the emperor's own bodyguards.

UNDERSTANDING PHILIPPIANS

Paul's letter was an invitation to the happiness that Jesus gave. Paul wrote: "I press on towards the goal to win the prize for which God has called me heavenwards..." Paul's prize was in heaven.

READING PHILIPPIANS

- *Chapter 1:1–11*: Hello and thank you.
- *Chapter 1:12–26*: Problems aren't a problem with Jesus.
- *Chapter 1:27–2:18*: Living like Jesus.
- *Chapter 2:19–30*: Two of Paul's friends.
- *Chapter 3:1–11*: What makes a Christian.
- *Chapter 3:12–21*: The goal is Jesus.
- *Chapter 4:1–23*: The secret of happiness.

A Roman soldier

PLAGUES AND PASSOVER

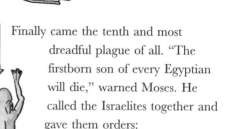

Hopping frogs

T he Israelites lived far away from their own land, in Egypt. They had been made slaves to the Egyptians, and worked in brickyards. An Egyptian scribe wrote: "The small builder carries mud...He is dirtier than...pigs from treading down his mud. His clothes are stiff with clay." (See also the pages headed Joseph and Moses.)

An Israelite slave

THE BURNING BUSH

One day, Moses saw a burning bush that kept burning. God spoke out of the bush. He said, "Bring my people out of Egypt. I will take them to a new land."

Moses did not like the idea of leading the people. "I'm no good at public speaking," he said. "Your brother Aaron will speak for you," said God.

Burning bush

GOD VERSUS PHARAOH

Moses kept asking the pharaoh, the ruler of Egypt, to let the Israelite slaves go free, but the pharaoh refused. So God sent ten disasters, or plagues, to warn the pharaoh. But he was proud and greedy. He would not give in to God. The first nine plagues were:

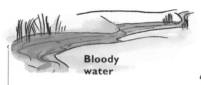

Bloody water

1. All the water in the River Nile turned to blood.
2. Millions of jumping, hopping frogs.
3. Gnats everywhere, crawling on people and animals.
4. Swarms of crawling flies.
5. All the animals died of plague.
6. Boils and sores covered the people.

Boils and sores

7. A massive hailstorm smashed down the crops.
8. The land was black with gobbling, greedy locusts.
9. Total darkness for three days.

Total darkness

Finally came the tenth and most dreadful plague of all. "The firstborn son of every Egyptian will die," warned Moses. He called the Israelites together and gave them orders:
- Kill a lamb and put its blood on your doorposts.
- Roast the lamb with herbs.
- Make bread quickly without yeast.
- Eat the meal and pack all your things.

That night, the angel of death came to Egypt. But whenever he saw a house with lamb's blood on the doorpost, he passed over the house and no one died.

(To find out what happened next, see the page on the Israelites' escape, the Exodus.)

THE PASSOVER

Each spring every Jewish family eats a Passover meal of roast lamb and bread made without yeast. They do this to remember how God acted to set them free.

Bible Search

- Burning bush: *Exodus 3:1–22*
- Jesus eats the Passover meal: *Mark 14:12–26*
- Slaves in the brickyards: *Exodus 1:8–14*

Telling stories over a meal

PLAYS,
BOOKS AND ENTERTAINMENTS

In Bible times, people did not go out in the evening for entertainment, as people may do today. They relaxed over meals, making music or telling stories.

Religious festivals drew big crowds at holiday times, and by New Testament times, the Greeks and Romans had introduced big sports contests or gladiator fights.

THEATRE

The Greeks loved the theater. Some Greek writers wrote clever comedies; others wrote serious plays to make people feel very sad, angry or scared.

Greek theaters were all open-air. The audience sat on rows of stone seats, built in a semi-circle, which faced a stage made out of stone.

A Greek theatre

PLAYS

Most Jews refused to go to Greek plays. We know of one Jewish writer of plays. His name was Ezekiel, and he lived in Alexandria in Egypt, before Jesus was born. He wrote plays based on Bible stories.

Bible Search

- A dancing display: **Mark 6:22**
- A public meeting: **Acts 19:29**
- Party music: **Amos 6:5**
- Prizes for riddles: **Judges 14:12–13**
- Music and dancing: **Luke 15:25**

ONE-MAN THEATRE

Jewish teachers, or rabbis, gave talks in public places. If a teacher didn't have a voice which carried well, he had a herald who repeated what he said, rather like a human loudspeaker.

These talks were not boring lectures. The speakers used poetry, short stories, proverbs, humor, rhymes and catchy sayings to get over their main points. The teacher Gamaliel once used 300 examples to illustrate one point.

The best example of this sort of speaking is Jesus' talks to the people.

LIBRARIES

In Palestine in Jesus' time, there were private libraries of Old Testament scrolls and other religious writings, but no public libraries.

PARTIES

The Jews often had parties. When all the food was cleared away, there was music and dancing. Men and women danced separately. People told stories, jokes and riddles, and talked for hours.

At big Roman parties, there would be entertainment between the courses of the meal. This might be prose and poetry readings, music, and dancing displays.

Men and women danced separately

240

POTTERS
IMPORTANT CRAFTSMEN

E very village had a potter. He was important because of the useful things he made: jugs, bowls, pots, storage jars, lamps and seals for letters.

Clay was dug from the ground and stamped on to get all the air out of it. It was then mixed with water and some grit.

SHAPING CLAY

Working with clay

Clay was shaped by hand. The first clay bowls were made by putting long coils known as "worms" of clay on top of each other to build up a shape. The sides were then smoothed down. The pot was left to dry, then decorated and baked in a kiln.

Some potters used a potter's wheel. The wheel was a stone which was placed in another hollowed-out stone. One man turned the top stone while the potter worked the clay.

A potter's wheel that could be turned by foot was not invented until about 200 years before Jesus' time.

Potters sometimes pressed clay into wooden molds. Seals and oil lamps were made in this way.

Bible Search

- Trampling clay: *Isaiah 41:25*
- Jeremiah: *Jeremiah 18:1–6*
- A seal on clay: *Job 38:14*

Using a potter's wheel

DECORATION

These were some methods of decorating a pot:

- A woven rope was pressed into the wet clay.
- When the clay was dry, but not hard, the pot could be chiseled or engraved.
- Colored clay might be added in bands or zigzag patterns as the pot was being made. Red and black were popular colors.
- A pot could be burnished to make it shine. Before it was fired, the dry pot was put on the wheel, and turned while holding a piece of pottery or bone against it.

FIRING

Once a pot had been dried and decorated, it was baked, or fired. A simple kiln might be shelves over a fire. Some kilns were dome-shaped clay ovens in a 4 feet deep, 10 feet wide hole in the ground.

241

PRAYER THE LORD'S

Jesus talks to his friends

O ne day, Jesus' friends asked, "Lord, teach us to pray." Jesus replied, "When you pray, say…" and he gave them the prayer we call "The Lord's Prayer".

The Lord's Prayer is very short. Jesus said, "When you pray, don't keep babbling on." He meant that it is better to say a few words and really mean them.

THE LORD'S PRAYER

Our Father
We can trust God to take care of us. He is the father parents ought to copy.

God's example shows us how to be a good parent

In heaven
Heaven, here, means the place where everyone obeys God. It is where the angels are, and where we go when we die. There is more to life than just the world around us.

There is more to life

Hallowed be your name
Hallowed means holy, and *name* means "nature." God is absolutely good and completely different to us. With these words, we give him our reverence and love.

Your kingdom come, your will be done, On Earth as it is in heaven
Kingdom means God's rule. We are praying that we may obey God, and carry out God's plans in the world.

Don't worry about the future

Give us this day our daily bread
Daily means "for the coming day." It reminds us not to worry about the future, but to pray for the next day. *Bread* means "food." God gives us everything we need.

Forgive us our trespasses
As we forgive those who trespass against us
Trespass means debts (things we should have done). We are asking God to forgive us, as we must forgive other people.

And lead us not into temptation, but deliver us from evil
Temptation means tests. We are asking God to keep us from difficulties that are too hard for us to cope with. The prayer also asks God to keep us safe from the clutches of evil.

Bible Search

- The Lord's Prayer: *Matthew 6:9–13; Luke 11:1–4*
- The Devil: *1 Peter 5:8*

PRAYER QUESTIONS

P rayer is asking God for things such as help and forgiveness. Prayer is talking to God: thanking him, praising him, and telling him how we feel. And prayer also means being silent with God and giving our love to him. "I look at him and he looks at me," said one old lady. Sometimes people give rules about prayer, but Jesus never did that.

"I look at him and he looks at me."

Bible Search

- Jesus prays:
  Mark 1:35; Luke 6:12;

- About everything:
  Philippians 4:6;
  I Thessalonians 5:17

- Hezekiah's letter:
  Isaiah 37:14–20

- With others:
  Acts 2:42

WHY PRAY?

Sometimes people ask what point there is in praying, because God knows everything anyway. God is our father. Parents want to hear from their children what they have been doing, even when they already know. They want to talk to their children, and find out what their thoughts are.

Parents like to talk to their children

WHERE TO PRAY?

Find a quiet place to pray

Jesus often prayed in quiet places: in a garden, on a hillside, in the country. But he also prayed with his friends. Nehemiah prayed while he built the walls of Jerusalem, which was a very noisy spot. It's not always easy to find a quiet place to pray, but we can make a quiet place in our minds wherever we are.

PAUL IN CORINTH

There are no rules about how long a prayer should be. Sometimes Jesus made quick 'arrow prayers', and sometimes he prayed all night.

We don't have to get on our knees to pray. The best position is one which you find comfortable. People often say, "Close your eyes and put your hands together." This is to help you concentrate.

WHAT TO PRAY?

Paul said, "Do not be anxious about anything, but in everything, by prayer and petition, with thanksgiving, present your requests to God." We can pray about anything, from the smallest thing to something very important. King Hezekiah prayed about a difficult letter.

WILL I HEAR GOD SPEAKING?

God doesn't use a human voice when he speaks to us. But he speaks by giving us a new idea, or with words in the Bible, or through things that happen.

God does not have a human voice

PRAYER PROBLEMS

Praying is one of the most important things Christians can do. That's why people say, "When Christians pray, the Devil trembles."

Sometimes, people find it difficult to pray. These are some of the problems they experience.

NOTHING HAPPENS

Often, nothing seems to happen when we pray. But later, we notice changes. Someone said, "When I stop praying, the coincidences stop happening."

Sometimes the change is not in the things around us, but in the way we understand them. This happened to David (look at Psalm 73).

Sometimes nothing seems to happen

- A widow: *Luke 18:1–8*
- Prayer in Jesus' name: *John 15:16*
- A loving Father gives good gifts: *Matthew 7:7–11*
- Showing-off prayers get nowhere: *Matthew 6:5–6; Luke 18:9–14; James 4:2–3*

HOW DOES A PRAYER WORK?

How prayer works is a mystery. But often it's as if God waits for us to pray, so that we can have the happiness of seeing him at work in the world, and of sharing in that work. James said, "You don't have, because you don't ask God."

Jesus told a story to encourage people not to give up on prayer. There was once a wicked judge. A poor widow kept coming to him, saying she'd been wronged. The judge took no notice. In the end, he was so fed up with her that he gave her what she wanted. Jesus meant that if a wicked judge could help a widow, how much more God would help his people.

ANSWERING PRAYERS

Sometimes we ask for wrong things in our prayers, so God won't answer them.

Jesus said that prayer asked "in his name" would be answered. This means prayers that match what Jesus is like. Sometimes Jesus asks us to wait for our prayers to be answered. Once, a message was brought to Jesus to say that his friend Lazarus was ill. Jesus did nothing. Lazarus died. But then, Jesus showed his power by bringing Lazarus to life again.

Jesus learns Lazarus is ill

CONCENTRATING

Some people find that their mind wanders while they are praying. The best thing to do is to try to make these thoughts part of their prayers.

The wicked judge

PREJUDICE
FIGHTING AGAINST

Prejudice means disliking people for no good reason, usually because they are different to you in some way, such as by their sex, race or religion. To know what the Bible teaching is on this, we have only to look at the life of Jesus. He fought against prejudice of every kind.

We are all different to each other in many ways

MONEY

Poor people were often treated as though they were very unimportant. But Jesus didn't think that money made a person important. He chose to be poor.

James wrote: "Suppose a man comes into your meeting wearing a gold ring and fine clothes, and a poor man in shabby clothes also comes in. Don't treat the rich man better than the poor man. God has chosen the poor in this world to be rich in faith."

A rich man

A poor man

FOREIGNERS

The Jews were especially prejudiced against Samaritans. But Jesus told a story in which the hero was a Samaritan.

A Jewish man was traveling to Jericho, when he was attacked by thieves and left by the roadside. A powerful priest came past, but took no notice of the man. Some time later, a Levite came along the road. He too ignored the injured man. Then a Samaritan came by, and immediately went to help the man.

WOMEN

In Bible times, women were treated like servants. They had no rights. Jesus showed this was wrong by his actions. For example, the first person Jesus appeared to, when he was brought back to life, was not Peter or John, but Mary Magdalene.

Jesus had many friends who were women, and he treated them with great kindness. He often spoke to women he didn't know in public: this was against Jewish custom.

BACKGROUND

Jesus grew up in Galilee. People who came from Galilee had a distinctive accent, which was looked down on by people in other parts of the country.

Some of Jesus' friends were uneducated and poor, but he was also friends with powerful and clever people. Jesus was not prejudiced against anyone.

SUMMING UP

Paul wrote: "For Christians, there is no difference between people of different races. There is no difference between male and female. You are all the same to Jesus."

Bible Search

- The first witness: *John 20:10–18*

- Rich and poor: *Luke 21:1–4; James 2:2-5*

- A woman in public: *John 4*

- The Good Samaritan: *Luke 10:25–37*

Jesus speaks to a woman he doesn't know

PRIDE
AND HUMILITY

A proud person might think, "I am in control of my own life. I don't need or want God." A humble person says, "I am weak, and do wrong things. I need God's help." The Book of Proverbs has wise words about pride: "Pride leads to arguments, but those who take advice are wise. Pride goes before destruction, and a haughty spirit before a fall."

Pride goes before a fall

MARY'S SONG

When Mary knew that she was going to be the mother of Jesus, she sang a song in praise of God: "God has scattered those who are proud in their innermost thoughts… but has lifted up the humble."

Mary praises God

JESUS

Jesus described himself as gentle and humble in heart. This didn't mean he was weak, but that he had great strength, controlled by God. When Jesus was on trial before his enemies, they made fun of him, but he didn't let them make him angry.

RUDE GUESTS

People who think they are good are in for a nasty shock. This was the point of Jesus' story about rude guests. A rich man invited important guests to his feast, and they all made excuses. So he invited blind people, cripples and beggars: people who were usually despised.

Jesus was making the point that proud people may refuse God's call to join him. But people who don't think they deserve God's love will be thrilled to find that he cares for them.

PAUL

Paul had a problem with pride. He had a lot to be proud about. He boasted that he had been a perfect Jew. He boasted about how much he had suffered for Jesus. God had to keep on pulling him down to size!

Paul wrote about how stupid he felt in the town of Damascus. There were guards at the city gates waiting to arrest him. The only way Paul could escape was by being let down over the city walls in a basket.

Paul wrote: "God chose the weak things of the world… so that no one may boast."

Bible Search

- Paul boasts: *2 Corinthians 11:16–33; Philippians 3:3–10*
- Jesus: *1 Peter 2:23; Matthew 11:29*
- Rude guests: *Luke 14:16–21*
- God chooses weak people: *1 Corinthians 1:26–28*

The rich man welcomes his guests

PRIESTS AND PROPHETS

A poor man and his pet lamb

I n Old Testament times, people depended on prophets and priests to teach them what God wanted. In the time of Moses, all priests came from the family of Aaron (Moses' brother); later other members of the tribe of Levi also took on priestly duties. The job of High Priest (the leader of the priests) was passed on from father to son.

PRIESTS

The main work of a priest was to explain God's laws; offer sacrifices and pray for the people; look after the Tabernacle and, later, the Temple. Priests were divided into twenty-four groups, which took turns doing a week's Temple duty.

The High Priest wore a special breastplate, which had twelve precious stones set in gold.

The High Priest

PROPHETS

Prophets gave advice

Prophets were men and women chosen by God to give the people his messages. They told people how they should live in order to please God.

Some prophets were king's advisers; some went to war (like army chaplains today); some gave guidance about problems. Sometimes prophets lived together in groups.

Bible Search

- The breastplate:
  Exodus 28:15–30
- Zechariah on duty:
  Luke 1:5–10
- Groups of prophets:
  1 Samuel 10:10; 2 Kings 4:1
- Nathan: *2 Samuel 12:1–10*
- A priest's work:
  Deuteronomy 33:10

When King David fell in love with Bathsheba, he had her husband sent into battle where he knew he would be killed.

The prophet Nathan came to see David. Nathan said, "A poor man had one pet lamb. It ate at his table, and slept in his arms. But a rich man killed it for a party. You are like that man." David realized how wrong he had been.

AFTER THE EXILE

During the Jews' exile in Babylonia, the work of teaching God's laws was taken over by scribes.

When there was no king, the priests became the leaders of the people. The High Priest was leader of the Sanhedrin (a council of religious leaders in Jerusalem), and the chief priests were members of it.

A scroll for teaching

PROMISES
AND AGREEMENTS

We rely on people to do what they say they will do. If people keep breaking their promises, it causes trouble. For example, when a husband and wife break their marriage promises, the marriage breaks down.

All through the Old Testament, we read how God promises to care for the people he loves, but those same people keep betraying him.

If you promise to play with your sister, then you should do so

NOAH

God often entered into a bond, or pact, with people, called a covenant. After the Flood, God made a covenant with Noah. God promised that he would never again destroy the Earth in such a way, until the end of time. As a sign of this, God made a rainbow.

ABRAHAM

God made a covenant with Abraham. He promised that Abraham would have as many descendants as there were grains of sand on the seashore. Abraham had only to believe God.

MOSES

The Ten Commandments

Through Moses, God made a covenant with the Israelites. God promised to look after the people, if they would keep his laws. If not, trouble would come. The people broke their promise to God, and God kept his promise about the trouble.

Bible Search

• Abraham:
Genesis 15; 22:17

• A new covenant:
Hebrews 8:7–13

• Jesus' death makes it possible: *Hebrews 9:15*

• Yes and no:
Matthew 5:37

A seashore

A NEW COVENANT

The prophet Jeremiah said that one day, God would make a new covenant with his people.

At the Last Supper, Jesus told his friends that he was about to bring in the new covenant. His death would make it possible. Anyone, man, woman and child, could enter into an agreement with Jesus. The agreement would be based on love.

Food at the Last Supper

KEEPING YOUR WORD

Jesus said that people must keep their word. There was no need to swear oaths (our modern version might be to say things like "cross my heart"). Jesus said people should say a simple "yes" and "no" and stick to it.

248

PROVERBS THE BOOK OF

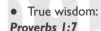
- True wisdom:
  Proverbs 1:7
- Trust in God:
  Proverbs 3:5–6
- Talking:
  Proverbs 11:13;15:1
- The way of life:
  Proverbs 19:23

Everybody wants to be wise. Or, to put it another way, nobody wants to be stupid! The purpose of the Book of Proverbs is to tell people how to be happy, wealthy and wise. The book has over 900 snappy sayings, and longer "thoughts" about everyday life.

WRITERS

Many of the sayings are by King Solomon and some are by King Hezekiah. Others are by teachers known as wise men. Along with prophets and priests, wise men gave advice about the right way to live. Wise men told people that they should do their job of work well, make the right choices, and live a life based on respect for God.

UNDERSTANDING PROVERBS

There are two ways of doing things: a right way and a wrong way. Wise people choose the right way of life. The Book of Proverbs shows how to find it.

READING PROVERBS

- *Chapter 1–9*: In praise of wisdom.
- *Chapter 10:1–31:9*: Wise words.
- *Chapter 31:10–31*: The ideal wife.

Apart from the passages on wisdom, the topics are mixed up. It's best to read a few at a time, without looking for any order.

- A good man takes care of his animals. (Proverbs 12:10)

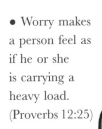

- Worry makes a person feel as if he or she is carrying a heavy load. (Proverbs 12:25)

- A happy heart is like good medicine. (Proverbs 17:22)

- If a person does not punish his children, he does not love them. (Proverbs 13:24)

- Don't praise yourself. Let someone else do it. (Proverbs 27:2)

- Wisdom is the most important thing. Like flowers in your hair, it will beautify your life. (Proverbs 4:7–9)

- Go and watch the ants, you lazy person. Watch what they do and be wise. (Proverbs 6:6)

- Depend on the Lord in whatever you do. Then your plans will succeed. (Proverbs 16:3)

- A gentle answer will calm a person's anger. (Proverbs 15:1)

PSALMS
THE BOOK OF

T he Book of Psalms is made up of 150 songs and poems. It is probably one of the best-loved books in the Bible. It is also the longest. The Israelites used psalms as hymns and prayers. Some were written to celebrate special events.

WHO WROTE THE PSALMS?

Many psalms, perhaps as many as seventy-three, were written by King David. He is described as the sweet singer of Israel. Psalm 90 was by Moses. Other psalms were by musicians and poets in the Temple. Their names are often given at the top of the psalms they wrote.

UNDERSTANDING THE PSALMS

The Book of Psalms was the hymn-book and prayer book of the Israelite people (who are called Jews in the New Testament). The Jews called it the 'Book of Praises'.

Musical instruments

SONGS

Many of the psalms are songs, or chants. Musical instructions are often given at the top of the psalms. Psalm 5 says, "for flutes," and Psalm 6, 'for stringed instruments'.

King David wrote many psalms

POETRY

Hebrew poems did not use rhymes. They were written in a style called parallelism. The first line made a statement or asked a question. The second line picked up the same thought, repeated it in another way, added to it, finished it or even said the opposite. Line 3 then gave a new idea, which was "paralleled," as above, in line 4. This continued in pairs of lines to the end of the poem.

Here's an example from Psalm 63:6-8:

"On my bed I remember you;

I think of you through the watches of the night.

(Repeat/add)

Because you are my help,

I sing in the shadow of your wings.

(Finishes)

My soul clings to you;

Your right hand upholds me."

(Opposite contrast)

SAY IT WITH PSALMS

Some psalms were specially written for big events. Psalm 45 was for a king's wedding.

Other psalms were for pilgrims to sing on their way to Jerusalem. Psalm 122 was one of these "songs of ascent."

'I rejoiced with those who said to me,
"Let us go to the house of the Lord."
Our feet are standing
In your gates, O Jerusalem.
Pray for the peace of Jerusalem.'

PSALMS A WAY TO GOD

In the psalms the writers tell God their feelings – whatever they may be! They pour out their problems and fears. They praise God, and sometimes shout at him.

Jesus often quoted from the Book of Psalms.

Bible Search

- Angry: *Psalm 35*
- Making a decision: *Psalm 37:1–11*
- Feeling sad: *Psalm 51*
- Happy: *Psalm 100*

PSALMS

Feeling ill or afraid
Psalm 23 tells us that God cares for us just as a shepherd cares for his sheep.

Feeling let down
In Psalm 41 David writes that a friend he trusted had turned against him. He asks God to help him.

Jealous
The writer of Psalm 73 looks at bad people around him who ignore God, and wonders why they are so well, happy and successful. Then he realizes that they will come to a bad end, whereas he has God to guide him.

Help from God
In Psalm 34, King David praises God for saving him from great danger.

God's power
Psalm 29 tells of a great thunderstorm. It makes the writer think of God's power.

Harvest
In Psalm 65, David is so happy that he feels as though the hills and fields are singing.

JESUS AND THE PSALMS

Jesus quoted from the Book of Psalms more often than from any other Old Testament book. On the cross, he cried, "My God, my God, why have you left me alone?" (Psalm 22)

'I HATE YOU!'

The psalms were written hundreds of years before Jesus. The writers hated God's enemies, and wanted them to suffer. But Jesus has shown us a different way of dealing with our enemies.

"I hate you!"

QUEENS
POWERFUL WOMEN

Kings and queens were powerful people. In the Bible, some well-known queens used their power for evil ends.

Jezebel tried to make the people of Israel worship Baal. Herodias had John the Baptist killed.

Jezebel

BATHSHEBA

King David fell in love with a beautiful woman called Bathsheba, but she was already married to an army general. David gave orders for Bathsheba's husband, Uriah, to be sent to the front line, hoping he would be killed in battle. Uriah was indeed killed in the next battle, and so David made Bathsheba his queen. But David had done wrong in God's eyes.

Bathsheba and David had a son called Solomon. When David was old, Solomon's half-brother Adonijah plotted to seize the throne. Just in time, Bathsheba found out and told David. At once, David made Solomon king.

JEZEBEL

King Ahab of Israel married Princess Jezebel of Tyre. The new Queen Jezebel worshiped the god Baal, and she tried to make this the only religion in Israel. But the prophet Elijah stood up to her, and the Jewish religion survived.

Jezebel came to a gruesome end: her enemies threw her from an upstairs window to a courtyard below.

QUEEN OF SHEBA

The Queen of Sheba came from Arabia to see King Solomon. She brought gifts of gold, jewels and spices. She may have come on a trading mission, but her visit turned out to be more than a business trip. When she saw how wise Solomon was, she praised Solomon's God.

The Queen of Sheba

HERODIAS

Strictly speaking, Herodias was not a queen. Her second husband, Herod Antipas, was a "tetrarch," ruling Galilee for the Romans. But everyone called him King.

"Herodias is breaking the law of Moses," John the Baptist thundered. "She has left one husband and married his brother." Herodias had John thrown into prison.

Herodias' daughter, Salome, danced for Herod at his birthday party. As a reward, he promised her anything she wanted. "Ask for John the Baptist's head on a plate!" said Herodias. John was beheaded in prison.

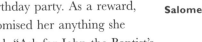

Salome

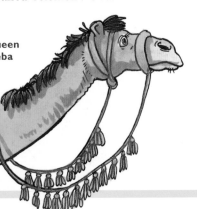

- Bathsheba:
  2 Samuel 11; 1 Kings 1

- Queen of Sheba:
  1 Kings 10:1–10

- Herodias:
  Matthew 14:1–12

Bible Search

A Hindu goddess

RELIGIONS
OTHER BELIEFS

In the city of Athens, there were statues to many gods and goddesses. One day, Paul visited Athens. When he started to preach he said, "I will tell you about the unknown God…this God wants people to search for him." Then Paul went on to talk about Jesus.

SEARCHING

People today are looking for God through many different religions. In his sermon, Paul showed that other religions may have glimpses of the truth, but he believed that Jesus brought the full truth about God.
John said: "Test the teachers to see if they come from God. Have nothing to do with those who do not teach the truth."

A Greek goddess

BUDDHISM

Buddhists follow the teachings of Buddha. Their aim is to find perfect peace (nirvana) by following an eight-fold path of right living.

Buddha

HINDUISM

Hindus worship many different gods. They believe that after death, you are born again in another body. The type of body you are reborn in depends on how good you have been in this life.

Hindus believe that you can be reborn in another body

ISLAM

Muslims believe that Jesus was a good teacher sent by God, but the greatest teacher was Muhammed.

JUDAISM

Jews believe God made an agreement with their ancestor Abraham, that Jews should teach God's laws to the world. They believe that one day God's messenger will come to change the world.

SECTS

Many religious groups say that they follow some, or even all, of the teaching of the New Testament. Two well-known non-Christian sects are Mormons and Jehovah's Witnesses.

Bible Search

- Testing: *1 John 4:1–3; 2 John 9–10*
- Trust: *Galatians 2:16*
- Obedience: *Matthew 7:21*

REVELATION
THE BOOK OF

John kept preaching about Jesus. The Romans didn't like this and arrested him. John was sent to the island of Patmos in the Mediterranean, where he may have been forced to work in the stone quarries. His enemies thought they had silenced him, but they would soon find out that they had not succeeded.

UNDERSTANDING REVELATION

One Sunday, John had an amazing vision. He also heard a voice saying, "Write what you see." The result is the Book of Revelation.

In many places, Christians were under attack. They were being tortured and killed. John wrote to help them to remain strong and not give in.

A bowl of plagues

SECRET SIGNS

The book is full of weird and wonderful things: a sea of glass, living creatures covered with eyes, a pale horse ridden by Death, angels with trumpets, a dragon, bowls brimming over with plagues, and even a wedding where the bride is a lamb.

FIND THE CLUES

Like a game, you have to pick up the clues as you go along, when you read Revelation. Stars are angels, and lampstands stand for churches. The lamb is Jesus himself.

A dragon

CRACK THE CODE

Revelation is full of numbers: 1, 4, 7 (the number seven is mentioned 52 times), 12, 666 and 144,000. They are all codes. They all stand for perfection or completeness, except 666, which stands for complete evil.

READING REVELATION

- *Chapter 1–3*: Letters to seven churches.
- *Chapter 4*: A glimpse of heaven.
- *Chapter 5–11*: Scrolls, seals and trumpets.
- *Chapter 12–14*: The last great battle.
- *Chapter 15–20*: Pictures of judgment.
- *Chapter 21–22*: A new heaven and a new Earth.

A FAMOUS VERSE

Jesus said, "Here I am! I stand at the door and knock. If anyone hears my voice and opens the door, I will come in and eat with him."

A creature covered with eyes

Bible Search

- John sees Jesus: *Revelation 1:9–18*
- A new song to Jesus: *Revelation 5:11–13*
- No more suffering: *Revelation 21:3–4*

ROMANS
LETTER TO

T he apostle Paul wanted to travel to as many places as he could to preach about Jesus. But most of all he wanted to go to Italy and visit Rome. Every time he tried to get there, something stopped him. In the end, he wrote a letter to the Christians in Rome. He wrote to say what his message was, and to announce that soon he hoped to be on his way. This letter was the Letter to the Romans.

ROME

Rome was the capital of the known world. Over a million people lived there. The rich lived in luxury in beautiful villas. But the poor had filthy rooms in crowded buildings.

Rich and poor people

NERO

Nero was the Roman emperor when Paul wrote his letter in A.D. 57. He was a cruel man and the first Roman emperor to persecute Christians.

Nero

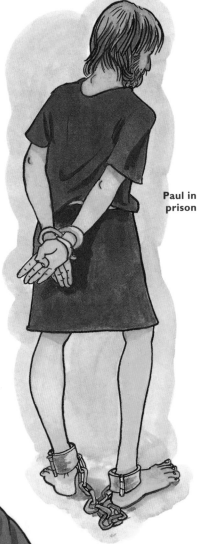

Paul in prison

PAUL IN PRISON

Paul finally made it to Rome, but not in the way he expected. He was a prisoner of the Roman government.

READING ROMANS

- *Chapter 1:1–7*: Paul's hello.
- *Chapter 1:8–3:20*: Everyone has done wrong things.
- *Chapter 3:21–5:21*: God's rescue plan: Jesus.
- *Chapter 6:1–8:39*: How to enjoy being a Christian.
- *Chapter 9:1–11:36*: What about the Jews?
- *Chapter 12:1–15:33*: How a Christian should live.
- *Chapter 16:1–27*: Paul signs off.

UNDERSTANDING ROMANS

We are not born good. We can't make ourselves as good as God wants. God gives us his goodness, and makes us his friend, when we trust Jesus. Anybody can be a Christian.

PAUL WRITES

Paul wrote: "We have been made right with God because of our faith. So we have peace with God through our Lord Jesus Christ."

Bible Search

- A gift: **Romans 5:7**
- Good out of bad: **Romans 8:28**
- On the winning side: **Romans 8:37–39**

RUTH
THE BOOK OF

The Book of Ruth is set in the times of the Judges. It is a beautiful story of the love of a young woman called Ruth for her mother-in-law, Naomi.

When famine came, families often moved to search for food. Naomi and her husband, Elimelech, left their home in Bethlehem and moved to the country of Moab. Their two sons married two local girls, called Orpah and Ruth.

Ruth and her mother-in-law Naomi

A PROMISE

Then disaster struck the family. Naomi's husband and two sons died.

Naomi said to Orpah and Ruth, "I'm going back home to Bethlehem. You two girls stay here in Moab and marry again."

Ruth did not want to be parted from Naomi, and said she would go with her. Her words to Naomi have become famous: "Where you go I will go, and where you stay I will stay. Your people will be my people, and your God my God. Where you die I will die, and there I will be buried."

Disaster strikes Naomi

Naomi and her family leave Bethlehem

HARVEST

When they got back to Bethlehem, Naomi and Ruth had no money. It was harvest time, and each day Ruth went to the fields where men and women were cutting the barley with sickles. The law said that some grain had to be left for poor people.

Ruth and Boaz

BOAZ

Boaz, a rich farmer, was a relative of Naomi. He spotted Ruth picking up leftover stalks of grain. He had heard of her kindness to Naomi. He told his workers to look after her and give her extra grain.

Boaz and Ruth fell in love, and were married. When their first son, Obed, was born, Naomi became the proudest grandmother in Bethlehem.

UNDERSTANDING RUTH

The country of Moab and the country of Israel were often at war. The story of Ruth showed that God loved people of every country, not just Israel. It also showed how God brings happiness out of sadness, when people do what is loving and right.

READING RUTH

- *Chapter 1:1–22*: Naomi and Ruth.
- *Chapter 2:1–2:23*: Ruth meets Boaz.
  - *Chapter 3:1–18*: Naomi's plan.
  - *Chapter 4:1–17*: A happy ending.
  - *Chapter 4:18–22*: A family tree.

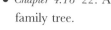

SABBATH A DAY OF REST

T he word sabbath comes from the Hebrew word for seven. The fourth of the Ten Commandments says, "Remember the Sabbath day by keeping it holy… On it you shall not do any work." The Jews took this command seriously. Every seventh day was a day for praise and worship.

THE SABBATH

The Sabbath began when it got dark on Friday evening, and ended at the same time on Saturday evening. (A new day started in the evening, not at midnight.) To let everyone know when the Sabbath had begun and ended, a trumpeter would go to the top of the tallest building and blow some loud notes.

A trumpeter

GETTING READY

Each Friday, houses were cleaned and food was cooked, because no cooking was to be done on the Sabbath. Then everyone washed and put on their best clothes. Lamps were lit and the whole family sat down for a meal.

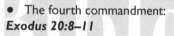

Food was cooked on Friday

- The fourth commandment: *Exodus 20:8–11*
- Jesus and the Sabbath: *Mark 2:23–3:6*
- Trumpets for alarm clocks: *Leviticus 25:9*

SATURDAY

In Jesus' time, on Saturday morning everyone went to the synagogue for Bible reading, teaching and prayers.

There were thousands of rules to stop people doing things which might be considered work.

- A writer could not carry his pen in case he 'worked' and wrote something.
- No one was allowed to eat an egg that a hen had laid on the Sabbath.
- If your donkey fell down a well, you could lift it out. But you could only help an injured person if his life was in danger.

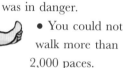

- You could not walk more than 2,000 paces.

ARGUMENTS

In the time of Jesus, teachers argued about these laws. Some said they were too strict; others said they were not strict enough. The Essene community (a group of very religious Jews) thought that it was better to let a man drown than to rescue him on the Sabbath.

One Sabbath, Jesus healed a man's hand. Jesus said, "The Sabbath was made for man, not man for the Sabbath."

Essenes believed that a drowning man couldn't be rescued on the Sabbath

SACRIFICES
AN OFFERING TO GOD

A sacrifice was something which was given to God to say "thank you" or "I'm sorry." It was also a way of making a promise to God. It was an outward sign of an inner feeling. Sometimes the Jews forgot this, and thought the outward sign was enough, without the need to feel sorry or thankful. This was wrong.

Sometimes the Jews forgot the need to feel sorry too

ANIMAL SACRIFICE

The Old Testament taught that sin must be punished. People believed that by killing an animal, their own sins would be forgiven. Only sheep, goats, cattle or doves could be sacrificed. They had to be young and perfect. These animals were known as "clean" animals.

The person making the sacrifice put his hands on the animal. Then he gave the animal to the priest. The priest killed it and sprinkled its blood on the altar. This showed the animal's life was given instead of the life of the sinful person. The worshiper was forgiven and could be at peace with God.

Offerings of grain were sometimes made as well. The first food harvested each year was also offered to God to give thanks.

TYPES OF SACRIFICE

● Burnt offering. A whole animal was burnt. This meant that you gave your life to God.

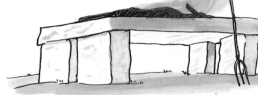

A burnt offering

● A grain offering was an accompaniment to fellowship and burnt offerings. Flour, bread, grain and incense were offered. The priest burnt some and kept the rest.
● A fellowship offering was a sign of friendship with God. The fatty parts of an animal were burnt. The priest kept some and the rest was roasted and eaten in a family meal.
● A sin offering allowed a sinner to be forgiven. An animal was killed and its blood was sprinkled on the altar.
● For a guilt offering, the fatty parts of the animal were burnt. The priests kept the rest. These offerings might be made by someone who had been stealing, or someone who had broken God's law by mistake, or by a leper who had been healed.

ALTARS

A sacrifice was made on an altar. At first, altars were a mound of earth, a block of stone, or a flat stone supported by other stones. In time, "horns" shaped like animal's horns were added at the four corners of a stone block.

A grain offering

Bible Search

● God's laws: *Leviticus 17:11*

● Jesus' sacrifice: *Hebrews 9:26–28*

● What God really wants: *Hosea 6:6*

Delilah cuts Samson's hair

SAMSON
A VERY STRONG MAN

Bible Search

- Samson's birth: *Judges 13*
- A wedding: *Judges 14*
- Delilah: *Judges 16:4–22*
- Samson dies: *Judges 16:23–31*

DELILAH

Samson fell in love in Delilah. The Philistine chiefs told Delilah that if she found out what made Samson so strong, they would give her a lot of money.

So Delilah kept asking Samson to tell her his secret. "It's my long hair," he said at last. When he was asleep, Delilah had his hair cut off. All Samson's strength left him, and he was seized by the Philistines.

Samson pulls a millstone

SAMSON DIES

The Philistines blinded Samson and set him to work pulling a millstone to grind corn. One day, all the Philistine leaders met together in their temple. "Let's have some fun," they said. They brought Samson out. His hair had grown again. "Lord, give me strength once more," Samson prayed. He felt for the pillars holding up the building and pushed hard. Down crashed the temple, killing all the Philistines, and killing Samson, too.

You can read more about the Philistines on the page on Samuel.

S amson grew up in Zorah. Around Zorah, the Israelites had given in to the Philistine enemy. Samson was a rebel who never gave in. He fought a one-man battle with the massive strength that God had given him. But he was weak in other ways, and cared more about himself than about God.

Samson was a judge. Judges ruled over tribal districts.

SAMSON'S MOTHER

An angel told Manoah's childless wife that she would give birth to Samson. "Your baby is to be a Nazirite," said the angel. A Nazirite was someone who promised to work only for God; sometimes for a short time, sometimes for life. As a sign of this promise, a Nazirite never cut his hair.

SLIPPERY SAMSON

The Philistines were Samson's sworn enemy. But every time they thought they had caught Samson, he escaped. Once, they locked the gates of a city, but Samson tore up the gates and the gateposts, and walked out. Their only hope was trickery.

Samson

SAMUEL
THE FIRST AND SECOND BOOKS

David leads the procession into Jerusalem

The First and Second Books of Samuel take up the story of the Israelites where the Book of Judges leaves off. Here we read about: Samuel, who was the last of the judges; Saul, Israel's first king; Jonathan, Saul's son; and David, Israel's greatest king.

Samuel is asked to find a king

SAMUEL

"We want a king," said the Israelites. "Everyone else has a king. If we have a king to lead us, we might stand a better chance in battle." God told Samuel to make Saul king.

SAUL

Saul started well as king, but slowly he stopped obeying God. One day, Saul heard the people singing a song in praise of their hero David, who had defeated the Philistine enemy Goliath.

Saul too had been proud of David's victory, and had begun to look on David as part of his family. But now he became jealous, and eventually David had to run away and hide. Jonathan, Saul's son, was a very good friend of David.

Saul

DAVID

David became king of Israel after Saul. He was commander-in-chief of the army and beat Israel's fiercest enemy, the Philistines.

When the Ark of the Covenant, (a holy box containing God's laws), was brought into Jerusalem, David led the procession, dancing and singing praises to God.

Like Saul, David at times disobeyed God. (David fell in love with a married woman called Bathsheba, and had her husband Uriah killed in a battle.) But unlike Saul, David was deeply sorry for his mistakes.

David's sling

- Jonathan's bravery:
  1 Samuel 14:1–13
- Saul's jealousy:
  1 Samuel 18, 19
- David and Goliath:
  1 Samuel 17
- David and Jonathan:
  1 Samuel 20

UNDERSTANDING THE BOOKS OF SAMUEL

God told Saul, "Because you have rejected the word of the Lord, he has rejected you as king." Saul failed in God's sight, but David was "a man after God's own heart."

The pages headed Samuel, Saul and David will tell you more. God's call to Samuel is on the page headed Children.

ANY QUESTIONS

1 Why was Saul no longer a good king?
2 Why did David have to hide from Saul?

READING SAMUEL 1 AND 2

1 Samuel
- *Chapter 1–8*: The life of Samuel.
- *Chapter 9–20*: The life of Saul.
- *Chapter 21–31*: David in exile.

2 Samuel
- *Chapter 1–10*: David as king.
- *Chapter 11–12*: David's great sin and his sorrow.
- *Chapter 13–20*: Suffering and trouble.
- *Chapter 21–24*: David's last days.

David

SAMUEL A GREAT JUDGE

Samuel

Samuel was the last and greatest of the judges, and one of the first prophets. Judges governed Israel before it had a king. He was a hero, not just in his own area, but to the whole country. He led the people back from idol worship to God. Thanks to Samuel, the Israelites beat the Philistines.

HARD TIMES

The Ark of the Covenant

Samuel was born after his mother prayed for a baby. To find out how God called him, turn to the page on Children.

When Samuel was young, there was a terrible battle. The Philistines captured the Ark of the Covenant (a holy box containing God's laws). The Ark was very important as it was a sign to the people that God was with them. The loss of the Ark left the Israelites at rock bottom.

IRON

Iron weapons were made by smelting iron ore in very hot furnaces. The Philistines first brought this skill to Canaan. Before then, "iron" chariots were wooden chariots studded with small lumps of iron. The Philistines sold iron tools to the Israelites, but not iron weapons.

PHILISTINES

The Philistines came from across the sea, from the country of Crete. They settled along the coast, in five cities ruled by five tyrant kings. One secret of Philistine power was that they knew how to make iron weapons, whereas nobody else did. Another secret was that the kings joined together to fight, which made them very powerful. In the time of Samuel, the Philistines wanted to take over the whole of Canaan.

A Philistine ship

KING-MAKER

Samuel's work was mainly to settle disputes between people. He also led their worship of God, and directed the army.

When Samuel was old, the people were afraid. Who would lead them when Samuel was dead? God told Samuel to anoint first Saul, and later the shepherd boy David, as king. (See the pages on Saul and David.)

Bible Search

- The great defeat: *I Samuel 4*
- Iron: *I Samuel 13:19–21*
- Samuel's regular work: *I Samuel 7:15–17*
- Victory: *I Samuel 7*

SARAH
HAGAR AND ISHMAEL

Sarah was Abraham's wife. Sarah and Abraham lived in Ur, but left to travel to Canaan, when God told them to.

Hagar was Sarah's Egyptian slave, and Ishmael was her son.

EGYPT

Because there was a famine, Sarah and Abraham left Canaan and went to Egypt. Sarah was beautiful, and when the ruler of Egypt, the pharaoh, saw her, he took her into his household. Abraham told a lie. He said Sarah was not his wife, because he thought the pharaoh might kill him. When the pharaoh found out the truth he was disgusted, and sent Abraham and Sarah away.

Sarah

HAGAR

Hagar was Sarah's Egyptian slave.

Sarah had no children so she told Abraham to marry Hagar and have a baby with her. Sarah planned to adopt Hagar's child.

Hagar

THE LAW OF THE LAND

More than 4,000 flat clay bricks covered with writing have been dug up from the ancient city of Nuzi in southern Mesopotamia. These were letters, business deals, contracts and wills. They describe daily life at the time of Abraham. We learn that if a woman could not have a child, she could give her servant to her husband and the servant's child became her own.

ISHMAEL

Hagar called her son Ishmael. Fifteen years later, Isaac, Sarah's son, was born. One day Sarah saw Ishmael making fun of his little brother Isaac. She told Abraham that she didn't want Hagar and Ishmael to live with them any more. Abraham was very sad, but God told him to do what Sarah asked. 'I will look after your son Ishmael,' God said.

Ishmael makes fun of Isaac

SAVED BY THE WELL

Hagar and Ishmael went off into the desert. Eventually they ran out of water, and Hagar thought they would die. But an angel appeared and showed her where there was water. They were saved. Ishmael grew up to be a great desert warrior, and the founder, it is said, of the Arab race.

To find out more, turn to the pages on Abraham and on Isaac.

A desert warrior

Bible Search

- Abraham and Sarah in Egypt: *Genesis 12:10–20*
- Birth of Ishmael: *Genesis 16:1–16*
- Saved by an angel: *Genesis 21:8–21*

SAUL AND JONATHAN

Saul was the first king of Israel. His story is one of the saddest in the Bible.

God told Samuel to find a king to rule Israel. When Saul came to the city where Samuel lived, God told Samuel to make Saul king.

GOD'S CHOICE

Saul was young, handsome and taller than anyone else.

Saul was looking for his lost donkeys when he met Samuel. Samuel told Saul that he was to be the first king of Israel.

When Samuel came to make Saul king, Saul had disappeared. Eventually he was found hiding among some baggage. Samuel anointed Saul by pouring oil on Saul's head. That was how a king was crowned.

Samuel anoints Saul with oil

Saul hides among some baggage

A WAR CHIEF

Spears

Men from the tribes of Israel gathered together into a small army, led by Saul. They won some victories, but Saul had two big faults: he looked at his problems instead of at God; and he got big-headed.

Weapons of war

SAUL IN A MESS

A few years after Saul had become king, the Israelites were about to be attacked by the Philistines. Samuel told Saul to wait for him to make an offering to God, before the battle started. But, scared of the enemy, and in a panic, Saul did not wait for Samuel to offer sacrifices. He did it himself.

Samuel told Saul that he had disobeyed God's word, and that his descendants would not now rule Israel. Saul felt crushed. He began to have fits of misery and madness. (Read more about Saul on the page on David.)

JONATHAN

Jonathan was Saul's son. He was a brave warrior and a devoted friend to David, who became king after Saul.

DEATH ON THE HILL

All Saul's sons died in a terrible battle on Mount Gilboa. Saul was very seriously wounded too, and killed himself.

- Saul is made king:
  I Samuel 10

- God leaves Saul:
  Samuel 15

- Jonathan and David:
  I Samuel 18:1; 20

- David's sad poem:
  2 Samuel I

Bible Search

263

SCHOOLS
AND TEACHERS

Girls had to learn how to run a home

For the Jews, school meant learning about God. Every lesson was religious education. When Jesus was alive, school was not compulsory. Girls were not allowed to go to school, and had to stay at home and learn how to run a house.

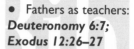
Bible Search

- Fathers as teachers: *Deuteronomy 6:7; Exodus 12:26–27*
- Jesus listens in on a lesson: *Luke 2:41–47*
- Paul in higher education: *Acts 22:3*

HIGHER EDUCATION

A father teaches his son

HOME EDUCATION

At home, mothers would tell their children stories from the Old Testament, and fathers might teach God's laws, the commandments, and the meaning of the religious festivals.

Learning at home

SYNAGOGUE SCHOOLS

At the age of five or six, boys went to school in the local synagogue. These synagogue schools were called "houses of the book," because all the lessons were from the Old Testament.

Each synagogue had one classroom. This was the room where the Old Testament scrolls were kept. The teacher sat on a small platform, and the children sat on the floor in front of him.

If there were more than forty children in the class, the teacher had to have a helper.

Children learned long passages of the Old Testament by heart. They may also have learned to read and write from the Bible.

Teachers were paid by the synagogue. They were considered to be very important people, and were called "messengers of the Almighty." But if they were too strict, they were sacked!

At thirteen, boys left school. Most started working with their father, joining him in whatever trade he followed. A father would teach his son the skills he needed for the job, which probably also included arithmetic. If a boy wanted to learn how to be a teacher, he had to go to Jerusalem, where teachers (mostly Pharisees) held lectures in the Temple courts. Learning was by discussion and argument.

Discussion and argument

SCIENCE
LOOKING AT THE WORLD

S cience is the study of the world around us, and the laws which control it. People study science for the excitement of knowing how things work, and use their knowledge to find ways to make life better on Earth.

We still use the Greeks' discoveries today

MESOPOTAMIA

In ancient Mesopotamia (the land Abraham came from), people loved to study maps and astronomy. Their number system was based on the number sixty. Our time measurements of sixty minutes to an hour, and sixty seconds to a minute, come from the Mesopotamian system.

The earliest picture we have of a wheel comes from southern Mesopotamia. It's a pictogram dating from 3500 B.C., and shows a sledge with wheels.

Studying the stars

EGYPT AND ISRAEL

The pyramids

The Egyptians were interested in sciences which aimed to ensure a good life in the next world, such as embalming and the building of pyramids.

The Jews were not very interested in science. They believed that only God knew the secret of why things were as they were. They believed it was more important to study the Bible than to study the world.

When Bible writers wrote about natural events in the world, they described them in poetry, not scientific language. The events were recorded in order to praise God.

GREEKS AND ROMANS

The Greeks were great scientists and mathematicians. In about 550 B.C., Pythagoras worked out how scientific investigations should be made: by looking carefully, doing experiments, and forming conclusions based on the results.

The Romans took up Greek ideas and discoveries, and became great engineers.

A Roman aqueduct

Bible Search

- God knows the law of the world: *Job 38*

- Astronomers: *Matthew 2:1–12*

- A poem: *Psalm 19:1–6*

265

SCRIBES
TEACHERS OF THE LAW

A scribe

Scribes were the readers, writers and accountants of ancient times, so they were important people. In the New Testament, the scribes are called "teachers of the Law," Rabbi, and "experts in the Law." (The Law was their Bible, and is now our Old Testament.)

WRITERS

Getting a letter written by a scribe

At first, only priests and scribes could read and write. People went to a scribe to get a letter written or read. A scribe always carried his writing equipment with him: reed pens in a pen case, and an ink horn hanging from his belt. He also had a knife for cutting paper.

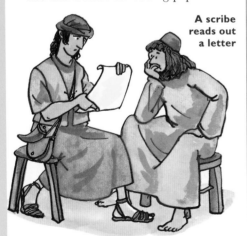

A scribe reads out a letter

KINGS' MEN AND LAWYERS

Kings depended on scribes to write up court records, to keep account of taxes, and make lists. Scribes also acted as their advisers.

Scribes would sit by the city gates, a spot where business was conducted. They acted as lawyers, and could write out a will or legal document there and then.

THE EXILE

When the people of Judah were taken as prisoners to Babylonia, although they no longer had their Temple, scribes copied out the Law and taught it to the people. The most famous scribe, who was also a priest, was Ezra. Without the scribes, the people of Judah might have lost their sense of being God's special people.

Bible Search

- Jesus: *Matthew 23*
- Shebna the scribe: *2 Kings 18:18*
- Gamaliel: *Acts 5:33–39* .

NEW TESTAMENT

In the New Testament, scribes are called "teachers of the Law." They worked out many rules, which they said people had to keep. These were passed on by word of mouth (called the "oral law").

They also trained young people to become teachers of the Law. Anybody, rich or poor, could join their classes, which were held in the Temple.

Some scribes were members of the Sanhedrin, a council of religious leaders in Jerusalem.

JESUS

Many teachers of the Law didn't like Jesus because he wouldn't keep all the extra rules. Jesus said, "You shut the kingdom of heaven in men's faces."

SERVANTS
AND SLAVES

S ervants were really slaves. A slave was his owner's property. Some owners looked after their slaves, but many did not.

Foreign slaves were bought in the slave market or captured in war. Thieves who could not pay back the money they had stolen, were forced to be slaves. Sometimes poor people sold themselves or their children into slavery to pay off debts. It was forbidden to force a fellow Israelite to be a slave against his will.

A cruel master

Selling children to be slaves

SLAVE RIGHTS

Slaves had certain rights. These included:

• A slave must not be killed.

• If an owner hit his slave so hard that the slave lost an eye, or a tooth, the slave had to be set free.

A lost tooth

The Sabbath was a rest day

• Slaves had to have the Sabbath as a rest day.

• An Israelite slave could buy himself free at any time.

• After six years, an Israelite slave was always set free, and had to be given money and help.

• A slave was not allowed to work more than ten hours a day.

• If a slave ran away, and hid with someone, that person could not hand him over to his master.

A runaway slave

IN NEW TESTAMENT TIMES

Laws to protect Jewish slaves were so strict that there was a saying, "Whoever buys a Jewish slave gives himself a master." Probably, most Jewish slaves in Palestine were former thieves. Rich Jews had foreign slaves.

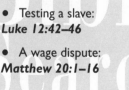

'Whoever buys a Jewish slave gives himself a master.'

ROMAN AND GREEK SLAVES

The Roman and Greek way of life depended on slaves. It has been said there were 60,000,000 (60 million) slaves in the Roman empire. Often, slaves were not considered to be people. A Roman called Varro said a slave was "a kind of tool that can speak." An owner could do whatever he liked with his slaves.

For Bible teaching about slavery, see the page on Freedom.

Bible Search

• Slave laws:
*Deuteronomy 23:15–16;
Exodus 21:26–27*

• Testing a slave:
Luke 12:42–46

• A wage dispute:
Matthew 20:1–16

SHEPHERDS
AND NOMADS

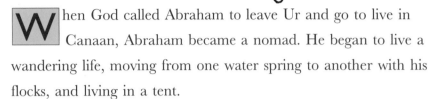

A trumpet made from a horn

When God called Abraham to leave Ur and go to live in Canaan, Abraham became a nomad. He began to live a wandering life, moving from one water spring to another with his flocks, and living in a tent.

When the Israelites settled in Canaan, their flocks were very important. The sheep and goats provided milk, food, and wool for clothes. Skins were made into leather, and horns were used as trumpets and containers for oil.

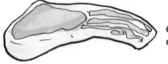

Goat's meat

Goat's milk

SHEPHERDS AT WORK

A shepherd's life was hard. There was danger from wild animals, robbers and enemy soldiers. If a sheep was hurt or tired, the shepherd carried it on his shoulders.

Today, shepherds often drive sheep along with the help of dogs. In Bible times, a shepherd led the way, and his sheep followed him. He often gave each sheep its own name, and the sheep came when he called.

A robber

TOOLS FOR THE JOB

A shepherd had certain equipment to help in his work:
- A strong club with flints (later nails) in the thick end, to attack marauders.
- A sling. This was used to fire stones at wild animals which threatened attack.
- A small leather bag to hold stones for the sling.
- A staff. This was a long stick with a curve at one end, to control the sheep.
- A pipe. Often a shepherd would call his sheep by playing a few notes on his pipe.

A shepherd

SHEEPFOLD

A shepherd sleeps outside his sheepfold

During the winter months, sheep were brought down to the village, and kept in a strong-walled sheepfold.

In summer, the sheep stayed out on the hills. At night they had to be kept safe. If the shepherd couldn't find a cave, he built a sheepfold from stones, with brambles on the top to make a roof. Instead of a door, the shepherd lay across the entrance.

PSALM 23

Psalm 23 is a poem about a shepherd's care for his sheep. In this psalm, God is compared to a loving shepherd. Jesus later called himself the Good Shepherd.

- Nomads: *Deuteronomy 26:5*
- Calling a sheep: *John 10:3–5*
- The door: *John 10:7*
- The good shepherd: *John 10:11–21*

SHOPS
AND TRADERS

Trading with other countries

King Solomon became rich from trading with other countries. His example encouraged people in Jerusalem and Samaria to start trading. The prophet Amos, writing about 760 B.C., said the tradesmen were so greedy for money that they hated holidays, because work had to stop.

BIG BUSINESS

About 600 B.C., Babylon was the trading center of the world. During the time the Jews were exiled in Babylonia, they learned business and banking skills. Archaeologists have found the records of some very rich Jewish traders.

MARKETS

In Bible times, there were no shops in small towns. People went to the city markets to buy olive oil, fish, figs, grapes, wine, animals, clothes, material and pottery. Market inspectors had the job of checking the traders' scales, and making sure that prices were fair.

Bible Search

- Greedy traders: *Amos 8:5*
- Putting money in a bank: *Matthew 25:27*
- Advice to businessmen: *James 4:13–15*
- Shopping in Rome: *Revelation 18:11–13*
- Personal loans: *Luke 6:34–35*

Shops in Jerusalem

MONEY-CHANGERS

People from all over the world came to Palestine, and money-changers were kept busy. They charged a fee which equaled about ten percent of the value of the money they changed.

All Jews had to pay a tax to the Temple in Jerusalem. Unfortunately, the money-changers in the Temple often cheated their customers. Jesus described the Temple as a robbers' den. Money-changers also lent money. The table on which they put their money was called a "bank." They lent money to people such as those setting up new businesses, shipbuilders, and international traders.

Checking a trader's scales

SHOPS

By the time of Jesus, there were probably small shops in Jerusalem and the larger cities, crowded side by side along the narrow streets.

Shops selling the same products would have been grouped together.

A bank

269

The Israelites camp at the foot of Mount Sinai

SINAI

A MOUNTAIN AND A PACT

The Israelites' escape from Egypt turned them from a mob of slaves into a nation. They became a people on their way to a land of their own. Events at Mount Sinai turned this people into God's people. They made a pact with God called a covenant. God promised to care for them and they promised to keep his laws.

MOUNT SINAI

In the middle of the rocky Sinai desert, there is a great range of granite mountains. Nothing grows on them. One of these mountains is Mount Sinai (also called Mount Horeb).

God told Moses to bring the people back to worship him at Mount Sinai. The people camped at the foot of the mountain. It was God's holy mountain. No one was allowed to touch it. If they did, they would die. For three days they waited.

FIRE ON THE MOUNTAIN

The mountain began to shake wildly. Lightning flashed. Fire blazed. A great cloud of black smoke rose and swirled. From the stormy darkness came a sound like a long trumpet blast, growing louder and louder. Moses and Aaron went up the mountain, and there God spoke to them.

Fire blazes on the mountain

THE TEN COMMANDMENTS

God gave Moses laws for the people to obey. These were the Ten Commandments, written out on two large slabs of stone.

God also gave Moses a long list of rules for living. These were examples of how the Ten Commandments worked in practice. There were rules for how to worship God, how to stay healthy, and how people should live together. Moses wrote these rules down.

Moses wrote down the rules

THE COVENANT

Moses made an agreement, or covenant, with God on Mount Sinai. The people promised to accept God as their ruler and king, and to obey his laws. God promised to look after the people.

To find out more about God's rules for living, turn to the page headed Ten Commandments. To find out more about what happened on the mountain, turn to the page on Aaron.

270

SOLDIERS
IN THE OLD TESTAMENT

The Israelites took the Promised Land of Canaan by force: they were the invading army. After that time, they themselves were often invaded by other armies, and beaten.

God sometimes chose unusual battle tactics to teach the Israelites to rely on him.

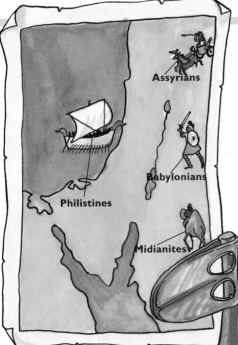

Assyrians

Babylonians

Philistines

Midianites

ENEMIES OF THE ISRAELITES

• Philistines. The Philistine warriors were the dreaded enemy at the time the Book of Judges was written. They took away all blacksmiths from the land, so that the people could not make iron weapons.

• Assyrians. The Assyrians often went on raids to get money to build magnificent temples and palaces.

• Babylonians. If an enemy would not give in quietly, the Babylonian army took them all off as prisoners of war, leaving behind only the very poorest people.

• Midianites. The Midianites and other desert fighters swooped in on camels.

The Midianites

WEAPONS

• For hand-to-hand fighting: axes, clubs, swords.

• For long-distance attack: slings, javelins, bows and arrows. The arrows were made out of reed, with metal heads. A quiver carried thirty arrows.

An archer

• For defense: chain mail (metal "scales" sewn to cloth), and shields (a wooden frame covered with leather).

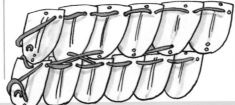

Chain mail

BATTLE TACTICS

• An ambush. The Israelites were particularly good at surprising and tricking their enemies (see, for example, the page on Gideon). King David conquered Jerusalem by sending a few soldiers up an underground tunnel.

• Laying siege to a town. Towns were protected by thick walls (sometimes by two walls), with towers and ditches round the outside. A town would be surrounded and the army either waited until the people ran out of food and gave in, or broke down the walls.

• One-to-one combat. Often, a battle between two armies was decided by a duel between one champion from each army, such as between David and the Philistine giant Goliath.

Bible Search

• Chain mail: *1 Kings 22:34*

• Spies: *Joshua 2:1–7*

• King Uzziah's weapons: *2 Chronicles 26:14*

• Invaders besiege Jerusalem: *Isaiah 36:1–3*

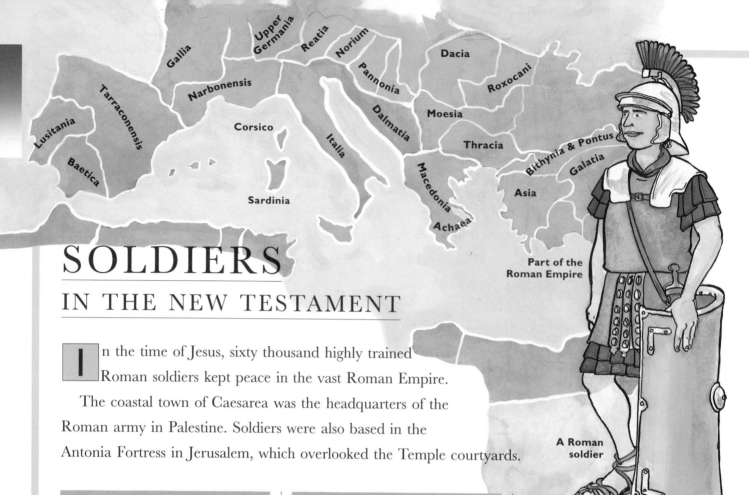

Part of the
Roman Empire

A Roman
soldier

SOLDIERS
IN THE NEW TESTAMENT

In the time of Jesus, sixty thousand highly trained Roman soldiers kept peace in the vast Roman Empire.

The coastal town of Caesarea was the headquarters of the Roman army in Palestine. Soldiers were also based in the Antonia Fortress in Jerusalem, which overlooked the Temple courtyards.

ROMAN SOLDIERS

Sword and dagger

A Roman soldier would have:
- A double-edged sword, used in hand-to-hand fighting.
- A dagger.
- A shield made from plywood, covered with leather and edged with metal.
- A bronze and iron helmet covering the neck and ears.
- Armor made from scales wired to each other and sewn on to cloth or leather.
- A spear.

Centurions were Roman officers in charge of a hundred soldiers. They were well-paid, intelligent men. Centurions made the Roman army into the successful force that it was.

JEWS AND WAR

Jews were not allowed to join the Roman army.

Jewish freedom fighters hid in the northern hills. The fiercest, the Sicarii, were a sort of assassination squad. Their name came from the short curved dagger which they hid under their cloaks. During festivals, they mixed with the crowds and stabbed Roman sympathizers.

The Jews were waiting for a Messiah (a king) who would rescue them from the Romans. Sometimes, somebody would come along claiming to be this great leader. He would collect a gang of followers and start fighting the Romans. But the Romans would send in their cavalry and squash the rebellion.

THE JEWISH WAR

In A.D. 66, about thirty years after Jesus died, the whole country rose up against Roman power. There was horrific fighting and bloodshed. The Roman army finally destroyed Jerusalem in A.D. 70. Jesus had warned his friends that this would happen, and had told them to escape to the hills.

Bible Search

- A centurion:
Luke 7:2–10

- Paul is rescued:
Acts 21:27–36

- False Messiahs:
Acts 5:35–39; Mark 13:21–22

- A warning of war:
Mark 13:14–19

SOLOMON A WISE MAN

Solomon was the son of King David and Queen Bathsheba. He was the third king of Israel. One night, in a dream, God offered him anything he wanted. He asked for wisdom. In later years, people looked back to his reign as a golden age. Solomon was a clever ruler, and brought wealth and power to Israel by trade and by marrying into the ruling families of other countries.

Trading with other countries

THE TEMPLE

Solomon built the first Temple. It was a magnificent building: "a glory of gold." Everyone was proud of it. It was not big: 90 feet long, 30 feet wide and 45 feet high. It was a house for God, not a cathedral for people.

Solomon's Temple

THE KINGDOM

In Solomon's time, the great empires of the world were weak. He made the most of this, and Israel became very rich. Solomon did not gain power by fighting, but by trade, and by marrying the daughters and sisters of other kings.

There were no wars, but Solomon was not popular. He kept his wealth for himself and his friends. He charged heavy taxes and made the people work hard without pay to build his sumptuous palaces, the Temple and other buildings.

TRADING

Camel trains were like our railroads. Solomon made camel trains from other countries pay when they passed through his land.

For the first time, Israel had a navy. Solomon's ships brought back gold, silver, jewels, ivory, expensive wood, baboons and other animals. Ships did not have to go through other people's lands and pay taxes!

Solomon built up an army of chariots to guard against attack. His 1,400 chariots were kept in six frontier "chariot cities."

WISE MAN

Solomon wrote 3,000 proverbs and 1,000 songs. His wisdom was the talk of the world. But he misused God's gift of wisdom. He studied "everything under the heavens," but he slowly forgot God. He began to worship the same idols as his 700 wives and 300 mistresses.

God said to Solomon: "You have not obeyed my commands. So I will tear your kingdom away from you."

- Solomon asks for wisdom:
  I Kings 3:1–15
- Silver in Jerusalem:
  I Kings 10:27
- The Queen of Sheba's verdict:
  I Kings 10:1–13

Bible Search

The people paid heavy taxes

273

A gazelle

SONG OF SONGS
THE BOOK OF

The name of the Book of the Song of Songs means "the greatest and best songs." The songs are love poems spoken by a man and woman to each other. The book shows the beauty and wonder of physical love. It used to be said that the book was by King Solomon, and it is possible that at least some of the poems were Solomon's.

The gift of love

A GAZELLE

Look! Here he comes,
bounding over the mountains,
leaping across the hills.
My lover is like a gazelle...

NIGHT

All night long on my bed
I looked for the one my heart loves.
I looked for him but did not find him.
I will get up now and go
about the city,
through its streets
and squares;
I will search for the one
my heart loves...

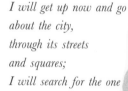

Searching for the loved one

UNDERSTANDING THE SONG OF SONGS

God has given the gift of love to men and women. If the love between a man and women can be so wonderful, how much more wonderful God's love must be.

Some people think that the songs were meant to be sung during the week-long party that would be held for a wedding.

SPRINGTIME

See! The winter is past;
the rains are over and gone,
flowers appear on the earth;
the season of singing has come,
the cooing of doves is heard in our land.

PICTURES

The poems in the Song of Songs compare the beauty of love with the beauty of nature. We read about the countryside in spring, and many plants and animals.

READING SONG OF SONGS

- *Chapter 1:1*: Title.
- *Chapter 1:2–2:7*: The first meeting.
- *Chapter 2:8–3:5*: The second meeting.
- *Chapter 3:6–5:1*: The third meeting.
- *Chapter 5:2–6:3*: The fourth meeting.
- *Chapter 6:4–8:4*: The fifth meeting.
- *Chapter 8:5–7*: Love as strong as death.
- *Chapter 8:8–14*: Conclusion.

Springtime

SPORTS AND GAMES

Wrestling

I n Old Testament times, archery and wrestling contests were popular. The Israelites were experts at using the sling as a weapon of war, and boys liked to play 'slings and stones'.

In New Testament times, the Greeks and Romans loved sports, and so did many of the Jews. Pharisees didn't approve of the Greek games, because they were religious events, held in praise of the god Zeus. Roman sports were bloodthirsty, and the Jews despised them.

GREEK GAMES

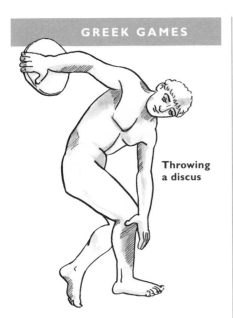

Throwing a discus

The Greeks thought physical fitness was as important as education. They held all sorts of contests. The pentathlon events were long jump, running, discus, javelin and wrestling. Greek boxing was a fight to the death. Instead of boxing gloves, arms and hands were bound with leather studded with metal.

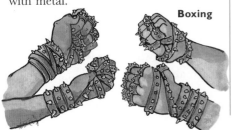

Boxing

OLYMPIC GAMES

Greeks held the first Olympic Games in the village of Olympia in 776 B.C., for the god Zeus. The games were held every four years, and while they took place, all warfare stopped. Only men were allowed to watch the Olympic Games: any woman who watched was put to death. After 392 B.C., the Games stopped. They were started again only a hundred years ago, in 1894.

Bible Search

- Sling shots: *Judges 20:16*
- Wrestling: *Genesis 32:22–32*
- Strict training: *I Corinthians 9:24–27*
- A race: *Hebrews 12:1–2*

ROMAN SPORTS

Chariot racing

In chariot races, a team of four trained horses pulled two-wheeled chariots for seven laps round a stadium. The drivers tied the horses' reins around their bodies.

Some Roman sports were very bloodthirsty. Gladiators fought with swords, or nets, or on horseback. Sometimes they fought in teams. The fight would not end until all the members of one team were dead. Criminals or slaves were often made to be gladiators.

Another cruel spectator sport was forcing people to fight wild animals. They were put into an arena, and a pack of starving animals was set loose on them. This was often the fate of criminals, but it also happened to Christians in Rome.

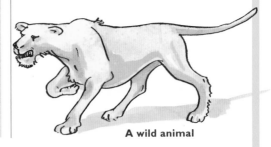

A wild animal

275

STEPHEN
DIES FOR
HIS BELIEFS

After Jesus had returned to heaven, the apostles at first stayed in Jerusalem. They preached to the people, and went to the Temple. But God had bigger plans for them than that, which he set in motion through three men: Stephen, Peter (see the page on Cornelius) and Paul.

God wanted his message spread all over the world

• God didn't need the Temple.
• They were the ones who had not kept God's laws.
• They had betrayed and murdered God's chosen leader.

Jesus carries his cross

STEPHEN

The twelve apostles were very busy, so seven men were chosen to be in charge of money and food. One of these men was Stephen. He was one of the first people to see that the Christian faith was for the whole world.

Stephen performed many miracles among the people. He also preached that trust in Jesus meant that the Temple, and many Jewish laws, were no longer needed. This was dangerous teaching! Stephen was arrested, and brought before the Sanhedrin (the council of religious leaders), just as Jesus had been.

Stephen was in charge of money and food

STEPHEN'S DEFENCE

Luke wrote that Stephen's face looked like the face of an angel. His speech to the Sanhedrin was so important that Luke quoted a long section of it in his Gospel. At first, the speech reads like a history lesson telling the story of the Jews. At the end of the speech, Stephen delivers three bombshells to the Sanhedrin. He told them:

DEATH

The council members were absolutely furious. Stephen said, "Look, I see heaven open and Jesus standing at the right hand of God." At this, they dragged Stephen out of the city and stoned him to death. As he lay dying, he cried, "Lord, do not hold this sin against them."

PERSECUTION

After this, many Christians were thrown into prison, and many left Jerusalem and went to live in other towns. Everywhere they went, they talked about Jesus. The more people tried to destroy the new faith, the more it spread!

Bible Search

• Choosing the seven: *Acts 6:1–7*

• Stephen: *Acts 6:8–15*

• Stephen's speech: *Acts 7:1–53*

• Death: *Acts 7:54–60*

SUFFERING

One of the hardest questions we ask is: "Why is there so much suffering in the world?" The Bible only gives hints, not full answers. It does say that God is good, that he comforts those in need, and that one day he will bring all suffering to an end. Here are some of the Bible's comments.

THE DEVIL CAUSES TROUBLE

Job was a good man, who loved God. Then the Devil decided to test his faith, and Job lost everything. His seven sons and three daughters were killed, as were his 7,000 sheep, 3,000 camels and 1,000 cattle. He became seriously ill.

Job's wife told him, "Curse God and die." But Job would not say anything against God. Eventually, God made him even happier and richer than before.

Job lost everything

SELFISHNESS CAUSES FIGHTS

Much suffering in the world is because God has given us freedom to choose, and human beings make other human beings suffer. James said the reason for fights and quarrels was wanting something and not getting it.

Selfishness causes fights

- Paul: *2 Corinthians 1:3–4*
- Causes of fights: *James 4:1–6*
- A blind man: *John 9:1–41*
- The end of suffering: *Revelation 21:4*
- God doesn't cause evil: *James 1:13–17*

WHOSE FAULT?

Some people think that illness is a punishment from God. This is not true. God can bring good out of it, but God does not cause it. A man who had been born blind was brought to Jesus. Jesus' friends said, "Who sinned? Was it this man? Or was it his parents?" Jesus replied, "His blindness has nothing to do with his sin or his parents' sin. He is blind so that God's power might be seen in him."

JESUS

God does not cut himself off from suffering. God sent his own son, Jesus, to die on the cross (a hideous way to die) so that he might destroy the power of sin, suffering and death.

Paul wrote: "Praise be to the God and father of our Lord Jesus Christ...who comforts us in all our troubles, so that we can comfort those in any trouble..." We are to share God's comfort with people who suffer.

SUNDAY
A DAY OF REST?

Sunday is sometimes called "the Lord's day." It's the day when most Christians go to church.

There are issues about Sundays which concern some Christians. How should they spend the day? Can they work on a Sunday? Should shops stay open?

Should I work on a Sunday?

Should shops open on Sunday?

BEGINNINGS

In Genesis, we are told that God made the world in six days, and rested on the seventh day. He said the seventh day should be a "holy day." This was written into the Ten Commandments. Jews call this day the Sabbath, and celebrate it on Saturday. (See the page on Sabbath.)

JESUS

One Sabbath, Jesus' friends picked and ate some ears of corn. But this counted as work, and when some Pharisees noticed, they told Jesus it was wrong. In reply he said, "The Sabbath was made for man, not man for the Sabbath."

Jesus disagrees with the Pharisees

SUNDAY

Jesus was brought back to life on the first day of the week: Sunday. The first Christians started to meet together every Sunday to praise God for Jesus' resurrection. They held a communion service (the Lord's Supper), and collected money for people in need. But Sunday was still an ordinary working day, not a holiday.

The writer of the Letter to the Hebrews said that Jesus set people free from having to keep Jewish laws. Every day was now filled with the peace of the Sabbath.

THE CHRISTIAN CHURCH

Christians wanted to show that they didn't follow the Jewish faith. So they gradually stopped keeping the Jewish Sabbath. As time went on, church leaders told Christians to keep Sunday as a day for rest and worship. Sunday began to be called the Sabbath.

Paul advised, "One man considers one day more important than another; another man considers every day alike… Do not judge your brother." (See the pages on Church, Work, and Worship.)

Bible Search

- Paul's advice:
Romans 14:5; Colossians 2:16
- Jesus: *Matthew 12:1–12*
- First Christians:
Acts 20:7; 1 Corinthians 16:2
- Singing:
Ephesians 5:19

SUPERSTITION
AND MAGIC

S ome people enjoy studying the mysterious, and turn to things such as magic, reincarnation, aliens, UFOs, and "new age" beliefs to bring meaning to their lives. Bible writers also had to deal with strange ideas, and they give us helpful guidelines.

Bible Search

- Jesus: *John 3:16; 14:6*
- A bonfire: *Acts 19:19*
- Forbidden magic: *Deuteronomy 18:9–13*
- God in control: *Psalm 37:3–5, 23–24*
- Useless astrologers: *Isaiah 47:13*

SUPERSTITION

A superstition is a belief, which is not based on anything true or real, that an object or an action will bring good or bad luck. Jesus set people free from superstition. He said, "I am the way, the truth and the life."

MAGIC

Magic, such as card and conjuring tricks, is harmless. But some people, who call themselves witches and sorcerers, practice black or white magic as a way of getting power. They try to use magic spells to control other people or events. This sort of magic is forbidden in the Bible. To use magic is the opposite of trusting God.

Conjuring tricks are harmless

Some people are superstitious about walking under ladders

FORTUNE-TELLING

Fortune-telling is trying to find out what is going to happen in the future by looking at some sort of object, and taking a meaning from it. In the Bible, fortune-telling is called "divination." The Greeks studied the insides of dead birds to find out the future!

Fortune-tellers today may use cards, or study the palm of a person's hand. Astrologers aim to tell the future from the position of stars, and produce horoscopes. We can read these for fun, but to rely on them shows a lack of love and trust in God.

Reading horoscopes can be fun

STRANGE IDEAS

John wrote to advise Christians how to tell which mystical ideas were harmless, and which were dangerous. If the people teaching these ideas disagreed with any of the following statements, said John, their ideas were wrong.

- Jesus is God and died and rose again.
- Jesus brings love, forgiveness and peace to those who obey him.
- God is in control of all that happens.

SYMBOLS
PICTURES IN WORDS

When two people meet, they often shake hands as a sign of friendship. Sometimes we talk of "waving the flag." It means we are standing up for our country.

These actions and words are symbols. They represent something else, usually an important idea or feeling.

Shaking hands

Waving the flag

THE BIBLE AND SYMBOLS

There are many symbols in the Bible. A rainbow was a symbol of God's promise that he would never flood the Earth again. God told Noah this after the Flood.

When the Israelites were attacked by poisonous snakes in the desert, Moses made a bronze model of a snake, as a symbol of God's power to protect and heal.

When people were baptized, they were washed in water. This was a symbol to show that God forgave them and made them clean from sin.

Bible Search

- Rainbow: *Genesis 9:12–13*
- Healing a blind man: *John 9:1–41*
- Bronze snake: *Numbers 21:4–9*
- Water into wine: *John 2:1–11*

JESUS AND SYMBOLS

Jesus' miracles were symbols in action. John's Gospel calls them "signs." When Jesus healed a blind man he was "saying" that he opened people's eyes to God.

A WEDDING

Jesus was a guest at a wedding in the town of Cana. At the wedding feast, the wine ran out. Jesus told a servant to fill some big water jars with water. The servant poured a drink from one of the jars and gave it to a guest. The guest cried, "You've saved the best wine till last." Only the servant knew that a few minutes before, the wine had been water.

John's Gospel sees this as a symbol that Jesus was bringing something new and exciting out of the old Jewish religion.

THE CROSS

The empty cross is a symbol. Sometimes it stands for the whole Christian faith. It shows God's great love, Jesus' victory over evil, and the forgiveness God gives us when we trust Jesus.

A FISH

ΙΧΘΥC

Early Christians often drew a fish as a symbol of Christianity. The letters of the Greek word for fish, "icthus," were the first letters of the words meaning "Jesus Christ Son of God, Savior."

A synagogue was often built on high ground

SYNAGOGUE

THE CENTRE OF JEWISH LIFE

T he word *synagogue* means a meeting place for Jews. The synagogue was the town hall, day school, law court, community center and welfare office. But chiefly it was the place where people went to learn about God and to pray.

IMPORTANT PLACES

When Jesus was alive, every village had a synagogue. Jerusalem had 394. The Jewish law said that a synagogue could be built wherever there were ten married Jewish men. So there were synagogues throughout the Roman world. Paul went to the synagogues on his travels, to tell people about Jesus.

- Guest preacher Jesus:
  Luke 4:16–21
- Guest preacher Paul:
  Acts 13:14–45
- Law courts:
  Luke 12:11
- Community centers:
  Acts 9:2

INSIDE THE SYNAGOGUE

Jewish teachers said that no one should live higher than a synagogue, so synagogues were built on high ground or part of the building was tall, such as a dome.

The synagogue leaders stood or sat on a raised platform with a reading desk facing Jerusalem. There was a large cupboard, with a curtain in front, called the Ark. Inside were the books of the Old Testament, written out on long scrolls. The Ark was placed to face towards Jerusalem. There were three doors, all facing Jerusalem. Only the men went in by the main door.

Inside a synagogue

GOING TO A SERVICE

Before the service, the floor was rubbed with water mixed with mint.

Men, and boys over thirteen, sat on benches or mats facing the platform. Women, girls and younger boys sat in a gallery, or on one side, behind a screen.

LARGER SYNAGOGUES

The seven-branched candlestick

In larger synagogues, there was a covered passageway with small rooms leading off it. These were used for classrooms or private rooms for guests.

The gallery where women and children sat was supported by columns. These were often decorated with simple paintings or carvings, perhaps of palms, vine leaves, or the seven-branched candlestick. Jews were not allowed to draw or carve people or animals.

TABERNACLE
GOD'S TENT

The Tabernacle

T he Israelites were camped at the foot of Mount Sinai. God told Moses, the leader of the Israelites, to make a special worship tent (*tabernacle* is an old word for tent). It was to be a central place to worship God, and to pray in. It would also be used to offer sacrifices to God.

Bible Search

- Building the Tabernacle: *Exodus 35–40*
- The craftsmen: *Exodus 35:30–36*
- God's glory: *Exodus 40:34–35*

THE TABERNACLE

The Tabernacle was about 45 feet long, 13 feet wide, and 15 feet high. Long upright poles were joined by cross poles made of acacia wood covered with gold. Four layers of coverings were stretched over the top, back and sides. The first was decorated linen. Next came a covering made from goats' hair. Rams' skins, which had been dyed red, were put on top of this and then covered with animal skins to make it all waterproof. Four posts covered with gold and draped with a woolen curtain, made a door.

Inner curtains were woven from blue, purple and scarlet linen.

The Tabernacle was surrounded by an open courtyard. In it was an altar made of wood covered with bronze, used for sacrifices, and a great bronze basin for the priests to wash in.

INSIDE THE TABERNACLE

Inside the Tabernacle was the Holy Place, containing a gold-covered altar, a golden lampstand holding seven lamps, and a gold-covered table. Only the priests and their helpers, the Levites, could go in here.

The Ark of the Covenant was a wooden box covered with gold. Inside were the Ten Commandments, Aaron's rod, and a golden jar of manna (special food sent by God). The Ark of the Covenant was kept in a special area known as the Most Holy Place (also called Holy of Holies). Only the High Priest ever went into the Most Holy Place, and then only once a year.

TASK COMPLETED

The Tabernacle took a year to make. It was set up in the middle of the camp. Then a cloud covered the tent, showing that God was there. The beauty of the tent taught the people about the holiness of God. (See also the pages on Sacrifices and Priests.)

A priest

282

TAX-COLLECTORS
AND TAXES

Paying tax

A tax is money paid to the government towards the cost of ruling a country. In New Testament times, tax-collectors collected taxes for the Romans. There were three sorts of tax: two (called direct and indirect) which were paid to the government; the third was a religious tax which was paid to the Temple at Jerusalem.

Tax-collectors

DIRECT AND INDIRECT TAXES

In Galilee, King Herod charged taxes on all sorts of things: on fishing, salt, olive oil, and on clothes.

In Judea, there was a tax on every male over thirteen. One day, Jesus' enemies asked him if they should pay the tax. They thought that if he answered "Yes", the Jews would hate him. If he said "No," the Romans would arrest him. Jesus said, "Show me a coin." It had Caesar's head on it. "Give to Caesar what belongs to Caesar," he said. "And to God what belongs to God."

Indirect taxes were taxes on goods people wanted to sell. Tax kiosks were set up on bridges, at town gates, at markets and crossroads.

Bible Search

- A tax riot: *Acts 5:37*

- Matthew the tax-collector: *Matthew 9:9*

- A tricky question: *Matthew 22:15–21*

- John the Baptist's advice to tax-collectors: *Luke 3:13*

TAX-COLLECTORS

The Romans divided the country into areas. In each area, businessmen made bids for the right to collect the taxes. The highest bidder agreed to pay the Romans a sum of money every year. Any money he took on top of that was his own. There was massive over-charging. Tax-collectors were loathed because they worked for the enemy, and were often thieves as well.

YOUR CART TOO

If you went to the market to sell figs, you were charged tax. If you didn't have many figs to sell, the tax-collector might decide to charge you for your cart, and for each wheel on your cart! He made up taxes to suit himself, and no one could prove that they weren't real taxes.

To find out more about taxes and tax-collectors, see the pages on Matthew, Priests, Levites, and Zacchaeus.

Market taxes

TEMPLE
IN THE NEW TESTAMENT

- Watch your step: *Ecclesiastes 5:1*
- Jesus' friends admire the Temple: *Mark 13:1–2*
- The curtain split in two: *Matthew 27:51*

Bible Search

I n 19 B.C. King Herod began to rebuild the Temple in Jerusalem. He didn't do it in order to worship God, but to make the people think he was a great man. His Temple was magnificent. In A.D. 56 it was finished. In A.D. 70 the Romans destroyed it.

First, Herod built an enormous stone platform across the flat top of Mount Moriah. It was the largest structure in the ancient world.

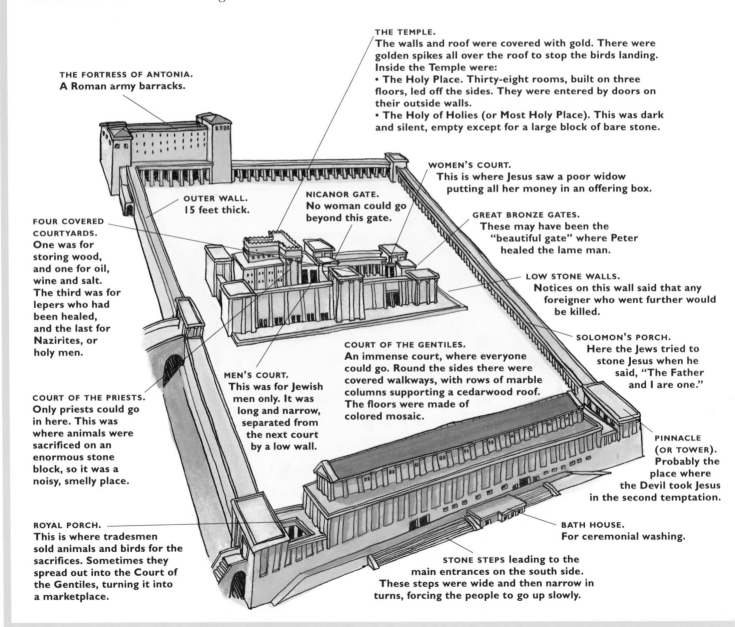

THE TEMPLE.
The walls and roof were covered with gold. There were golden spikes all over the roof to stop the birds landing. Inside the Temple were:
• The Holy Place. Thirty-eight rooms, built on three floors, led off the sides. They were entered by doors on their outside walls.
• The Holy of Holies (or Most Holy Place). This was dark and silent, empty except for a large block of bare stone.

THE FORTRESS OF ANTONIA.
A Roman army barracks.

OUTER WALL.
15 feet thick.

NICANOR GATE.
No woman could go beyond this gate.

WOMEN'S COURT.
This is where Jesus saw a poor widow putting all her money in an offering box.

GREAT BRONZE GATES.
These may have been the "beautiful gate" where Peter healed the lame man.

FOUR COVERED COURTYARDS.
One was for storing wood, and one for oil, wine and salt. The third was for lepers who had been healed, and the last for Nazirites, or holy men.

LOW STONE WALLS.
Notices on this wall said that any foreigner who went further would be killed.

SOLOMON'S PORCH.
Here the Jews tried to stone Jesus when he said, "The Father and I are one."

MEN'S COURT.
This was for Jewish men only. It was long and narrow, separated from the next court by a low wall.

COURT OF THE GENTILES.
An immense court, where everyone could go. Round the sides there were covered walkways, with rows of marble columns supporting a cedarwood roof. The floors were made of colored mosaic.

COURT OF THE PRIESTS.
Only priests could go in here. This was where animals were sacrificed on an enormous stone block, so it was a noisy, smelly place.

PINNACLE (OR TOWER).
Probably the place where the Devil took Jesus in the second temptation.

ROYAL PORCH.
This is where tradesmen sold animals and birds for the sacrifices. Sometimes they spread out into the Court of the Gentiles, turning it into a marketplace.

BATH HOUSE.
For ceremonial washing.

STONE STEPS leading to the main entrances on the south side. These steps were wide and then narrow in turns, forcing the people to go up slowly.

TEMPTATION

Temptation is when an idea comes into our mind to do something we should not do. Jesus himself was tempted. The New Testament says: "He was tempted in every way, just as we are, yet was without sin." This verse shows that it's not wrong to be tempted, only to give in to the temptation.

THE CAUSE

James wrote, "Never say 'God is tempting me… God does not tempt anyone.' " Temptation comes from evil outside us, or from our own mixed-up natures. (Look at the page on the Devil.)

THE TEMPTATION OF JESUS

The Bible shows us two times when Jesus was tempted, and how he beat the temptation:
• With the Bible.
For forty days, Jesus prayed by himself in the lonely desert, and there the Devil tempted him. Each time a temptation came, Jesus hit back with a verse from the Bible. He used the Bible like a sword.

Jesus prays

• With prayer.
On the night Jesus was captured, he lay on the ground in the Garden of Gethsemene, and prayed to God. He asked God to spare him the death that was to come, if possible. But only if that was what God wanted.

CRASH

Everybody, except Jesus, gives in to temptation. What then? John told his friends what to do: if they confessed their sins, God would forgive them. We can trust God. He does what is right. He will make us clean from all the wrongs we have done.

If we confess our sins, God will forgive us

PETER

The night Jesus was arrested, the disciples became very scared. Peter was asked by three different people if he knew Jesus. But three times he swore that he did not. Later, Jesus forgave him and helped him to start again. Peter became one of the leaders of the Christian Church.

Three times, Peter denies knowing Jesus

Bible Search

• Jesus is tempted: *Matthew 4:1–11; 26:41*

• Jesus understands: *Hebrews 2:18; 4:15–16*

• Forgiveness: *1 John 1:9*

• The sword: *Ephesians 6:17*

Jesus used the Bible like a sword

TEN COMMANDMENTS

GOD'S LAWS

It is wrong to steal

God rescued the Israelites from slavery in Egypt. Now they needed guidance on how to live as God's people. Moses went up Mount Sinai, and there God gave him the Ten Commandments.

The commandments fall into two groups. The first four are about how to live with God. The second six are about getting along with other people.

THE TEN COMMANDMENTS

1. You shall have no other gods before me.
(God must come first in your life.)
2. You shall not make for yourself an idol in the form of anything in the heaven above, or the earth beneath, or in the waters below. You shall not bow down to them or worship them.
(You must not make any images to worship. God is invisible. You must worship only God.)

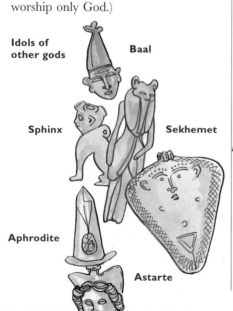

Idols of other gods

Baal

Sphinx

Sekhemet

Aphrodite

Astarte

3. You shall not misuse the name of the Lord your God.
(God's name is not a magic charm.)

4. Remember the Sabbath day by keeping it holy.
(One day in seven is for rest and worship.)

5. Honour your father and mother.
(Respect your parents.)

Respect your parents

6. You shall not murder.
7. You shall not commit adultery.
(Do not have a love affair with someone else's husband or wife.)

8. You shall not steal.
9. You shall not give false testimony against your neighbour.
(You must not tell lies about anyone in a court of law.)
10. You shall not covet your neighbour's house....or anything that belongs to your neighbour.
(You must not long to have something that is not yours.)

A SUMMARY

One day, Jesus was asked which was the most important commandment. He quoted from two places in the Old Testament:

• "Love the Lord your God with all your heart, and with all your soul, and with all your mind, and with all your heart."

• "Love your neighbor as yourself."

In these words, Jesus summed up the Ten Commandments.

Bible Search

• Ten Commandments:
Exodus 20: 1–17;
Mark 12: 28–31

• Written on stone:
Exodus 24:12

TENTMAKERS
AND TANNERS

I n Greece and Rome, the rulers looked down on everyone who had to work for a living. It was the opposite in Palestine. "He who does not teach his son a trade teaches him robbery," they said. The apostle Paul wrote with pride that he earned money for himself and his friends by making tents.

Although Jews thought that it was good to work, some jobs were regarded more highly than others. Tanners were at the very bottom of the list. They had to work with dead bodies of animals, which the Jews thought were "unclean" (made you unfit to worship God). Also, it was very smelly work! Tanners had to work outside towns and villages, in places where the wind would not blow smells back into the town.

A tanner would prepare a hide like this:
- Skin the animal.
- Remove hairs from the skin (by scraping, soaking and rubbing in lime).
- Soak the skin in water.
- Rub in animal manure.
- Hammer until soft and flat.

HOW TO MAKE A TENT

This is how Abraham and his sons might have made a tent.
- Get some goat or camel skins.
- Sew them together. Attach wooden toggles around the edges.

- Drive poles into the ground.

- Place the skins over the poles.

A tent

- Tie a rope to the wooden toggles. Tie the other end of the rope to tent-pegs sunk into the ground.

GOATS' HAIR

In New Testament times, goats' hair was used to make tents. It was woven into very long strips. The hair of goats and camels was particularly good for making tents, as it was waterproof.

Paul came from Tarsus, close to Cilicia. Here the very best goats' hair, called cilicium, was found.

LEATHER-WORKERS

Even after tents were no longer made from animals' skins but from goats' hair, tentmakers were usually also craftsmen in leather. They made items such as water-bottles, belts, leather slings, helmets, shields and sandals.

A tanner at work

Bible Search

- Paul: *Acts 18:3; 20:34*
- Peter: *Acts 9:43*
- Black goat's hair: *Song of Songs 1:5*
- Don't be idle: *2 Thessalonians 3:6–13*

THANKS AND PRAISE

The words *thanks* and *praise* often come together in the Bible. We thank God because everything is a gift from him. Praising God means sharing in and showing the greatness and joy of God.

A psalmist wrote: "Sing to the Lord with thanksgiving… He covers the sky with clouds; he supplies the earth with rain and makes grass grow on the hills. He provides food for the cattle… ."

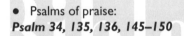

Bible Search

- Psalms of praise:
  Psalm 34, 135, 136, 145–150
- In prison:
  Acts 16:16–40
- Thanks for everything:
  Ephesians 5:20

THANKS FOR EVERYTHING

Paul and Silas were beaten and thrown into prison. In prison they prayed and sang hymns to God. Paul wrote: "Give thanks in all circumstances, this is God's will for you." He also said, "Make music in your hearts to the Lord, always giving thanks to God the Father for everything… ."

PAUL IN CORINTH

Jesus died on the cross and rose again. He did this to set us free from the power of evil. Paul said, "Thanks be to God! He gives us the victory through our Lord Jesus Christ." And Peter said, "…declare the praises of him who called you out of darkness into his marvelous light."

PRAISE FOR COMFORT

Paul wrote: "Praise be to the God and Father of our Lord Jesus Christ…who comforts us in all our troubles, so that we can comfort those in any trouble with the comfort we ourselves have received from God."

PRAISE FOR HEALING

One day Jesus healed ten lepers. Nine went rushing off, but one came back to thank Jesus. "Where are the other nine?" Jesus asked. "Did they not want to praise God?"

SACRIFICE OF PRAISE

The Letter to the Hebrews says: "Through Jesus, therefore, let us continually offer to God a sacrifice of praise… ." This means a sacrifice where we let go of what we want in order to do something for God.

THANKS FOR FRIENDS

Paul often wrote to his friends, "We always thank God for all of you…", meaning that he thanked God for the good things about friends.

THESSALONIANS
THE FIRST AND SECOND
LETTER TO

T he apostle Paul went to the city of Thessalonica in Greece with his friend Silas. He stayed about three weeks, teaching Christianity in the synagogue. He was so successful that the Jews hired a mob to get him into trouble. Paul had to escape in the dark. Not long afterwards, when he was in Corinth, he wrote the first of these letters. The second was written about six months later.

Paul escapes from Thessalonica

THESSALONICA

The city of Thessalonica was the chief city of Macedonia (northern Greece). It was on the main Roman highway to the East, the Egnatian Way. Thessalonica was a busy, rich town, and a port.

Thessalonica

UNDERSTANDING 1 THESSALONIANS

Paul sent Timothy to help the Christians in Thessalonica. When Timothy came back, he reported that things were going well. Paul was so delighted, he wrote to the Thessalonians at once. He also answered some of their questions, such as what would happen to Christians that had died when Jesus came again? Paul answered that they would be with Jesus when he came again.

UNDERSTANDING 2 THESSALONIANS

In 2 Thessalonians, Paul answered more questions about Jesus' return. For example:
- "When is Jesus coming again?" "Has he already come?" "Will he come soon?"
- Paul's answer: 'He has not come yet. Before he comes again 'the lawless one" will appear. The lawless one is the leader of the last rebellion against God. He will be unmasked, and then for a time all hell will be let loose. But Jesus will destroy him and his assistants."

The Thessalonians had many questions for Paul

READING THESSALONIANS

1 Thessalonians
- *Chapter 1–3*: Paul's congratulations.
- *Chapter 4–5*: Be ready for Jesus' return.

2 Thessalonians
- *Chapter 1*: Stand firm under attack.
- *Chapter 2*: Coming events.
- *Chapter 3*: Don't be lazy.

Bible Search

- A famous prayer: *1 Thessalonians 5:23*
- How to live: *1 Thessalonians 5:16*
- Paul in Thessalonica: *Acts 17:1–10*

289

TIMOTHY
THE FIRST LETTER OF PAUL TO

Paul wrote this letter to his friend Timothy in Ephesus. Paul had spent three years in Ephesus, and had left Timothy there to carry on his work. Paul sent good advice to Timothy in the letter. (Look also at the pages on Ephesians and 2 Timothy.)

"Don't argue all the time."

"Welcome strangers."

"Set a good example."

FACTFILE ON TIMOTHY

Grandmother: Lois (a Jew who loved God).
Mother: Eunice (also a Jew who loved God).

Lois

Eunice

Father: A Greek (who probably didn't love God).
Home town: Lystra (in modern-day Turkey).
Faith: Became a follower of Jesus through Paul's preaching.
Experience: He traveled with Paul on some of his missionary adventures. He was was with Paul when Paul was in prison in Rome.
Work: To choose and train Christian leaders.
Character: Shy and sensitive.
Health: Poor.
Later news: The Letter to the Hebrews tells us Timothy was in prison and then set free. Paul wrote a second letter to Timothy.

UNDERSTANDING I TIMOTHY

Timothy was young. He needed help and encouragement. Paul said: "Don't let anyone look down on you because you are young."

As the Christian Church spread, and as the first followers of Jesus died, it became important that the right leaders should carry on their work. Paul wrote that a church leader should have self-control, welcome strangers to his home, be a good teacher of the Christian faith, be gentle and peaceful, and have a happy

"Don't let anyone look down on you because you are young."

BEING A CHRISTIAN

Paul wrote a list of what Christians should and should not do. He said:

- Don't be a lover of money.
- Don't argue all the time.
- Do have faith.
- Do have love.
- Do be patient.
- Do set a good example.

READING I TIMOTHY

- *Chapter 1:1–11*: Warning about false teachers.
- *Chapter 1:12–20*: God's goodness to Paul.
- *Chapter 2:1–15*: Rules about public worship.
- *Chapter 3:1–16*: Leaders in the Church.
- *Chapter 4:1–16*: Dealing with false teaching.
- *Chapter 5:1–6:2*: People in the Church.
- *Chapter 6:3–21*: Living in the right way.

TIMOTHY

THE SECOND LETTER
OF PAUL TO

aul was in prison in Rome when he wrote this letter to Timothy. This time he was probably not under house arrest, as in his first imprisonment, but chained up in a dungeon. This is the last letter we have from Paul. He was beheaded by the Roman emperor Nero, probably not long after writing to Timothy.

Paul in prison

PAUL

Paul was lonely and cold. Twice he told Timothy to come to see him, and he asked him to bring his coat. Everyone had left Paul except Luke. But Paul said, "The Lord stood by my side and gave me strength."

UNDERSTANDING 2 TIMOTHY

Now that Nero was the Roman emperor, the small groups of Christians throughout the Roman empire were in extra danger. Paul saw trouble and suffering ahead. He wrote his letter to help Timothy not to be afraid.

Timothy was a young leader in the Christian Church. He found it hard to stand up to others. (See also Paul's first letter to Timothy.)

'Be brave!'

ATHLETE AND SOLDIER

Paul compared Timothy to an athlete and a soldier. An athlete has to keep to the rules of the race. Timothy was a "runner" for Jesus. His "rules" were goodness, faith, love and peace.

A soldier puts up with troubles, and wants to please his commanding officer. Paul told Timothy to be a good soldier of Jesus Christ, and not to be ashamed to tell people about Jesus.

FOOLISH ARGUMENTS

Ignoring arguments

False teachers were on the prowl among the Christians. Their poisonous teaching was spreading like a disease. Paul's advice was: "Don't have anything to do with foolish and stupid arguments, because you know they produce quarrels. And the Lord's servant must not quarrel."

READING 2 TIMOTHY

- *Chapter 1*: Fatherly advice.
- *Chapter 2*: Advice to Christian workers.
- *Chapter 3*: The last days.
- *Chapter 4*: Paul's last words.

Timothy was a "runner" for Jesus

- An athlete: *2 Timothy 2:5; 2:22*
- A soldier: *2 Timothy 2:3*
- Be brave: *2 Timothy 1:7–8*
- The Bible: *2 Timothy 3:14–17*
- False teachers: *2 Timothy 2:16–19*

Bible Search

TITUS THE LETTER TO

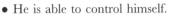

P aul was an old man when he wrote this letter to his friend Titus. Titus became a Christian as a result of Paul's preaching. He was one of Paul's best friends and helpers. Paul wrote to the Corinthians, "God comforted me by the coming of Titus."

Paul and Titus had visited Crete together, and Titus had stayed on to teach and help the members of the young Christian Church.

Titus

Bible Search

- Christian leaders: *Titus 1:5–9*
- Cretans are liars: *Titus 1:12*
- In a nutshell: *Titus 3:4–7*
- A holiday: *Titus 3:12*

- He is able to control himself.
- He wants to live in God's way.
- He agrees with Paul's teachings about Jesus.
- He knows how to teach and help other Christians.
- He can answer arguments of non-Christians.

He has only one wife and Christian children

He is not proud, selfish, or bad-tempered

He does not get into fights

He does not drink too much

CRETE

Crete is an island in the Mediterranean Sea, between Sicily and Cyprus. In Bible times, there was a saying about the people of Crete: "Cretans are always liars, evil brutes, lazy gluttons." They lied so much that the Greeks made up a new word: *Cretize*, meaning "to lie."

Cretans

UNDERSTANDING TITUS

Titus had to choose leaders for the Christian Church in Crete, and to teach the new Christians how to live as followers of Jesus. Paul wrote to give Titus advice. He gave Titus the following checklist for finding a Christian leader:

- He does not do wrong things.
- He has only one wife.
- He has Christian children.
- He is able to control his children.
- He is not proud.
- He is not selfish.
- He is not bad-tempered.
- He doesn't drink too much.
- He doesn't get into fights.
- He doesn't rob and cheat to get money.
- He invites people to stay at his house.
- He loves goodness.

READING TITUS

- *Chapter 1*: Qualities needed in Christian leaders.
- *Chapter 2*: Advice to young and old, men and women.
- *Chapter 3*: How to live as a Christian.

TOWNS AND VILLAGES

Most people lived in villages. Villages were often very small, with perhaps only a few hundred people living there. In Old Testament times, the difference between a village and a town was that a town had a wall around it. By New Testament times, the difference was that a town had a court of law and judges. Towns and villages were usually built on hills.

VILLAGE LIFE

In Old Testament times, most village people were farmers. They worked in the fields surrounding the village, and sold their produce in the town markets. If an enemy attacked, the village people escaped to the nearest walled town.

TOWNS OR CITIES

Nearly all towns (sometimes called cities) in Old Testament times were small, with about 250 houses and 1,000 inhabitants. Houses were crowded together: sometimes you could cross a town by striding from one flat roof to another!

There were a few streets, and a maze of alleyways twisted between the houses. These often got filled with garbage and trash.

Crossing the town

MARKETS

Markets were held every day by the city gates. Craftsmen and traders sometimes put their goods on show outside their workshops. In larger towns, craftsmen were often grouped together on the same street.

CITY GATES

The noisy, crowded area around the city gates was the heart of the town. Each town had massive wooden gates, often covered with iron and bolted with strong bronze bars. Here business deals were made, lawsuits agreed, and notices nailed up. Beggars pleaded for help, and the city leaders met to talk.

ROMAN-STYLE TOWNS

A narrow street

Some of the towns we read about in the New Testament were built like Roman towns. King Herod rebuilt Samaria and Caesarea with a wide main street lined with shops and theatres, and smaller streets crossing neatly at right-angles. There were public baths, and the houses were built in blocks of four.

A market

Bible Search

- Walls:
  Deuteronomy 1:28, 3:5
- A fortified city:
  Jeremiah 34:7
- Street of the bakers:
  Jeremiah 37:21

TRAVEL
BY LAND

Traveling was uncomfortable and dangerous. It was easy to get lost, and there were many robbers who attacked travelers.

ROADS

In Old Testament times, the only roads were tracks. The tracks were given grand names, such as "The Way of the Sea" and "The King's Highway," but they didn't live up to their names. In 1200 B.C., an Egyptian wrote that roads in Canaan were "filled with boulders and pebbles...overgrown with reeds, thorns and brambles".

When a king or ruler was traveling, someone would go ahead to repair the roads.

A road in Canaan

ROMAN ROADS

The Romans were the first to make good roads. Their 50,000 miles of straight roads made as much impact on their world as the inventions of the train, car and plane have in this century. Roman armies and messengers could now travel quickly to any part of the empire.

Only soldiers and government messengers were allowed to use the roads. Other travelers had to walk alongside!

The roads were made of a layer of sand, a layer of stone, and a layer of crushed stones mixed with cement. This was topped with large paving stones sloping to gutters on each side. Mileposts were put up every 1,480 miles.

Roman shops sold maps showing the network of Roman roads.

A Roman road

TRANSPORT

Most people walked, or rode donkeys. Camels were used to travel long distances across the desert to trade.

Carts, drawn by oxen, were not suited to the rocky hill tracks of Palestine, but they were sometimes used to carry farm produce.

TRAVEL FOR THE RICH

In New Testament times, wealthy and important people traveled by four-wheeled horse-drawn chariots. Very rich people could hire a two-wheeled chariot called an essedom, and drive themselves.

The most luxurious way to travel was in a litter carried by slaves.

You can read more about travel on the page on Letters.

Bible Search

- Road repairing:
  Isaiah 62:10
- Robbers on the road:
  Luke 10:30
- Donkey transport:
  I Samuel 25:18–25

TRAVEL BY SEA

Many Jews were frightened of the power of the sea. If you escaped being shipwrecked, then you risked being killed by pirates. Usually, the only people who traveled by sea were soldiers and traders. The Egyptians and Phoenicians were skilled boat-builders.

SOLOMON'S NAVY

Only one king of Israel ever built a navy: King Solomon. To do this, Solomon made a deal with the best sailors and boat-builders around: the Phoenicians.

FISHING BOATS

The Sea of Galilee is not a sea but a large inland lake. When Jesus wanted to cross to the other side, he went by fishing boat. All fishing boats had oars, and some had sails. Jesus and his twelve disciples could just squash into one boat. To find out more, turn to the page on Fishing.

A pirate

Bible Search

- Solomon's ships:
  1 Kings 10:22

- Paul's sea trip to Rome:
  Acts 27:1–44; 28:11–13

- Paul's adventures at sea:
  2 Corinthians 11:25–26

- Jesus in a storm:
  Mark 4:35–41

PAUL AT SEA

Paul had some hair-raising experiences at sea. Luke's account of the time Paul was shipwrecked is one of the best descriptions of a sea journey in ancient literature.

Paul would have traveled on a grain ship. It would have had a sculpted figure on the bow (front), representing the name of the ship. Sailors liked to think their boats were people. Often they painted an eye on each side of the bow.

A central mast supported a square mainsail and a small topsail. A small sail at the front, called a foresail, was used to help with steering.

The back of the ship, called the stern, was often built up into the shape of a goose's neck, topped with a goose's head.

Two large oars in the stern took the place of an underwater rudder. There were three heavy anchors.

CREW AND PASSENGERS

There were no passenger ships. Travelers slept on the deck of cargo ships, and brought their own mattresses, food and dishes. There were 276 people on Paul's ship.

There were no compasses. The captain judged his position by the stars.

Travelers brought their own mattresses

TREES IN THE BIBLE

Many hills in Israel that are bare today were covered with woods in Bible times. Trees were important for building and making furniture. Some trees were important as a source of food, especially fruit trees. "When you capture a city... do not cut down its fruit trees," said the laws given by Moses to the Israelites.

The Ark of the Covenant

FIG
Adam and Eve's first clothes were made from the large leaves of a fig tree. Dried figs were a source of iron in soldiers' rations.

CEDAR
The country of Lebanon was famous for its forests of giant cedar trees. The people of Israel thought that this beautiful evergreen tree was the greatest of all trees. The long-lasting, sweet-scented red wood of the cedar was prized for making furniture, carved panelling and important buildings. The cedar did not grow in Israel, so it had to be imported from Lebanon.

ACACIA
The acacia was one of the few trees that grew in the desert. Its wood was light and hard-wearing. Acacia was used to make the frame of God's desert worship tent (the Tabernacle) and the Ark of the Covenant.

POPLAR
The Israelites were taken to Babylonia as prisoners. They were too sad to sing in this new place. They hung up their harps on poplar trees, and sat crying by the riverside.

SYCAMORE
(This is a type of fig tree, different than our sycamore tree.) The sycamore was the tree that Zacchaeus climbed to see Jesus. Its branches grew low down, so it was easy to climb.

ANY QUESTIONS
1 Why did Zacchaeus choose to climb a sycamore tree to see Jesus?
2 Which trees were used as a source of food?

OAK
In Old Testament times, many peoples thought that oak trees were were holy. Arabs today still bury their dead under oak trees.

PALM
This was often used as a symbol for victory. People waved palm leaves when Jesus rode into Jerusalem as their king. Palm trees produced dates: an important food.

CAROB
This was a common tree. In Jesus' story of the prodigal son, pigs were fed on the sweet bean pods of the carob tree.

Bible Search

- Fruit trees:
Deuteronomy 20:19

- Dried figs:
1 Samuel 25:18

- Palms for victory:
John 12–13

- A sad song Babylon:
Psalm 137:2

TRINITY OF GOD

T rinity is a way of describing God. The word was first used by early Christians. They said, "God is one God. But he is not single. He is three: Father, Son and Holy Spirit." God the Father, God the Son, and God the Holy Spirit are often called "the persons of the Trinity."

- Jesus' last orders: *Matthew 28:18*
- Jesus speaks to Philip about God's three dimensions: *John 14:9–12*
- Paul's trinitarian prayer: *2 Corinthians 13:14*

ONE GOD

God gave Moses the Ten Commandments, to show the Israelites how they must live. The first commandment said, "I am the Lord your God...You shall have no other god."

Other countries had lots of gods. One of the things that made the Jews special, was the fact that they worshiped one God.

In the Bible, the Holy Spirit is often represented as a dove

Jesus prays

THE FATHER

Jesus often went to a lonely place to pray. And when he prayed, he spoke to God as "Father." He taught his friends that God was their loving father.

JESUS

Jesus at the Last Supper

The night before he was arrested, Jesus and the disciples ate a last meal together. During the meal, Philip said, "Show us the Father." And Jesus replied, "Anyone who has seen me, has seen the Father."

Slowly, the disciples became sure that Jesus was God. (See the page on Jesus is God.)

THE HOLY SPIRIT

Jesus' friends were praying in an upstairs room when the Holy Spirit came to them. They became sure that the Holy Spirit was truly God, carrying out his actions. (See the pages on the Holy Spirit.)

THE TRINITY

The Trinity is God the Father, God the Son, and God the Holy Spirit. The Trinity is not three separate gods, or one God with three different names. It means that God has three aspects, just as space has three dimensions of height, width and depth. The Hebrew word for God is *Elohim*, which is a plural word.

It is hard to understand the Trinity. But it is the only explanation that fits the facts in the Bible. Paul's prayer helps to make it clear. He said, "The grace of the Lord Jesus Christ, the love of God, and the fellowship of the Holy Spirit be with you."

TRUTH AND LIES

Truth is what is real. God is truth we can rely on. Many people can't face the truth about God. It was the same in Paul's day: "They exchanged the truth of God for a lie," said Paul.

Jesus said, "I am the truth." About the Devil, Jesus said, "There is no truth in him. He is a liar and the father (the starting-point) of lies."

It's my best one.

JESUS

After his arrest, Jesus was eventually brought before Pilate, the Roman governor. Jesus said, "Everyone on the side of truth listens to me." "And what is truth?" Pilate asked. He didn't need to hear a reply. He was staring at the truth: Jesus.

Jesus and Pilate

Bible Search

- What God wants: *Psalm 51:6*
- Lies instead of truth: *Romans 1:18–23*
- Word of truth: *Ephesians 1:13*
- Father of lies: *John 8:44*

LIVING TRUTH

Jesus said, "If you hold to my teaching you will know the truth, and the truth will set you free." The way to experience truth is to obey Jesus. Paul called the good news about Jesus 'the word of truth'.

LIES

I didn't do it!

God doesn't love me.

HYPOCRITES!

Jesus was furious with those Pharisees who said they loved God, but whose actions were unloving. Their lives were a lie. "You hypocrites!" said Jesus. The word "hypocrite" means "play-actor." The Pharisees often said long prayers in front of people, hoping everyone was admiring them!

A HAPPY MAN

When Jesus first saw Bartholomew, he was sitting under a fig tree. Jesus described him as "a true man in whom there is nothing false". This was the highest praise.

A psalmist said, "Happy the man in whose spirit there is no deceit (lies)." "God wants inner truth," said David.

The Israelites were very welcoming

VISITORS
A WELCOME FOR STRANGERS

In the time of Abraham, the Israelites lived in tents in the desert area of Canaan, which was a vast, lonely, dangerous place. The Israelites thought it their duty to welcome travelers. It was considered evil to turn someone away, as he might die in the desert from a lack of food and water. From this time on, welcoming visitors became a custom.

Bible Search

- Abraham: *Genesis 18:1–15*
- Moses: *Exodus 2:15–17*
- A neighbour: *Luke 11:5–13*
- Welcome visitors: *Romans 12:13; Hebrews 13:2*

STRANGERS IN TOWN

In Old Testament times, there were no inns or cafes. Later, there were some inns, but most were not pleasant places. A stranger arriving in town would sit by the town well, or by the city gates, and wait to be invited to someone's home.

A stranger by a well

IN A RUSH

Abraham was sitting at the opening of his tent when three strangers came into view. He rushed to meet them, but didn't ask them their names, as this would not have been polite. Abraham quickly chose one of his best calves, and his servant hurried to prepare a meal for the guests.

GREETINGS

When an important visitor arrived, the host made a low bow. Friends were kissed on both cheeks. Water was then provided to wash the visitor's hot, dusty feet. Refreshing, perfumed oil might be poured on the guest's head.

A meal was prepared and served, and the host stood while his guest ate. Introductions were only made at the end of the meal.

The host bowed when visitors arrived

Visitors' feet were washed

HELP!

Jesus told a story about a man who had an unexpected visitor late at night. To his horror, he discovered that he had no food to offer his guest. He rushed to his neighbor and woke him up. He would not go away until his angry neighbor gave him some bread. (Jesus used the story to show that God answers our prayers!)

A visitor who stayed more than two or three days was expected to contribute towards the cost of food.

WASHING AND TOILETS

Keeping clean was very important. Jewish teachers taught that to wash well was better than any medicine. Washing helped to prevent the spread of diseases. The Romans brought sewage systems and public baths to Palestine.

TOILETS AND DRAINS

Toilets did not have pipes leading to underground sewers. In towns, people emptied buckets into gutters, and the sewage drained away in open drains. But the Romans did have sewage systems. King Herod rebuilt Caesarea and Samaria using Roman towns as his model for a sewage system. Near Caesarea, archaeologists have found pipes which emptied sewage into the sea. There was also a drainage and sewage system in Herod's Temple in Jerusalem. Toilets were 'flushed' by a small stream which flowed under them.

- Abraham's first words to his visitors:
  Genesis 18:3-5

- Rudeness to Jesus:
  Luke 7:44

- Kinds of soap:
  Jeremiah 2:22

The ruins of Herod's bathhouse

FOOT WASHING

Today, when people come in from a journey, they often freshen up by washing their hands and face. In Bible times, people washed their feet. It was extremely bad manners not to wash the feet of your guests. If you were rich enough to have a slave, this would be the slave's job.

BATHING

Bathing was done at the public baths, if the town had one, or in the river or a spring. By the time of the New Testament, more and more towns followed the Roman custom and built public baths.

People also washed as a sign that they wanted to be fit to worship God. You can read more about this on the page on Worship.

CLEANING TEETH

There were no toothbrushes. 'Scented pepper' was used to sweeten the breath. This was probably a variety of aniseed.

SOAP

A very rough soap was made from sodium carbonate and fat, or fat mixed with the ashes of plants that had soda in them. To make themselves smell nice, people rubbed herbs, such as rosemary or marjoram, on their bodies.

WATER
FOR LIFE

There was no rain at all from June to September. In October and March, there was some heavy rain, but it only lasted for a few days. Light rain fell in hilly areas from October to May. So, there was not much rain, and water was very precious. The lives of the people depended on springs, wells and streams.

- Friendship: *John 4:7-15*
- Hezekiah's tunnel: *2 Chronicles 32:30-31*
- Enemies: *Genesis 26:15*
- A well-digging song: *Numbers 21:17-18*

KING HEZEKIAH'S TUNNEL

Jerusalem had no spring. People had to go outside the city to get water. King Hezekiah was worried that if an enemy army surrounded the city, they would be cut off from their supply of water. So he instructed his builders to cut an underground tunnel through solid rock. His workmen started digging from both ends and met in the middle. You can still see the tunnel today. It was a brilliant piece of engineering.

WELLS

In the earliest times written about in the Old Testament, no one had found a way of storing large supplies of water. It had to be fetched from a well in jars. Every town had many wells. Older girls were often given the job of collecting well water.

A quick way of declaring war was to fill your enemies' wells with earth and rocks.

CISTERNS

A cistern was a pear-shaped pit for holding water. At first, cisterns were cut out of limestone rock. Later, people found out how to dig pits in the ground and waterproof them with plaster made from lime.

MAKING FRIENDS

Do you want to show you are friends with someone? Today you might say, "Have a cookie." In Bible times you asked for, or offered, a drink of water.

UNDERGROUND POOLS

In New Testament times, some towns had giant man-made pools, or reservoirs. The water from the reservoirs flowed to the towns through canals and stone or clay pipes.

The Romans built aqueducts (canals that went over bridges) to bring water from mountain springs to the towns.

WEATHER
AND TIME

The cold, wet winter

There were only two named seasons: the cold, wet winter, called the rainy season, and the hot, dry summer, called the dry season. There were twelve months in a year. By the time of the New Testament, the Jews followed the Babylonian system of naming the months.

The hot, dry summer

YEARS

Every country had its own system for dating years. This was rather confusing. At first the Jews used important events, or the reign of kings, as a dating system. In Jesus' time, some Jews dated the years from the date the Romans took over the land. Other people dated time from the year we would call 3761 B.C., when they thought the world began.

MONTHS

For the Jews, a month began on the first day of the new moon, which gave 354 days a year. This was too short, because the Earth takes 365 days to go round the sun. So every few years, the Jews added an extra month.

A new moon

DAYS AND WEEKS

A week of seven days goes back to the very earliest times, and was made law by Moses. A new day began at sunset, when the day's work was over. Every seventh day was called "the Sabbath," and the day before was "he Preparation." Other days were known by numbers: the first day of the week, the second, and so on.

A new day began at sunset

Bible Search

- New Year's Day: *Leviticus 23:24*
- Hours: *Matthew 20:1–6*
- Dates: *Amos 1:1*
- Days: *Matthew 27:62; 28:1*

HOURS

There were no hours in Old Testament times. Time was described more generally, such as morning, middle of the day, or the time of the evening sacrifice.

When Jesus was alive, a day was divided into twelve hours. Because daylight lasted longer in summer, an hour in summer was longer than an hour in winter.

Nights were not divided into hours but into "watches," that is, a fixed period of time when a sentry was on duty. In New Testament times, there were four watches in a night: evening, midnight, cockcrow and dawn.

The Greeks and Romans told the time with sundials or with water clocks.

A sentry on watch duty

Weaving

WEAVERS
AND CLOTH

Clothes were made from wool

I n Bible times, most everyday clothes were made from wool. Many women made their own clothes. Sometimes they made the material too, by spinning wool into thread, dyeing it, and weaving it into cloth!

A long spindle was used to spin the wool into thick thread. The spindle was a stick of wood with a hook at one end and a whorl (a heavy stone or piece of clay) at the other.

FULLER

A fuller's job was to wash wool and cloth. When a fleece was shorn from a sheep, it needed to be clean. The fuller dipped the material in water, beat it, washed it and bleached it in the sun. Fullers worked outside the town, close to water.

A fuller

DYEING

Often, thread was left in its natural colors of white, brown and black. Sometimes it was dyed. The most expensive color was purple. Purple was a sign of power, and religious teachers did not approve of it.

WEAVING

Nearly every home had a loom for weaving cloth. Early looms were horizontal, and were pegged out on the ground. The shuttle which held the thread was passed from side to side, first of all going over and then under the large warp (vertical) threads. Later, vertical looms were invented, and weights were attached to the warp threads to keep them taut.

EMBROIDERY

Clothes were often decorated with embroidery, and the Jews were probably very skilled at this work. Complicated patterns were stitched in the popular colors of green, black, yellow and red. Gold thread, made from real gold, was sometimes used. Archaeologists have found many needles used for this type of work.

In the Bible, the word *embroidery* may also describe patterns made as the material was woven, or quilting and tapestry work.

Bible Search

- Purple cloth: *Acts 16:14*

- Jesus' seamless tunic: *John 19:23–24*

- Embroidery: *Exodus 26:36; 39:3*

A vertical loom

WEDDINGS
A BUSINESS DEAL

A marriage was a business deal fixed up between two families. Love came second. Girls could be betrothed when they were about thirteen, and boys at about fourteen. Often, they were married a year later.

AGREEING THE PRICE

The girl's family lost a worker when she left home to marry. So the boy's family paid a "bride price." There were long talks about payment.

A betrothal was more like a marriage than an engagement. A betrothal could only be broken by legal means, similar to a divorce.

PRESENTS

A father gave his daughter a present, perhaps servants or land. The groom gave the bride jewelry and clothes. In New Testament times, this included a circlet of silver coins, which was fastened to the bride's headdress.

THE WEDDING

Weddings were not all alike, but this is what often happened. Before the wedding, a contract was drawn up and signed or spoken before witnesses. The best man, called the 'friend of the bridegroom', was in charge. He had to make sure that everything went smoothly.

WEDDING CLOTHES

The bride and groom were dressed in rich clothes. The bridesmaids braided the bride's hair with jewels. The bride and groom wore crowns of flowers. The bride wore a veil. Sometimes guests were given wedding clothes to wear.

THE EVENING BEFORE THE WEDDING

The groom and his friends came to the bride's house. Her parents "gave her away" with a prayer. There was a torchlit procession to the groom's home, with tambourines, singing and dancing. Later, the bride went to her room with her bridesmaids, while the groom had a party.

THE WEDDING DAY

The groom spent the day merrymaking and playing games with his friends. Sometime during the evening, he came for his bride.

A great feast was held for all the guests. The bride and groom sat under a canopy decorated with flowers. They were treated like royalty.

The bride and groom spent their first night together in a specially decorated 'bridal room'. There was no honeymoon, but the feasting went on for a week.

- Foolish bridesmaids
  Matthew 25:1-13

- A near disaster at a wedding:
  John 2:1-11

- Wedding guests:
  Matthew 22:1-12

Braiding the bride's hair

WEIGHTS AND MEASURING

Our modern Bibles translate the measurements of Bible times into terms we understand, so we don't have to struggle with mental arithmetic. The first weights were stones. Distances could be measured by arrows, donkeys and soldiers.

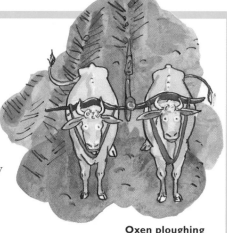

Oxen ploughing

YOU CHEAT!

In Old Testament times, weights were not exact, and it was easy for traders to cheat people. Careful shoppers carried their own weights about with them so they could check what they were sold. By the time of the New Testament, weights had become more standard, and a different system of weights and measurements was in use.

WEIGHTS

The first weights were stones. Archaeologists have found hundreds of small stones with weights marked on them. Later, bronze and lead weights were used. Weights were sometimes carved into animal shapes: these were easy to recognise and handle.

The most common weight was the shekel, which was used to weigh silver. The heaviest weight was the talent.

Weighing was done on scales. Before coins were invented, silver was weighed on scales and used as money.

Scales

Money stones

MEASURING

Palm

In the Old Testament, the unit of measurement was the human body!
- A cubit was $17\frac{1}{2}$ inches. • A finger was $\frac{3}{4}$ inch.
- A palm was 3 inches.
- A span was 9 inches.

DISTANCES

In the Old Testament, a distance was measured by how far an arrow could be shot, or how far a caravan of donkeys could travel in a day. A day's journey was about 18 miles.

ROMAN MILES

The word *mile* comes from the Latin word for a thousand. It referred to the distance covered by a marching soldier: one thousand paces was about 1,478 meters. A pace was the distance covered by a left and a right step.

OTHER MEASUREMENTS

Farmland was measured by how much land two oxen yoked together could plow in one day.

Water was measured in fathoms. A fathom was 6 feet.

A caravan of donkeys

Foods and drinks were measured in containers: pots, baskets or by the donkey-load.

- An attempt at a common standard: *Genesis 23:16*
- Cheating: *Micah 6:11*
- An arrow shot: *Genesis 21:16*
- A day's donkey ride: *Jonah 3:3*

Bible Search

Measuring distance

Marching soldiers

WILDERNESS
LESSONS

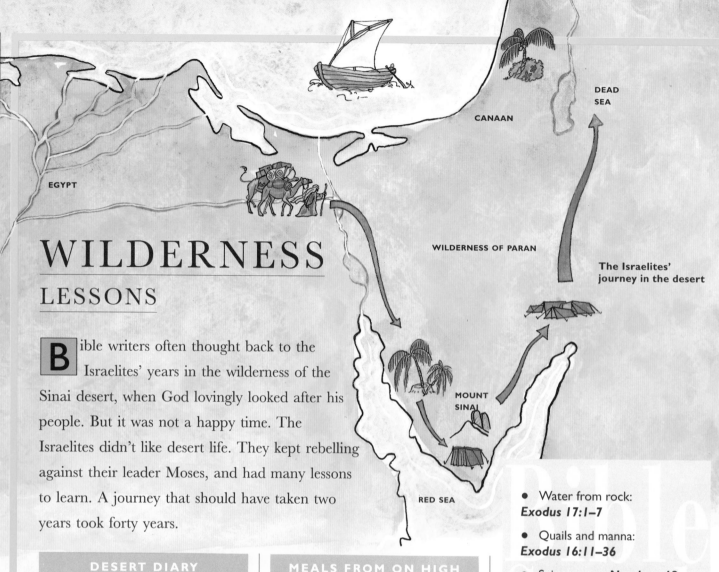

EGYPT

CANAAN

DEAD SEA

WILDERNESS OF PARAN

The Israelites' journey in the desert

MOUNT SINAI

RED SEA

Bible writers often thought back to the Israelites' years in the wilderness of the Sinai desert, when God lovingly looked after his people. But it was not a happy time. The Israelites didn't like desert life. They kept rebelling against their leader Moses, and had many lessons to learn. A journey that should have taken two years took forty years.

- Water from rock: *Exodus 17:1–7*
- Quails and manna: *Exodus 16:11–36*
- Spies go out: *Numbers 13*
- Moses dies: *Deuteronomy 34*

DESERT DIARY

- Journey to Sinai (3 months).
- At Mount Sinai to get God's Law and build the Tabernacle (12 months).
- Journey towards the Promised Land of Canaan (about 8 months).
- A wait at Kadesh, while some of the Israelites go ahead to spy out how the land is in Canaan (about 40 days).
- The spies report that there are strong cities in Canaan. "We'd rather die in the desert," the people moan.
- Waiting. The slaves grow old and die in the desert (38 years).
- Finally, their grown-up children march into Canaan.

MEALS FROM ON HIGH

After five weeks in the desert, the Israelites were starving. "God will make food rain down from heaven," Moses replied. Probably no one believed him, but flocks of quails appeared, which the people caught and ate.

The next morning, the people found little, white, sweet-tasting flakes of food lying on the ground. They called it manna, which meant "What is it?" They ate this every day.

All the water came from water-holes. When they dried up, there was panic. At Massah, God told Moses to hit a rock with his rod, and water flowed out.

MOSES DIES

After forty years in the desert, Moses knew that he would soon die. He told Joshua that he would have to lead the Israelites into Canaan instead. Then Moses climbed to the top of a mountain, and God showed him the green and beautiful land of Canaan. Moses died on the mountain, his work done. (See the page on Joshua.)

Quail

WISDOM
"WISE AS SERPENTS"

A serpent

W isdom has nothing to do with being clever. It means that in our choices and actions, big and tiny, we should know and do what God wants.

Wise people were popular in Old Testament times, and advised people on many practical matters.

BE WISE

"Be innocent as doves, and wise as serpents," said Jesus. Today we might translate this as "keep your head screwed on the right way." And the right way is God's way.

How can we know what wisdom is like? Jesus shows us. Paul wrote: "In Jesus are hidden all the treasures of wisdom."

The wise and foolish bridesmaids

THE WISE AND FOOLISH BRIDESMAIDS

Jesus told a story about ten bridesmaids. Ten young women were bridesmaids at a wedding. They were all due to carry lamps to light the wedding procession. Five bridesmaids were wise, and carried extra oil for their lamps. The other five were foolish and forgot to take any.

While the bridesmaids waited for the groom to arrive, the oil in the lamps ran out. The foolish bridesmaids had to go and buy more oil, and missed the wedding.

Jesus' story showed people that they should be well prepared for going to heaven.

- The start of wisdom: *Proverbs 9:10*
- Solomon's wisdom: *I Kings 3:5–28, 4:29–34*
- A gift: *James 1:5*
- The cross: *I Corinthians 1:20–24*

Bible Search

SOLOMON THE WISE

When David died, his son Solomon became king of Israel. One night God spoke to Solomon in a dream. "Ask me for whatever you want," God said. What an offer! Solomon asked God for the wisdom to rule his country.

The Hebrew word for wisdom means "a listening ear." The first step towards wisdom is to hear what God is saying.

A CASE STUDY

Soon afterwards, two women came to Solomon for advice. They were having a violent argument over a baby. Each woman said the baby was hers.

"Cut the baby in two," said Solomon.

"That's fair," said one woman.

"No. Give her the baby," said the second woman.

Solomon then knew that the second woman must be the real mother, and gave the baby to her.

Two women fight over a baby

WOMEN

Women and girls form half the world's population. Yet they own less than one hundredth of the world's property. In many parts of the world, women do not get an education.

The teaching of the New Testament states that women and men are equal, and must be given equal rights.

Bible Search

- Adam and Eve: *Genesis 1:27–28*
- No difference: *Galatians 3:28*
- Priscilla: *Romans 16:3*
- Witnesses: *Mark 16:1–8*
- Mary: *Luke 10:42*

A female priest

ADAM AND EVE

In the first chapter of the Bible we read that God made both Adam and Eve in his image. They were both told to look after the world. Eve was called Adam's helper, but this did not mean that she was less important than him.

IN GOD'S SERVICE

In the Bible we learn of some female leaders, in charge of both men and women.
- Deborah was a judge of all Israel.
- Miriam was a prophetess, speaking God's word to the people.
- Many women helped the apostle Paul in his preaching work, including Priscilla. Paul described her as his coworker.

Miriam

Paul and Priscilla

WOMEN IN THE CHURCH

Some Christians are against having female priests and ministers. They refer to a few Bible passages which speak of male "headship." and point out that Jesus had twelve male apostles.

Other Christians say that some practical rules in the New Testament about women not teaching were to avoid unnecessary offence to customs of the time. For example, one of the apostles' jobs was to preach, and Jewish law would not allow women to preach.

JESUS

Women were among the close group of friends who traveled around with Jesus. By welcoming women into this group, Jesus was doing something revolutionary.

In Bible times, women were considered less important than men. They were not allowed to be witnesses in a court of law. Yet the first people to witness Jesus' resurrection were women. This was a sign to all men! "Go and tell the disciples," said the angels.

Jesus and Mary

WORK

A workaholic

Work is an activity that earns money (or that trains you to earn money, like schoolwork!) Work is also any activity undertaken for a purpose. For example, in Christian life it is an activity that has spiritual results. True prayer is work.

A GIFT

Work was never meant to be a hard burden. It was a gift. The Garden of Eden was a place of perfect happiness, and God put Adam and Eve there "to work it and take care of it."

For Christians, what matters is not what you do, but the way you do it. Paul said, "Whatever you do, work at it with all your heart as though you were working for the Lord and not for men." And Paul wrote those words to slaves!

Work which is a call from God to serve him in the world, is called a vocation. Priests, nuns, ministers and preachers are all following a vocation. Sometimes this is paid work; sometimes it is voluntary.

A nun

UNEMPLOYMENT

Not having a job is depressing

Millions of people today can't get jobs. This is wrong, because work is an important part of human life.

Unemployment makes many people feel useless, but there are still things they can do. Our importance does not come from the job we do, but from our friendship with God. Every Christian can pray and serve God. This is work we can do for the whole of our lives.

ANY QUESTIONS
1 What is a vocation?
2 Why is it important for people to work, besides earning money?

REST

One day Jesus said to his friends: "Come with me by yourselves to a quiet place, and get some rest." Some people are workaholics, which means they can't stop working and rest. This is as bad as being lazy.

The writer of the Book of Proverbs made fun of lazy fools: "A little sleep… a little folding of the hands to rest, and poverty will come on you like a bandit!"

Lazy fools

Bible Search
- A wicked lazy man: *Matthew 25:26*
- A gift: *Genesis 2:15*
- Hard work: *Genesis 3:17–18*
- Advice to slaves: *Colossians 3:22–23*
- Your aim: *1 Thessalonians 4:11*

WORSHIP IN BIBLE TIMES

- Singing at family worship:
  Mark 14:26
- Music in Temple worship:
  Psalm 150; 1 Chronicles 25:6–7
- Guest preacher:
  Luke 4:16–21
- A family sacrifice:
  Luke 2:22–24

F or the Jews, religion was a way of life, not just reserved for special times when they went to the Temple or the synagogue. Laws about matters such as the food they could or couldn't eat, showed that every part of life belonged to God.

PRAYER

Three times a day, in the morning, at midday and in the evening, every adult male Jew stopped what he was doing. He had to turn towards the Temple in Jerusalem and say the Shema (Deuteronomy 6:4-9 and 11:13-21; Numbers 15:37-41). Women, slaves and children did not do this.

There were also set prayers, called the eighteen blessings, which were said two or three times a day. Prayers were usually spoken aloud with hands raised to God, while standing or kneeling.

When they prayed, men wore a prayer shawl with long fringes, and a phylactery (a small box containing Bible verses).

Stopping work to pray

A priest

TEMPLE

Every morning and evening at the Temple, a priest sacrificed a lamb. Then he stood on the steps above the Men's Court. He recited the Shema and read aloud a passage from the Law (the first five books of the Bible).

At three o'clock every day, a priest took a short service which included a Bible reading and prayers. Sometimes a choir chanted psalms and played music.

Thousands of people went to the Temple to pray. They bought lambs or pigeons from the Temple traders to make their own private sacrifices.

(See also the pages on Sacrifices and on Festivals.)

A lamb and pigeons for sacrifice

SYNAGOGUE

An hour-long service was held each Sabbath in every synagogue. There were opening prayers, including the Shema and the eighteen blessings. These were followed by a reading from the Law, which was divided into 153 parts, with a set reading for each Sabbath.

There was a reading from the prophets, which was then discussed. Often the congregation chanted psalms. The service ended with prayers and a collection of money.

Chanting psalms

ANY QUESTIONS
1 How and where did people pray?
2 How did people worship on the Sabbath?

Objects of worship?

WORSHIP TODAY

T o worship someone or something means to be devoted to that person or object, giving them your greatest possible respect and love. Human beings have a built-in need to worship. Whatever people put first in their lives, is their object of worship.

Bible Search

- Keep meeting together: *Hebrews 10:25*
- Pray all the time: *1 Thessalonians 5:17*
- Worship with our lives: *Romans 12:1–2*
- Places don't matter: *John 4:21–26*

TRUTH

One day, Jesus sat down by a well and talked to a woman about worship. He said that the important thing was not where we worship, but our spirit of true love for God.

Jesus at the well

TRUE WORSHIP

Paul wrote: "We are members of God's family, and I ask you to remember two things: keep God's kindness always in your minds; and give yourselves heart and soul to him, your energy, your heart and your mind. You belong to God, and it is service (worship) like this that makes God glad."

Paul wrote that we should worship all the time. We are worshiping God when we try to please him in our lives, in our work, and in our choice of friends.

IN CHURCH

Christians belong to a family. They meet together with other members of the Christian family to worship God in church by:

- Singing.
  - Prayer.
    - Learning from Bible readings and sermons.
    - Remembering the life, death and resurrection of Jesus.
      - Sharing. Giving money to the collection is a sign that we want to help with God's work in the world.

Singing hymns

DIFFERENT FORMS

Worship in church can take many forms. Some services are very formal, some are very free. Many churches make the Holy Communion the center of their worship.

Singing hymns or songs, listening to a choir, joining in prayers, watching a ceremony, are all part of worship. If one kind of worship does not appeal to you, another kind might.

ZACCHAEUS
AND OTHERS JESUS MET

'Don't bother me now, I'm busy!'

We often say, "Don't bother me now, I'm busy!" But Jesus never said that to anyone. He had time for everybody, even those that most people didn't like, such as tax-collectors. Tax-collectors were hated because they worked for the Romans, and often overcharged people.

A TAX-COLLECTOR

Zacchaeus could not see Jesus

Zacchaeus was the chief tax-collector in Jericho. He longed to see Jesus when he came to the city, but there was a crowd, and Zacchaeus was not very tall. Zacchaeus knew that the crowd would not let him get near Jesus, so he ran on ahead and climbed into a tree.

Jesus stopped right under the tree. "Come down, Zacchaeus. I must stay at your house today," he said, to Zacchaeus' great surprise.

Zacchaeus was overjoyed, and said, "Lord, here and now I'm giving half my money to the poor, and if I've cheated anybody out of anything, I'll pay it back four times over." Jesus was very happy. He said, "I've come to seek and save the lost."

- A widow: *Luke 7:11–17*
- Bartimaeus: *Luke 18:35–42*
- Zacchaeus: *Luke 19:1–10*

A WIDOW

Jesus was going into the town of Nain, when a funeral procession came out of the town gates.

The dead person was the only son of a widow. Jesus felt extremely sorry for her. He said, "Don't cry." He went up to the coffin, which didn't have a lid, and said, "Young man, get up." The widow's son was brought back to life.

A JERICHO BEGGAR

Bartimaeus gets his sight back

When Jesus was on his last journey to Jerusalem, he had to go through Jericho. King Herod had built a fine new town to the south of the old city of Jericho. A blind beggar called Bartimaeus was sitting by the roadside just outside the new town.

Bartimaeus started to call out to Jesus. "Oh, be quiet!" the crowd said. Jesus stood still. "What do you want me to do?" Jesus asked. "Sir, give me my sight back," Bartimaeus said. "Your faith has healed you," Jesus replied.

Jesus brings the young man back to life

ZEALOTS
AND OTHER GROUPS

In every country, people belong to different religions and political parties. Some people feel very strongly about the political party they belong to, but many other people are busy with their own lives, and don't get involved. It was just the same in the time of Jesus.

ESSENES

The Essenes move to the desert

Essenes also hated the Romans, but instead of fighting, they went away and set up small communities in the desert. One group lived to the northwest of the Dead Sea. (See the page on the Dead Sea Scrolls.)

SADDUCEES

The Sadducees were small in number, but had a lot of power because they were the ruling party in the Sanhedrin. The Sadducees came from the wealthy families of Jerusalem.

Most of the priests were Sadducees. They liked the Romans, and saw Jesus as a threat. They were worried that if Jesus started a riot, the Romans would blame them for not keeping order, and then they would lose their jobs.

The Sadducees saw Jesus as a threat

ZEALOTS

Zealots were terrorist freedom fighters. They wanted to get rid of the Romans by force. In the time of Jesus, there were lots of small groups who often fought each other as well as the Romans. One fierce group was called the Sicarii, which meant "dagger men."

Many zealots came from Galilee. At first, they supported Jesus, until they found he didn't want to lead an armed rebellion against Rome.

Zealots

APOCALYPTISTS

Apocalyptists thought that very soon there would be a great battle, when God would put an end to the evil in the world. They wrote books describing their weird visions and dreams about future events.

The Apocalyptists wrote books

HERODIANS

Herodians were a group of people in Galilee who were friends of Herod Antipas. Herod was kept in power by the Romans, so the Herodians supported Rome. They were against Jesus, because they thought he was a dangerous troublemaker.

- Sicarii: *Acts 21:38*
- Jesus for king: *John 6:14–15*
- Deserting Jesus: *John 6:66*
- Herodians: *Mark 12:13*
- Sadducees: *Mark 12:18*

WORD INTO WORD

AMEN A Hebrew word meaning "Truly," or "Let it be that way."

ANOINT To pour or rub oil on a person's head or chest. Anointing was a sign that someone was set apart to do a special job for God. Objects could also be anointed.

APOSTLE The word *apostle* meant someone who was sent out as a messenger. After Jesus' death, the twelve disciples became known as apostles. They were messengers of the teachings of Jesus.

ARAMAIC The language spoken by Jesus.

ARK OF THE COVENANT This was a special box covered with gold, with gold cherubim on top. It was carried on poles. The Israelites made the box while they were in the wilderness, to hold the Ten Commandments. No one knows what happened to it.

ATONEMENT In the New Testament, this meant being made "at one" with God, that is, to be able to know him as a friend. Jesus atoned for our sins by dying on the cross.

BEATITUDE This comes from a Latin word meaning "happy." In the New Testament, The Beatitudes are part of Jesus' Sermon on the Mount. They contain eight descriptions of a person with true inner happiness.

BETROTHAL An agreement, or contract, made between a man and a woman to get married.

BLASPHEMY Using God's name in wrong ways, or acting in a way that insults God. In Old Testament times, the punishment for blasphemy was to be stoned to death.

BLESSING Special happiness given as a gift from God. In Old Testament times, this often meant money, land, or children. In New Testament times, it often referred to the inner happiness given by Jesus.

CHRIST A Greek word meaning "The Chosen One." It is used in the New Testament as a name for Jesus. See also Messiah.

COVENANT An agreement. In the Old Testament, it was the agreement God made with the Israelites. Jesus set up a new covenant between God and human beings.

DISCIPLE A person who follows, obeys, and learns from a teacher. Jesus had many disciples. He chose twelve men to be with him all the time, to share his life and work. See also Apostles.

ETERNAL LIFE A new life of friendship with Jesus. It is given by God as a gift to those who trust Jesus. It begins in this life, and goes on for ever.

FELLOWSHIP Loving, sharing friendship between people who share the same beliefs.

FRANKINCENSE A type of incense. It was one of the gifts brought to the baby Jesus by the wise men.

GENTILE Someone who is not a Jew.

GOLGOTHA An Aramaic word meaning "the place of the skull." This was the name of the hill where Jesus was crucified.

GOSPEL The word means "good news." The Gospels are four books of the Bible, written by the apostles Matthew, Mark, Luke and John. They are accounts of the life of Jesus. Sometimes the word is also used to mean "the Christian message."

HADES A Greek word meaning "the world of the dead."

HEBREWS One of the names given to God's chosen people. They were also called Israelites, the people of Israel, and later, Jews.

INCENSE A material which makes a sweet smell when it is burned. It is often used during services of worship.

JEHOVAH A word used in some translations of the Bible to mean the God of the Israelites. It has been translated from the Hebrew word "Yahweh."

LEVITE A descendant of the tribe of Levi. Levites helped priests with their duties.

MAGI A Greek word meaning "wise men."

MANNA A food provided by God for the Israelites, when they were starving in the wilderness. The word is Hebrew and means "What is it?" It was small, white flakes, which tasted sweet.

MESSIAH A Hebrew word meaning "The Chosen One." In the Old Testament, the Messiah meant a future great leader to be sent by God, who would set the people free from their enemies. See also Christ.

MYRRH An expensive, sweet-smelling gum. Myrrh was rubbed on the body of a dead person before burial.

NAZIRITE A person who promised to work only for God; sometimes for a short time, sometimes for life. A Nazirite did not cut his hair, and did not drink wine, or eat vinegar or raisins! Samson, who was a very strong man, was a Nazirite.

PARADISE Another word for heaven, the place where Christians go when they die.

PROPHET A person called by God to preach his message to the world. Many prophets warned of unpleasant future events which God would bring about if the people did not live as he wanted them to.

RABBI In Bible times, a teacher of Jewish law. Today the word means the chief religious leader of a synagogue.

SAMARITAN A person who came from Samaria, a land in the middle of Palestine. Samaritans and Jews did not like each other.

SANHEDRIN A council of religious leaders in Jerusalem. It had the power to judge, punish and imprison people brought before it.

TESTAMENT An old word for covenant, or agreement. In the Bible it is used for the two halves of the Bible: the Old Testament and the New Testament. The Old Testament was written before Jesus was born, the New Testament afterwards.

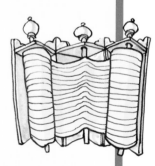

YAHWEH The Hebrew name for God, used by the Israelites.

INDEX

319